God's Honest Truth
Channeled Teachings and Messages from Angels and God

The majority of this book came to us through
Channeling, Meditation and Automatic Writing.

We were simply the catalysts used to bring this
information to Earth.

Love & Light to you!

Charlene Hill

Denis Hill

Susan Eagen

Charlene Hill
Denis Hill
Susan Eagen

God's Honest Truth

Channeled Teachings and Messages from Angels and God

This book is dedicated to:
Our Spirit Guides, all of the Angels, The Archangels
and to Almighty God.

Thank You for allowing us to help You get
Your Messages to the Earth.

Forward

In 1997, after my book, *The Messengers* became a New York Times Best Seller, I received dozens and dozens of requests to write the forwards for other authors who had created manuscripts spiritual in nature. This is not unusual that an author hoping to be published would call upon another author that had a best seller and ask for their endorsement.

Only three times in the past did I agree to write an endorsement for I felt those three, who were all well known authors, had distinguished themselves from many hundreds of other authors wanting to be published and recognized. I would agree to write their forwards, not because of their reputations, but because of the quality of the new manuscripts they had provided to me.

When the author of this book, Charlene Hill, contacted me explaining to me she had a manuscript that included channelings from angels, I thought, "Oh no, here we go again". There are so many people that believe they are channeling, or pretend they are channeling, that it usually takes me only a few pages to recognize the information is not coming from where they think it is, or claim it is being transmitted from. Allow me to explain the phenomena of channeling.

I am not a clairvoyant, for I cannot see into the spirit world, the world beyond our mortal world. I am not clairaudient, in that I cannot hear into the spirit world. But I do have clair-cognizance, which means being able to receive information from the spirit world, How is the information transmitted? It can be provided to the person who is the recipient either in thought placed into their conscious mind, that they can then retrieve, just as remembering what they had for breakfast that morning and describing it in words. Or, it can come through the handwriting of the receiver, as if they were taking dictation.

Who is sending the information? It is coming from the spiritual dimension and can either be from a spiritual master, which is a soul that previously lived on earth in a mortal body, or by an angel, who has never lived in the material world that we are now in. I don't know how they transmit this information to the person receiving it, other than it is by some form of mental telepathy.

When I received Charlene's manuscript, I had little enthusiasm to begin reading it. I have a spiritual website, nickbunick.com with many hundreds of people around the world conversing on it, as I teach them the lessons I am given, and converse with them daily on the site. I am also in the

4

process of writing my own fifth book, so her manuscript sat on a large table along side of many other books and manuscripts that I had discarded.

One day I picked up her manuscript, *God's Honest Truth*, and it rocked my boat. The narrative of how it all began for Charlene was interesting and well written, but it was when she began to share the messages she was receiving from the angels, that I knew this is real. This is profound. This indeed, is coming from the angelic realm. I finished the manuscript in one week, and I e-mailed Charlene, making a commitment to her that I would write this forward.

I began to test her work, by providing one or two paragraphs a day on my website, nickbunick.com, and the response was overwhelming. My spiritual brothers and sisters who visit my site daily posted over and over again, "Nick, we want more. This is wonderful information. Keep it coming".

We are all on a spiritual journey although most people do not know it. Our goal is to become at one with God and Christ Consciousness. Charlene's book, *God's Honest Truth*, will help you on that journey. It will give you the motivation and support you need to evolve, spiritually, on your journey to become at one with God. It does not make a difference if you are a true beginner, on your first steps on that pathway, or if you have ascended half way up that pyramid of 1000 steps, where God and Christ Consciousness reside on the top of the pyramid; or if you are near the top. This book is the road map that will help you ascend, that will inspire you and provide you the tools you need to evolve higher and higher.

Thank you Charlene, Susan and Denis for sharing this wonderful book with us. And thank you to your angels for allowing you to be conduits to us. God bless you all, as you continue on your journey.

Nick Bunick

Author of *Time for Truth*, *The Commitment* and co-author of New York Times best seller, *The Messengers*

God's Honest Truth

Channeled Teachings and Messages from
Angels and God

Contents:

Preface...A Bit of Background
Charlene Hill (Charlie)

I came into this life knowing things...perhaps I was allowed to remember more about the other side, because of the work that I am doing here. I have always had an open, constant communication with God and I have always known that the love of God is unconditional. I am not now, nor have I ever been, motivated by fear or guilt. Although it has taken much work because of things I was taught as a young child, I no longer believe that I am unworthy. I know who I am and why I am here on Earth.

I was born in Utah, the second of six children and the oldest female child. My parents are devout Mormons and I was raised according to church doctrine until I was old enough to make my own choices. By the time I was ten years old, I was already on a personal quest for my own truth. My family has held up my Spiritual work and lifestyle for ridicule and judgment, and I have been rejected by them because of my beliefs.

Even as a child, I had promptings by the still small voice that resides within me, and learned very early to pay attention to it. When I was eleven years old, sitting in school, I had a very strong "knowing" that I needed to go home. My mother was expecting a baby in a month and a half, but I knew I needed to get to her quickly. I told my teacher that I was leaving, that something was wrong, that I would be back if I could and I would stay in for recess to take the spelling test. Then, without any argument, I walked out of the school. We lived a mile and a half from the school, mostly uphill all the way. I hurried as fast as I could go and I found my mother hemorrhaging. I called my father, ran to the neighbor's to make sure that she could continue watching my four-year-old sister, and waited for my father to get home. When he arrived, he scooped my mother up and took her to the hospital in the car. They told me to go back to school, which I did. The baby was born that night. My teacher was much nicer to me after that; I think she was a little bit scared of me.

I met the love of my life, Denis Hill, when I was fifteen years old. We married young and started our family. Even prior to our marriage, we often had deep and lengthy discussions about God, religions, the purpose of life, etc. Denis and I were constantly reading and considering different theories and stayed up nights discussing them. The books we read were Spiritual in nature: A Course in Miracles, books by, Sylvia Browne, Dr. Wayne Dyer, etc. and we continued searching for answers and for truth. We learned Transcendental Meditation and we introduced our children to it at an early age. We learned how to do Automatic Writing and through this and meditation, we communicated with God on a daily basis. I have always begun each day by asking God to make me His instrument in doing His will.

Like many women, I lost myself in my husband and three children. I felt that it was my responsibility to make sure that all of their needs were met and that they were happy. As time went on, however, it became apparent that Denis was not happy. He began to criticize me about everything and I felt that I had failed him. I found that there was nothing that I could do to make him happy and I became depressed. We went for counseling several times. Things got progressively worse after Denis had a heart attack. He was only 47 years old and we had been told for years that he was in great health, with the heart of a bull. His heart attack caught us both by complete surprise. Denis said he felt that his body had betrayed him and he had a difficult time dealing with his feelings. He became increasingly verbally abusive to me and I grew more and more depressed. Thus began my "Dark Night of the Soul." I became extremely suicidal, even planning several scenarios as how to make my pain end. Finally, I cried out to God for help. I had never been in such emotional pain and turmoil. Eventually, I was able to completely surrender my will to God's. As a result, I was taken out of the marriage and Denis and I divorced.

I was devastated! I was lost! After years of living my life for my family, I found myself all alone. Throughout our marriage, Denis' company had transferred him to many different locations. Every time we moved, as I was starting over anyway, I had learned a new skill. I became a Cosmetologist, a Real Estate Broker, a Photographer, and an Artist. When I found myself on my own, I had an independent Real Estate company but I was my only employee. I wanted to paint and create, but I needed to figure out how to survive financially. Those years were very difficult but they were very important. I learned that I was much stronger than I had thought. I learned, finally, to stop playing the destructive "tapes" from my childhood. I learned how to love myself and take care of me. As you will see when you read this book, I can be very stubborn and sometimes wanted to take back the control that I had given to God. It took me awhile to learn not to do that anymore! Denis and I never stopped loving each other and we communicated nearly every day but we both had growth that needed to happen alone. We were, eventually, able to remarry and we are closer now than we have ever been. I have included much about my pain from our divorce in these pages, in an attempt to help others who may be going through their own difficult situation.

I met Susan Eagen through my Real Estate business. She was employed by a Title Insurance company and we did business together. We had an instant connection and became great friends. I knew Sue to be one of the most honest, true people that I had ever met. We found that we were both on "Spiritual Quests for Truth", and shared much with one another. We began the channeling contained within these pages thirteen years into our relationship, as a natural progression of our shared quest. We continue to speak to each other several times a day, no matter where we are at the time. The learning never stops...

My reason for sharing this information is to let everyone know that God has not stopped speaking to us. He has never stopped loving us. He has never abandoned us. God's Love is totally unconditional and unending. If you have questions, ask God. Ask with a pure heart, with no preconceived ideas as to the answers, and God will give you the answers you seek. As you read the information contained here, please do so with an open heart. If you have questions about what is in this book, ask God. He **will** let you know. If there are things here that you do not resonate with as truth for you, that is perfectly alright with me. Each of us is on our own Spiritual path and what is truth for me might not be truth for you. Please take what you can use and leave what you cannot.

Always remember to "**Expect a Miracle!**"

I wish you joy, happiness and Love.

Love and Light to you!

Denis Hill

I am a husband, father, grandfather, businessman and musician (drummer). After spending 23 years working for a major retail chain, I opened my own business, a Sales Rep. firm based in the Denver, Colorado area. As far as my music career is concerned, I am the Band Leader and Drummer for a "Classic Rock" band. Besides my wife and family, music is my passion. It feeds my Soul and continues to regenerate my Joy.

I am not a "Holy Man", nor do I profess to have all of the answers... especially when it comes to organized religions. I am just a regular guy who is hungry for knowledge and is willing to listen with an open mind and heart. Like many other men, I had a huge ego and many unrealistic ideas of how a man should behave. I had a lot of pent-up pain and anger that I needed to find a way of letting go of. Over many years, I had built a wall around my heart to protect me from feeling pain. Unfortunately, it prevented me from feeling anything else, as well.

I began my search for Spiritual truth at a very young age. This was because the things that I was hearing and being taught, simply did not resonate with me. Just as a guitar string that is out of tune, the harmonic vibration of this information didn't harmonize with what my Spirit knew to be true. I am not saying that the organized religions that I was exposed to in my early life were wrong for everyone, but they failed to be inspiring or comforting to me. I have never been a follower. I began to understand that being "religious" was not the same as being "Spiritual".

I met Charlene (My Wife) at a very young age and it was instantly LOVE. We married and began our journey together. As we added to our family, it intensified our knowledge of God's power and His unconditional love for us.

We read nearly every book we could find on Spirituality and had thousands of discussions. We also attended seminars presented by some of the best-known speakers and teachers on the planet. It seemed that everything was leading us to the fascinating material contained in this book.

As you read through this journey of our Spiritual Quest, you will see the Power of God and the thousands of Angels who guide us (you, too, if you choose). You are being invited to experience very personal conversations between Charlene, Myself, Angels and God (yes... God). We were working with a very dear friend, Sue, who is a Spiritual Channel. We were, eventually, Initiated into The Language of Light and began to channel messages, ourselves. This, along with a process called Automatic

Writing, intensified our ability to communicate directly with the Spiritual Realm in a two-way relationship.

Part of this journey was extremely painful. Charlene and I had to do our individual Spiritual work, separately, without the distractions of everyday life together. We were actually pulled apart (divorced) for five years so that we could accomplish this work. The rest of our journey has been very joyous and deeply rewarding.

I realize that your truths and belief structure may be completely different than mine.
I ask that you take what you want from this book and leave the rest. Please read it with an open mind and heart and understand that it is not fiction.

God Bless...and Enjoy!!

Susan Eagen (Sue)

I believe that God wants us to love, to learn, and to be who we are. We are Eternal Spirits, made of His/Her likeness, having a human experience. It is man, not God, that has established all these silly "church" rules, and regulations. God, our Heavenly Creator, simply wants us to be the best we can be, learning along the way, helping others as we go, and staying out of our own way!

Our Loving Heavenly Father did not just dump us on this planet and say, "Wing it, and good luck My Dear Child." No....not even close! First, we incarnate by choice. That's right, we have made the choice to be here now, at this time, on this planet. We have agreed to incarnate in the family units we are in, for various reasons.

We all created an outline of the life we wanted on Earth and we actually wrote in the struggles we wanted to face and conquer. God gave us each at least one personal Guide as well as personal Angels. Even though we can't "see" the help God gave us, they are with us always, just as God is always with us.

How does one go from being brought up in Catholic Schools in the Chicago suburbs to channeling Angels and God in Denver, Colorado? How did my experiences of losing a baby, my near-death, divorce and raising three boys as a single mother lead me here? It is a long story, and one for another book.

May this book and our experiences help you with whatever you are going through in this lifetime.

With Love and Light, God bless you!!

God's Honest Truth

Channeled Teachings & Messages from Angels and God

Introduction:

But if any of you lacks wisdom, let him ask of God, who gives to all liberally and without reproach; and it will be given to him.   James 1:5   World English Bible

This is a book of Channeled Teachings and Messages received directly from Angels and God.

Although our experiences may differ from yours, know that you, too, have the ability to go directly to God for answers. Within these pages you learn how to do so.

As you read the information contained within these pages, there are some things to keep in mind:

1- There are no coincidences, so you would not be reading this book unless you were meant to read it. Nothing about the authors is any different from you.
Between every Channeling or Automatic Writing contained in this book, we were all continuing to pray and meditate, read and study on a regular basis. Many times the Angels would begin their messages by answering things, or making comments concerning things that we had been discussing among ourselves.

2- Angels and Spirit Guides cannot read your mind, unless you give them permission to do so. You can give them permission for a few minutes, or a day, if you choose to do so. Only God can read your mind, as He knows every thought that you have before you do. He knows every tear you shed, every joy you have, every temptation you face and every challenge you conquer.

3- One of the most surprising and endearing facts about the Angels and God is, they have great senses of humor! They even teased us, lovingly, on occasion. I guess it shouldn't be such a surprise, after all, God created us in His own image. Although our Angels are always with us, they are unable to help us unless asked, other than in a life-threatening situation...so ASK!

4- In the channeled dialogue, the **bolded** words are to give the emphasis where it was given during the channeling. Although all Channeling comes through the filters of the Channel, the text for these messages is as close to what was given, as is humanly possible.

5- Some names have been changed to protect privacy...and NO Channeling that we did for others has been included in this book. We did not even keep a copy of the tapes we made for them.

6- Prior to every Channeling, we said a prayer and spoke the Language of Light. The Language of Light helps us "tune in" to the frequency that makes channeling easier. It is not translatable into English. Everyone has their own Language of Light, as it is the Language of the Heart and we all sound different. Ours sound similar to indigenous languages, like Hawaiian or Aboriginal. The Language of Light is the Universal Language.

If you want to speak your Language of Light:
Say a prayer to protect yourself.
Focus on Love.
Focus on God's Light.
Pull all of the Love of the Universe into your heart.
Start softly saying "Love, Love, Love..." over and over.

You will tune in to the correct frequency to reach the Angels and God.
Simply speak whatever comes into your heart.
If you choose to you may just continue to softly say, "Love".
Remember that you cannot do it wrong.

7- Many of the messages contained in these pages are from our Automatic Writings.

To do **Automatic Writing:**

Say a prayer to protect yourself.
Address your question to God or the Angels.
Write down your question in detail.
Thank God or your Angels for helping you.
As soon as you have written your question, begin your answer page.
Simply start by writing," My Dear Child",
or whatever comes into your heart to write.
Do NOT edit!
Simply write down whatever comes into your heart and mind to write.
Remember that you cannot do this wrong!
When you are finished, you might want to take a quick break, and then begin reading your answer.

8- Every time you open these pages, you will find new messages, as you are ready to receive them.
God Bless you!

9- You may contact us at email address: chill@estreet.com

I'm Not In Charge, and It's OK!
By Charlene:

It was the Friday before Memorial Day weekend, May 22, 1998. I was driving Denis' little red convertible Mazda Miata because he had borrowed my big car to carry his drums for a gig. The weather had been strange all afternoon. It had rained a little, and even hailed a bit, but things were calm now; overcast and cloudy, but calm. I was traveling in the slow lane, having just entered onto the crowded Colorado Interstate-25, Southbound. My passenger and friend, Ruby, asked me to get off at the next exit so we could swing by the bookstore and pick up the book that they were holding for her, so I was staying in the far right lane. We were talking about how heavy the traffic was for 1:30 in the afternoon, even for the day before a big weekend.

Suddenly, my car was unexpectedly propelled forward, spinning to the left, directly into the holiday traffic! I attempted to correct by pulling the wheel to the right, but we were not on the ground, and the car continued spinning to the left. BAM! My head hit the metal frame of the soft top. BAM! "Well, this must be it; we are going to be killed. I have no way to get out of this." I expected to be lifted up above the traffic, watching my body below me like you see in the movies. BAM! "Whew! That was hard, but I guess not hard enough because I'm still here." BAM! The car was still spinning around left to right, and I was still trying to drive! I saw the body of the car come in toward me with each impact, and my body felt the blows. BAM! "Wow! That was hard...I guess not hard enough though. I'll bet the car looks like crumpled up aluminum foil by now! Den is going to be so upset that I wrecked his car!" BAM! Wow! I wondered when the BIG one was going to hit. BAM! A big red car crashed into us head-on. I felt each collision, yet I was not in the least bit afraid. BAM! "This is fascinating! What's next?" There was no noise except the noise from each concussion. BAM! "Ok, this is starting to be less interesting now." BAM! "We are going to hit that big grey car...there is nothing I can do about it." I telepathically communicated with the woman on the passenger side, and she acknowledged that she understood that there was nothing I could do to avoid hitting her. My car was still spinning to the left. Screech! The sound of grating metal was loud as we seared the side of the big grey car. "Ok, this is not fun anymore!"

"God, **help** us!" I commanded out loud.

No sooner did the words leave my mouth, than we stopped. It was a gentle stop, not even the least bit jarring. I looked over at Ruby, amazed that she was still alive. I hadn't heard any sound from her since the ordeal began, and was sure she had been killed. She was equally surprised that I was alive. We embraced each other, and assessed our situation. I was giggly and giddy with gratitude that we were still alive! Ruby, on the other hand, began spewing profanities. She was livid! It was as if we were experiencing directly opposite reality.

"They hit us!" she said. "Those f****** people in that grey car hit us!"

"No,' I assured her. "We hit **them**. It's ok, calm down."

The Miata had come to rest approximately sixty feet behind the big grey car. We were now in the lane adjacent to the fast lane, and we were facing the wrong direction on Interstate-25! All of the cars in front of us, headed South, the correct direction, had stopped in a perfectly straight line approximately one hundred feet in front of where we were. They weren't even staggered. The Miata was not running, so the car phone didn't work. I turned the key, and the car started! I turned on the phone and called 911, and told the dispatcher that there had been a huge multi-car pile-up on Interstate-25. I told her that there were at least ten cars involved, and that she had better get emergency equipment on the way immediately!

A tall man dressed in white got out of a white truck that had parked behind the big grey car, and came over to us. Ruby rolled down the window and he asked if we were alright and did we need him to call for help. We explained that we had already done that and that we were fine. We thanked him for his concern, and he went back to his truck but he stayed there and did not drive away.

Some of the cars facing us began to slowly creep around us and proceed down the Interstate. Ruby held her right hand out the window and stopped the traffic, and I drove in a big U-turn over to the other side of the freeway; to the shoulder of the slow lane. We were now facing in the correct direction. I pulled the car well off onto the shoulder, stopped, put the car in neutral, and called my husband, Denis. I told him that we had been in an accident on I-25 and were just South of the Dry Creek exit. He said he would be right there. Ruby called her husband, Jack, and he asked if she needed him to come. She told him that we were alright and that she would call him after the Paramedics checked us out.

As we waited for what seemed like a very long time for the Paramedics we checked each other out. Ruby complained that her thumb hurt, and that she had broken her thumbnail by holding on so tightly to the handle.

"What handle?" I asked.

"This handle," she replied, but there was no handle there. She swore that she had held on to one right there! Her nail was, indeed, broken.

A Police car had pulled up behind the grey car, across 3 lanes of traffic in the fast lane of the freeway. Ruby was very upset when she discovered that my head was bleeding. She jumped out of the car and holding her hand out to stop traffic, proceeded to walk across the crowded freeway! She began to shout to the Police officer that her friend was hurt and that he had better get some emergency equipment here fast! He motioned to her and yelled that she should not be out of her vehicle. With her arm outstretched to stop the traffic again, Ruby walked back across the busy freeway and got back into our car.

The Paramedics finally arrived and the Police officer allowed the Paramedics to check us out before talking to us. One of the Paramedics gave us a cursory evaluation and instructed me that I might want to go to the hospital and see if I needed stitches in my head. He told us that we might be a little stiff and sore for a few days. No one got us out of the car or checked our heart rates or anything. We could not understand their cavalier attitude. The tall man in white from the white truck was there, standing behind the Paramedics. He asked, again, if we were alright. We assured him that we thought that we were ok, thanked him and he went back and sat in his truck. The Police officer asked me what had happened and gave me some forms to fill out and to write my statement on, but nobody talked to Ruby or took any statement from her.

It was about that time that I noticed that our Lottery ticket was gone. We had just been to a luncheon meeting with our friend, Sue. The three of us had been talking about the fact that we wanted to build a Spiritual Center, where we could teach and heal and bring in speakers and healers from around the country. We had discussed the fact that we needed money to do this, and had decided to try to win the $12 million Lottery drawing that Colorado was having the next night. Sue had gone back to work and Ruby and I had gone to purchase the Lottery ticket just prior to getting on the Interstate. I had placed the Lottery ticket on the console but it was no longer there. We looked all over. We searched our bags, under the seats and all around the tiny interior of the car, but there was no ticket to be found. Ruby said that maybe when she had gotten out it had blown out of the door, so she went outside to look around. It had started to rain a little bit, but she stomped through the weeds and the mud along the shoulder of the Interstate searching for the ticket.

The big grey car limped across the freeway and parked about eighty feet in front of us. The Paramedics got everyone out and appeared to check them over very thoroughly. There was a man and a woman and a little boy who looked like he was probably three years old. After the family had been checked out, the Paramedics left and I drove up and parked closer behind the grey car. I walked to the car while Ruby searched for the Lottery ticket.

The little boy was screaming and crying very hard and his parents could not seem to calm him. As I walked toward him he ran to me, threw his arms around my legs and hugged me. I bent down and held him and told him that everything was okay. He stopped crying but continued to hug me. I asked the man and the woman if they could please tell me what they had seen.

They said they had been traveling in the fast lane and that there was a big blue semi-truck in the middle lane signaling that the driver intended to move to the right, where my car was. As they were passing the semi-truck, they said that our little red car flew **over the top** of the semi and hit them! They said that they were amazed that we were alive! I asked them if they had seen us spinning, and they said that they had not seen us at all until we flew over the semi and hit them. I thanked them and made sure that they had someone coming to get them, and walked back to my car.

As I approached the Miata, I noticed that there was hardly any damage on it! There was a small dent with blue paint on it on the left rear fender, and horizontal scratches on the front. None of the other collisions that we had experienced were evident on the vehicle! None of the windows were broken, and neither air bag had been deployed. No wonder that the Paramedics had treated us like this was "no big deal"! I got back in the car, and tried to figure out what was going on.

Denis arrived, parked behind me and asked if we were okay. I explained everything to him as best I could, and told him that Ruby was searching for the Lottery ticket. By this time she was about a half of a block behind the car, just in case the ticket had been blown that far. I needed to go to the Police car and answer more questions, so I asked Denis to search the Miata for the Lottery ticket. He could tell that the mysterious disappearance of the ticket was very upsetting to me, so he searched while I was gone...for about ten minutes. When I got back he told me that he had lifted the seats up and everything but there was no Lottery ticket in the car.

It was raining harder by then. Denis went to ask the Police if we could leave as Ruby returned, dejected, to the car. When she opened the passenger door she screamed, "You FOUND it!" There on the floor right in front of us was the Lottery ticket! It had **not been** there a second before. We squealed with delight, as we were certain that this was a **sign** that this Lottery ticket was going to win! We showed it to Denis when he returned,

21

and he could not believe it either! He knew that it had not been in the car! I secured the ticket safely in my purse, and we waited for the go ahead from the Police so we could leave the area.

It had taken nearly two hours for the Police to finish with us. The Miata still drove so I opted to drive it home and Denis followed behind in my car. We called Sue as soon as we exited the Interstate and told her what had happened. She was upset that we had been through such a thing, but very glad that we were not hurt worse. When we got to our house I parked the Miata in the garage. My head was still bleeding and we decided that it would be a good idea to go to the hospital and have the cut examined. Ruby called Jack and he said that he would meet us at the hospital. Denis took some of his drums out of my car and drove us to the hospital.

We entered the Emergency room and were reunited with the family from the grey car. It turned out that it was a Cadillac and that it had been "totaled". The family group had grown though, as they now had the mother and the grandmother of the man with them. When the little boy saw me he ran over and climbed on my lap and gave me a big hug. The man and the woman could not get over the fact that we were alive. They said that they thought that we should have been killed!

I remembered that Denis had a gig that night, and still had to go back home and get the rest of his drums out of the garage. I told him that he had better go, or he would be late meeting the other members of his band. I told him that I didn't feel like being alone, so I would go home with Ruby and her family. Denis said that he would pick me up from Ruby's when he was finished with his gig...around 2:00 A.M. He kissed me good-bye and left.

Eventually Ruby and I were evaluated and put into examination rooms. My head wound was cleaned and I was told that stitches were optional. I opted not to get them. Something irregular was evident in my heartbeat, so I was waiting for the Doctors to return and do an EKG, when Denis appeared in my room with our daughter, Teresa. He had gone to her Studio to meet his band members there and had told her that I had an accident and was in the hospital. Teresa had insisted that he bring her to the hospital. Her husband came about an hour later, and I told her to go ahead and leave with him, and that I would go home with Ruby. After about five hours in the hospital, we were released. On the way to Ruby's, I began to get stiff and sore and thought about how nice it would have been if I could have gone home to my own house and had a long warm bath and been held and comforted; but no one was there and I did not want to be all alone.

When we got to Ruby's, Jack ordered pizza, and we ate and talked until very late into the night. Ruby and I kept going over every detail of the experience we had been through. It didn't make any sense! It was **truly** a miracle! We should have been killed! We discussed the fact that each hit had been the same duration in between, and wondered if we had been a pawn in some sort of universal Ping-Pong game. Ruby said that maybe she had been held in her seat by an Angel. Her midsection was bruised. We joked that we were like Thelma and Louise in the Flying Miata! We talked about the man in the white truck and decided that he was probably an Angel sent to make sure that we were alright. We talked about the fact that we had been shown in no uncertain terms that we are not in charge and that there is indeed a "Higher Power" who is in charge and that it is more than ok. Jack finally went to bed around midnight, but Ruby and I talked until Denis came to get me, around 2:30 in the morning. By then, I was very sore and stiff.

The next morning, I got a call from the Police. They said they wanted to come and look at the Miata because none of the reports from the accident made any sense. I told them that I would be happy to meet with them on the following day, Sunday. I talked to Ruby, and she said that she wanted to talk to them, too.

That Saturday night was the Lotto drawing for which we had purchased the ticket. Ruby, Sue and I were **sure** that we were going to win because of the events that had transpired. We waited excitedly while the Lotto numbers were drawn...but much to our disbelief, we did **not** have the winning ticket! We were disappointed, but more than that, we were confused. What had been the message we were supposed to understand from the disappearance and reappearance of the ticket? Was it simply a demonstration of the fact that we were not **in any way** in control of our reality? Were we not yet ready to begin the Spiritual Center that we had intended? We did not know what the reason was, but we were certain that everything was happening exactly as it was supposed to...perfectly.

Ruby and I were ready when two Police officers arrived at my home on Sunday. We told them what had happened, and they wrote everything down. Ruby gave them a written statement, too, as she had never been questioned. The Police officers took pictures of the Miata and told us that they would continue their investigation because some things didn't make any sense to them. They shared with us the fact that there were no skid marks at all on the highway; none of the cars had skidded when they had stopped, even. There was **no way**, they said, given the position of the dent in the rear fender of the Miata, that we could have been propelled **over** the semi-truck. We should have gone **underneath** it, not over it. Had we gone underneath the truck, we would certainly have been decapitated. The Police officers seemed very confused as they drove away.

I spent the next few days resting and trying to process all that had happened. I had a bump approximately 8 inches long with a 2-inch gash in the middle of it on the left side of my head. My body ached all over but I was so happy! I wanted to be outside every minute to see the glorious colors in nature! All of nature was vibrant and I could even see energy coming off leaves and rocks! I was filled with love and gratitude to God for being alive!

A few days later, I was talking to my daughter and she said, "Mom, I think it was really awful of Dad to leave you at the hospital and go play his gig. Doesn't it make you feel bad that he only cares about his band? You would **never** have treated him like that. When he had his heart attack, you never left his side for over six months! Don't you think he should treat you better?"

It did make me feel bad. I had been increasingly concerned because I had been feeling more and more unloved for several years. I had expressed my feelings to Denis, but he got mad whenever I tried to discuss it with him. I guess he felt that I was attacking and blaming him, when in fact I was attempting to find a solution to my uneasy feelings so that I could feel happy in my marriage. I had felt suicidal off and on for four or five years, going for counseling only to be told that my depression was "situational".

A couple of days after my conversation with Teresa, on May 28, 1998, I was still feeling disconnected by the wreck. Even though I was sore, I wanted to be held and comforted. That night as we lay in bed, I told Denis that I needed to be held and made to feel loved and secure and protected.

"I'm upset about something. I feel like it was very insensitive of you to leave me at the hospital and go play your gig. You didn't even know if I was ok or not when you left," I said.

"You were fine. You told me to go, why are you getting all upset about it now?" he replied defensively.

"I was glad to be alive and I was probably in shock. You didn't know if I was ok or not, because **I** didn't even know how I was," I replied.

Silence...

"You **did** show me how important I am to you though; apparently, not very."

"Oh here we go again!" Denis stopped holding me, rolled over and put his hands under his head.

Several silent minutes passed.

Our ensuing conversation resulted in my leaving the house. I stayed with our son for two days, and then I returned to find that Denis was still very angry at me, and not at all remorseful for his behavior. I attempted to get reconciliation and counseling for another month, to no avail. I found a new place to live and moved out on the sixth of July. Although Denis began getting counseling the day I moved out, we filed for divorce and it was final in September, 1998.

I was totally heart-broken and devastated. I did not know why I had been taken out of my marriage and would not find out for a few years.

God really does work in mysterious ways, His wonders to perform!

2

Sue's Wonderful Surprise!
By Charlene:

Though we were apart, Denis and I talked to each other often. We both continued to do our own Spiritual work and worked hard to learn the things that we needed to know in order to live our best lives. We got together for various events, including things that we felt would enhance our Spiritual growth. In the summer of 2000, there was one such event that would change our lives. On occasion, I had attended a little church that promoted Spiritual growth. I heard that there was a special teacher, Michelle, who was coming from Arizona to give a speech about channeling and I asked Denis and Sue to attend it with me.

June 5, 2000

We were all three sitting close to the front of the church, Sue on the aisle, myself in the middle and Denis was on my right. Michelle is a dynamic speaker, and we were enjoying the evening very much. Michelle began to explain the way she communicates with Angels is through the Language of Light. The Language of Light is the Language of the heart. She explained that it is easier for Angels to communicate with humans this way. Human language is, sometimes difficult because things sometimes get misinterpreted through dimensions. She said that it had been her experience that whenever anyone spoke the Language of Light, there would be someone present that would be able to translate it. She said that since she is a conscious channel, and usually could translate as it came through her, she did not, generally, use a translator.

As Michelle was speaking, I saw Sue close her eyes and all of a sudden her right arm began waving wildly in the air and she had the happiest, sweetest smile on her face! Michelle walked over to Sue, and acknowledged her. Sue started speaking the most delightful words in a language that I had never heard before. It sounded like pure joy! She was smiling and gesturing in the cutest manner ever, still with her eyes closed and still sitting in her seat. Michelle began to translate the language that Sue was speaking to the crowded church: She said that Mother Mary was coming through, with a message for us to take care of the children of the world. She said that all of the Angels in Heaven as well as Jesus and God were very happy that we were all there to witness this wonderful event. She spoke of the importance of releasing fear and of the power of surrender. She said that if you surrender, you can connect with this Language of Light. She said that the Dove of Peace, which is the Holy Spirit, was returning to the planet, and we were all helping to anchor it here. She went on for a few minutes, all the while smiling and gesturing in that adorable manner. It was truly one of the most remarkable things I had ever witnessed! When Sue was finished, Michelle called a brief intermission.

Michelle was staying with a member of the church, Shirley, and asked us if it would be possible for us to go to Shirley's home the following day so that she could discuss what had happened with us. The next morning Denis, Sue and I went to see Michelle at Shirley's home. The following is the transcription of the tape we made of Michelle's explanation:

June 6, 2000
Michelle's Translation of Sue's Channeling from the night before:

Sue, I am here to translate what you channeled last night. I remember what was said, because I am a conscious Channel. When you channeled the Language of Light, you opened up the pockets of energy for the class. You began talking about how there is so much fear in the people and on the planet and that with the armor and the boundaries that people hold on their bodies, they can't channel the Light. So, what you did energetically is help people release their armor when you said that.

You said that everybody is very bored; that they are looking for a greater sense of satisfaction and that they do not realize how much Joy there is in connecting with God. You were opening up pockets of Light and energies from within the heart. You were talking about how we have forgotten our connection and we have forgotten who we really are. You were helping people reconnect in their heart and you were setting up the energy with your Higher Self. You were channeling the Elohim, which is a group consciousness of Archangels and you were setting up the energy in the room.

You are going to be a very important Channel in channeling the Language of Light. It is a healing energy that is also an activator of Light. It doesn't matter if you don't always understand what you channel. Just know that it comes from the purity of the heart in order to set the Light up. The biggest thing that you are helping people to do is to release fear. Releasing bondage, is what you also talked about. You told them to release the chains from their wrists, and the bondage in their hearts, and to release, let go and surrender.

You spoke about the power of surrender through voice, and by being an example, that if you surrender you can connect with this language. You said that the Dove of Peace was ascending and coming through you, and the Dove of Peace is returning to the planet. The Dove of peace is the Holy Spirit, which is returning and you were bringing and anchoring that

27

into the planet. You were bringing it in and anchoring it into the class last night. Thank you very much for assisting and opening up the pockets of energy last night.

You need to continue to channel and even if you don't understand it, that's OK. You will find someone who can interpret for you. Someone will show up who can interpret it. If you speak the Language, ask someone to close their eyes and tune in with you, and they'll start to channel it in English to translate what is said because it is very powerful. Thank you, Sue!

After speaking with us and explaining what had taken place, we each had individual readings with Michelle. Denis and Charlene were initiated into the Language of Light, then we thanked Michelle and went on our way.

Later that afternoon, Sue and Charlene decided to try to see if Sue could channel again. We wondered if maybe Charlie would be able to translate...if Sue did not remember what she had said.

The following is our very first attempt at what has become the way we live:

3-
Our First Channeling...Love Yourself & Judgment

June 6, 2000 at 1:12 P.M. Charlene and Sue:
We are going to say a short prayer. First, we want to thank our Heavenly Father for bringing us together, to do whatever work we need to do. Thank you for the lovely gifts, the lovely day and the friendship. We ask Christ's assistance in every way. We invite our Angels and our Guides to join us, giving us information that is important to us today, as we tune into the Realm of the Angelic Field. We ask for protection from anything that is not of the Highest Vibration.

Sue spoke in the Language of Light for a brief period and began to Channel in English:

Thank you for listening to what you were told today. We want you to **record everything** that you are doing together. The tapes will be used for future reference. Put the recordings away. You can listen to them, but they will be used for a specific purpose, which will be **told to you** at a later date.

Did you **Love yourself** today? Have you given yourself a big pat on the back? You know **Love** is the greatest gift. Love is the greatest **gift** that our Heavenly Creator gives us. It is important that we spread Love and that we start with **ourselves**. We have to properly Love **ourselves** before we Love others. Begin each day with Loving yourself. **Practice** it. It is a thing to be practiced daily. You have **many** things that you will be doing here in the near future. Start with practicing Loving. Practice Loving **yourself**; you do not Love yourselves **enough**. In fact, you get very hung up on trivial things. Love is **important**. That is what is **most** important right here right now; the beauty of Love as it truly **radiates** from your very Soul. It radiates from your very **heart**. People around you **feel** it. They see it. They know it. **This** is how you will help share this.

You spend **so** much time worrying about things that are **so** unimportant. When you wake up in the morning, and it's raining, do you say "Oh how lovely that it is raining today! I

29

hear the glorious sound of the rain! I can practically watch as the grass turns green and the flowers soak up the beauty of the water!" As you know, there is **balance** in everything in this world. The sun comes out. It dries out the rain. Do you say "Oh how lovely! How wonderful to feel the rays of the sun on my skin and on my face!" As you know, **everything** is **balanced**. See the beauty in **all**. See the **beauty** in the rain, see the **beauty** in the sun, see the **beauty** in the balance. There is **balance** every-where. Work on **seeing** the balance. Figure out what is **not** balanced, and how to correct it. If you need our help, we are **always** here to help you. Very often you forget to ask yourselves that question. You simply get hung up on the fact that some-thing does not **appear** to be balanced, rather than saying "It is balanced. It is balanced by the **opposite** of what is happening." So, you forget to **see** the balance.

Look at yourselves in your own lives right now. Figure out what is balanced and what is **not** balanced, and how do you **correct** that? Again, we will help you with the balance factor. Sometimes you forget to even **look** at it because you get hung up on the **trivial** rather than taking a look at the obvious. Sometimes, something is very large and very big and very great, but you don't see it because you are hung up on the fact that an "i is not dotted". Go back to the simplistic. Look at what is **simple**, look at what is obvious, look at what is large. Stop digging for the trivial, and look at the very obvious. The **answers** to your biggest questions are in front of your face. We are **here** to help you see when you get blinded by the fog or blinded by the trees. We are here to **help** you, but you forget to **ask** for help. Remember to **ask**! All you have to do is **ask**, and **all** can be given to you!

So lesson #1 today: **Love Yourself**. Love yourself **completely**. Once you know how to do this, it automatically just falls right off of **you**, onto others. There is no trying. There is no effort. It is automatic! Now consider the greatness if **all** did this. If **all** woke up in the morning and

Loved themselves, and started the day out with a Love...how could the day go wrong? How **could** you come across anyone who would be cranky or angry? They **couldn't** be cranky or angry because they are full of **Love**! This begins with you.

We need to concentrate now, on another lesson. The lesson is **judgment**. You do not want anyone to pass judgment on **you**; this is not your nature. You do not pass judgment on **other** people; this is not your nature.... simply **Love**. However, **pay attention** to that which is around you and you will see things that weren't as obvious before. You will then have people that are placed in your path and you will help train them; train and teach. For **that** is what Jesus did; He trained and taught. He did **not** pass judgment. No, no, that is **not** what took place! Nor shall **you** pass judgment. You shall help train and teach. You will pay attention to those people around you and you will notice things that you can do to help them. Very **gingerly** will you go to them, and very **gingerly** will you share certain information.

You will be sharing information that they will either jump all over and ask for assistance, or they will turn their back. Do not take it **personally**. Do not be **upset** by it. For when someone turns their back on you, send them Light and Love. Again, please, please, **no** judgments. For you know **no** **judgments** are placed upon you, and you shall **not** learn to place judgments on others. You will be doing some very, very, very important work. There will be people who **will not** appreciate it. And there will be people who not only **appreciate** it; they will Love you so **dearly** for it because you will **help** them. Simply Love everyone. Just start your day with Loving **yourself** and let it flow over to **all**. And you will start the Loving Circle...and **that** is how it begins.

Soon there will be a **group** of you; you will start forming a group. This will happen soon, and you will be doing **prayer** services together. You will be doing **healing** services together. And those people will come across your path and you will understand and know that they **are** to be invited into your group. Your group... you two have started a **group**. Not to worry about those that **you** think **should** be included, but cannot come for one reason or another. What is meant to be **will** be, as you know, and those that **need** to be here will be here. You will be **surprised** sometimes, that those you would never **anticipate** asking, will end up being with you. So follow Spirit's signals, as you have done. You have done very well. Continue following Spirit's signals, Spirit's words. The initiatives you are given, you **take**. Continue to do so, for you **know** and you **understand** when Spirit is speaking. Do use your **discernment** in things that come in front of you, for Love attracts many different things and many **different** people and many **different** feelings. Be aware, be protective, but don't **ever** stop being Loving.

Settle, settle, settle. All happens, not on **your** time frame and it will happen as it is **supposed** to happen. People will be put in front of you as they are supposed to be. You may not **hurry** the clouds as they roll by. You may not **hurry** the sun as it shines it's lovely rays. You may not **hurry** the moon as it goes across the sky, nor may you **hurry** the growing of the grass and flowers. **This** is no different, My Dears, no different. For you see, **you** are both still **growing**... just as the flowers grow from a bulb, and they grow to a beautiful bloom. You are simply a bud. Wait until your bloom is full. Please, you cannot **rush** these things. Stop trying. Enjoy your days; enjoy what is put in front of you **each** day. Enjoy the fact that you get up and Love **yourselves**. And Love those that are in front of you, whether you are in a grocery store, whether you are in an office, whether you are in a meeting. It doesn't matter. For you see, Love does **not stop**, depending on where you are.

This is your goal. Your goal is to **start** your day in a Loving manner, and end the day **full** of Love. Not hurt, not anger, not despair... but Love. Love **grows**. It does not divide and get smaller. It grows, it **multiplies**. Let it multiply within **you**.

By **doing** this, your small bud will grow into a glorious blooming flower. Your flower **will stay** glorious and blooming the rest of your lives. And through this beautiful blooming flower that you will be, you will attract many, for you are glorious and beautiful. Your **aura** will attract many. Be aware; don't be frightened just be aware, for there is **no** fear in God's World, just be aware. And remember that those that are **not** of your like, send them Love, send them Light and **send them away**.

Do not **get hung up** with the wrong entities. Use your **discernment**. Again, Love **does** conquer all. Use your Love, use your discernment, use your Light. This is the time that you will find that you **might** try to pass judgment. Please don't. We will help you. We will help you remember the balance that we discussed. Remember that there is **balance** in the world. Very often, something that is darker than the beautiful Light that you are, is there to **teach** you something. Maybe what it is there to teach you is **judgment**... **not** to pass judgment. Remember...just send Light and Love. Light and Love; those are what you need to remember those two items; **Light and Love**. And when you find yourself uncomfortable, call us, for we are **always** here. Remember to **ask** for any help whenever you feel a need. If you feel over your head, if you feel buried, **call** us. We are **here**. We will always, always be here. We are **always** here for you, and we help at all times, but you must remember to **ask**. In the meantime, will you please Love and **enjoy**? Enjoy every day. Enjoy the beauty of every day, and remember the beauty of every day. See the **positive**, see the happy, see the good. Concentrate on all the good.

Yes, there are so many dark things in your world right now. They can be conquered with Love. Can **you** do it alone? No, probably not, but you can **start**. Start by Loving **all** that are put in front of you. Remember everyone who crosses your path and comes onto your path, is there for a **reason**. Is it to **teach**, or is it to **learn**? Remember, **everyone** has something to teach, and **everyone** has something to learn. And you **take turns** with one another. You take turns learning, and you take turns teaching. So remember those items...they are very important. There is never a **mistake**. There is **never** a **coincidence**. Everything happens for **a reason**. If you are unsure of that reason, **ask** us and we will tell you. Just **ask** us. It is not difficult.

You will find there are some people who are placed in your path who will ask you some interesting questions. Never be afraid of the **truth**, for the **truth is healing** and the **truth frees your Soul**. Don't forget to be thankful. Remember to say "**Thank you**" to your Heavenly Creator who has given you more gifts than you are aware of yet, but will be unfolded in the next two years. Much will be unfolded, so much! You are not **capable** yet, as a bud, but you **will** be capable as a full, blooming flower, to understand and comprehend all that is in front of you. Not to be fearful but to be excited; to be grateful and **excited** for you have much excitement in front of you. And it will be **fun**, and you will **enjoy** it! And so you have much to look forward to. You are learning and you are growing, and you're not finished...and you'll **never** be finished. You need to get some more understanding, some more **basics**, and some more **teaching** under your belt, and then you will be ready. And it will all **fall into place**, not to worry, not to fear.

Never worry about an Earthly job, for **that** will all fall into place, too. Do what you **Love**. Do what you **Love**...the money **will** come. For Our Heavenly Creator takes care of the birds in the sky...have you seen any birds in your back yard and you say, "Oh Heavens! That poor bird hasn't **eaten** in days." I don't think you've ever said that. Therefore, do you think Our Creator would take care of **you** in a lesser manner? I think not! So **not** to worry! Just have faith, believe and have fun and Love! For every winter the tree loses his leaves and he goes to sleep, and in the spring he blossoms once again with beautiful colors of green until he is full bloom once again. He is given the correct water, he is given the correct minerals from Mother Earth and he lives a beautiful life for many years. He is taken care of. You, My Dear, are **far** more glorious and important and loved than the tree!

The time has come and the time is soon that this will be revealed, that **all** will be revealed as to what it **is** that the two of you are doing. Don't have fear, have faith. Freedom...you will have **freedom** with this knowledge coming out. You will feel much **happier** and all will be well. You will be free as a butterfly, for like the butterfly, **you** are coming out of your cocoon. You are an **attractive** caterpillar. You will be a **beautiful** butterfly! But you are an **eternal** butterfly for you will never die...for your sweet Spirits will live forever.

That is what **you know** and that is what you will teach. Not **everyone** is as aware as you that there is **no death**. That will be one of your very, very **important** teachings. **Many** are **unaware** that there **is no death**. They believe that when their body dies, they **are** no longer. They don't **understand** the power of God. You are going **beyond** the boundaries of the churches on this Earth. You are **not** held back by walls. You are **not** held back by rules, for there **are** no rules. There is **one law** of nature; there **are** no rules. God puts **no limits** on you what-so- ever, you have **no** limits! Remember you have **no** limits. And in your teachings you will teach others that they have **no** limits.

How do you explain the **Bible**? The Bible is an important book. There are many, many good things that are written in the Bible. The men who have written the Bible...did you hear me? The **MEN** that have written the Bible... many were inspired by **God**! They were inspired deeply, and they wrote what they **believed** they heard. You must understand; even with **us** there is a **barrier**. The barrier is **language**, for it is very, very hard for us, sometimes to communicate with you; which is why, at times, you **hear** what you hear. You see with your **mind,** rather than your eyes, what we want you to see.

And you speak as you **think you hear** what we say to you. However, there is a **language barrier**. We **try** very hard to connect and communicate properly. We **feel** we do a very good job, but it is **possible** that things get misinterpreted sometimes. It is sometimes **hard** to properly communicate. Imagine...so imagine...as these men are interpreting the Words of God...and it has **then** been translated to **how** many languages? Do you think, perhaps, some of it got **confused**? Do you think, perhaps, some men have their **own** agenda and occasionally **that agenda** gets intercepted along with the message given? Yes, this happens. Yes... it happens frequently. Yes, it even happens today. So bear in mind, much of what is in the Bible is **wonderful,** and much is **totally incorrect**. You must use your **discernment** when you read anything written by anyone. Feel it with your **heart**, for your heart **always** knows the **truth**.

You are both dealing with **many** people who have a set agenda. You will not be reinventing the wheel. You will use your discernment, in the things you share and how you share it. You will learn by **doing**. You will simply begin to **do** it. As long as you follow your heart, you **cannot** make a mistake, you **cannot** make an error, you **cannot** feel you have done something incorrect. This will not happen, for there are **no** errors, there are **no** mistakes, and there are **no** coincidences. Keep it in mind and **remember** that. For a time will come when you will feel" Oh my goodness, I have made a dreadful mistake." No, no, no you have not made **any** mistakes. You will feel at times, you have given **too much** information. No, no, no you have **not**, for people will digest that which they can. Just as a baby is given formula...if you, by accident, give the baby a steak, he will spit it out. For he **cannot** chew and digest it. You are **not** to worry about giving **too much** information. It simply will be **spit out** and it will not be digested.

It is now time to end. It is now time to continue on with your daily routines. Have a marvelous, wonderful day. You are

surrounded by Love and Light. You will get together as **often** as you can, and you will **record** each series, each session, completely. You will **date and document**, and put the **time of day** on it, also. When you first begin your classes, we would also like you to record that. You will be **told**. You will be **told** what to do and when to do it. You have been very **good** at listening... continue. We **thank** you, we Love you. You will begin spreading the Light and Love and it will start soon. Continue to **grow**, continue to blossom. Continue to give yourself plenty of water, for just as the flower needs water, so do you. And with that I say to you, "I leave you in Love".

Thank you. Thank you.

-4-
The Language of Light

June 16, 2000, 3:15 P.M. Charlene and Sue:
Prayer of Protection and The Language of Light...

You are here together, and it is so **nice** to see you back together. We've been waiting for you both, as it is **lesson time** and it is good to see you. And it is good to see your happy faces and your happy hearts. For with **joy** you can learn much and you can learn it much **happier** and much **faster**! **Keep** joy in your hearts. And as we begin today, I am beginning with a message and a lesson plan for you.

First, we will be discussing the **Language of Light** itself...the need for it, the purpose of it, what it is, and why you are doing it. Do you know it is the **Universal Language**? You stumble over your **words** sometimes. With the Language of Light, you don't stumble. Do you know why? Because, you see, language is an **intellectual** communication skill. The Language of Light is not. The Language of Light is an **Angelic Language** that comes from your **heart**, not your head. Other languages on your planet, in your dimension, come from your **head**, not your heart. Do you see the difference? For you will now be learning and teaching and getting a great skill, using your **heart**, instead of your head. You have come this far in your life by using your **head** instead of your heart. You are now going to **reverse** that process. You will let your **heart** be the leader.

With the **heart** as the leader, you will then speak the Language of Light, and you **cannot** stumble, you **cannot** make a mistake, you **cannot** use incorrect words and there can be no miscommunication... which is **why** it is so good. For when we use your language **we** stumble over words, but we do not with the Language of Light. The Language of Light is the **language of the heart**. It is the Universal Language. It is understood by **all**, for there is **no** language barrier. It is the

heart speaking. It is the heart, and you are **heart people**, heart entities; you are **Light Entities**. And now, lead with the **heart** and not the head. Lead with the **heart** and not the brain, for your heart is really where the **center** of life is.

The Language of Light is **important**. It is time, now, that you start teaching it. How do you begin? You begin by **speaking** it. By speaking it, you will then **trigger** the information and the forces within each heart that need to be triggered. Each person sounds **different**, just as each voice is different; just as each voice in **your** reality is different. It is the same with the Language of Light, for each **heart** is different. There are no two hearts that are identical. There are no two Souls that are really identical. So, what **is** there to compare oneself to another? You are your **own** self, you are your **own** person; you are your **own** individual self. **You cannot do this wrong**!

You will not need to solicit people to come to you, they just **will**. As things happen, as things open up in your life, it will simply happen. There will be **no** solicitation needed. You will be together in **different** groups, with different people. As you meditate together, as you channel together, this will simply happen. And then you will speak the Language of Light together. The two of you need to do this **together**, for you will have information that each of you, **individually**, will understand; which is **why** you need to do it together.

Together, you will then form a **group** and you will then be teaching classes, initiating **other** people into the Language of Light. It is important, as it changes the **vibration**. The vibration is changed drastically, and it will continue. It will continue at a very great speed, and you will notice this and you will **know** this because things will change in your own lives. Things will change; your needs will change, your wants will change, and the things that you need to do will change. The things that are **unimportant** will change, and the **importance** of things will change. Change is **good**. You are transforming. You are out of your cocoon; not quite...almost, and you are breaking into your butterfly. With transformation is **change**, and change is good. You say, "Ah yes, I want **change**, but don't change **me**! Ah yes, I want **change**, but don't let it effect **me**!" That is not true... you are **very** affected, and you will **continue** to be affected. You will be affecting others with the changes that **you** are making **within** yourselves.

Now we shall have you end your session today, knowing that we want you, **both together**, to practice the Language of Light. You will be practicing it together. Sue, you are to help Charlie, with initiating the Language of Light to others. Again, Charlie, there are **no** errors. Your heart is so, so **pure**. And you need to increase your vibration, which will happen with the Language of Light. We will speed up your vibration. It is helpful for you...for your **growth**. Nothing to fear; nothing is wrong, nothing **can** be done wrong. There **is** no wrong; there is **no** wrong. Stop using your brain, stop using your head and use your **heart**.

And with this, we will say "Good-bye", no, we will say "**Enjoy!**" and we will talk soon. We are here to talk whenever you are wanting to talk, and don't forget, if you choose, pick up a pencil and **write** down things, as you did today, or **record**. It is **easier** to correct when you write. When you record, we will correct it as we have to. Now, we will say "Good-bye" for the moment, as you continue your lessons alone...know you are not alone. We are **here**, but now your lessons are with **each other**. And I tell you, you are protected and you are very, very on the right path. You are very, very **intuitive** as to what you are to do. Now you just need to continue doing it. We Love you. Have a good rest of the afternoon.

Thank you. Thank you.

June 20, 2000... Tuesday morning, in the car...Sue alone.

Stop worrying about where you **are**. You are right where you **should** be. You are in the center, in the middle of your path; the path that you are **supposed** to be on. What you must remember is that not **everyone** is on the same path. They are on the path that **they** are supposed to be on. Therefore, you must stop worrying about where someone else is on his path. Sometimes the very **best** example is a silent one. You **cannot** be pushy. You cannot **push** anyone into the path of Spirit, or into the path that **you** think they should be on, for it is not your choice. It is **not** about you. You are simply the **conduit** and you are the **example**. You are the gentle person, not the **pushy** one, not the **loud** one. Instead of answering questions that are not asked, wait until they are **asked** of you. Sometimes you try to assume what the questions are, and answer them **before** they are asked.

Please don't do that, be silent and listen, for listening is a true, true skill, and one that you do well at. So, **listen** carefully before you talk. As language does get in the way as it passes through dimension to dimension, it truly **does** get in the way when it is on the same dimension! So **try** to be silent!

Now, let's **not worry** what tomorrow brings, let's enjoy today. Enjoy each day to it's fullest, for there is much joy in this world, and you need to **see** it, and you need to **feel** it, and you need to **enjoy** it. Why don't you take a moment, now, and simply enjoy! Remember to see your day with the Love of your **heart**, and remember that you are shining the Light of God. You have **much** Love, you have **much** happiness, and you have **much** help. So, be patient, My Dear, and continue your daily routine, in the loving way that you are intended. Have a lovely day.

Thank you. Thank you.

5-
Watch Out for Energy-grabbers! & Listen!

Wednesday, July 5, 2000 6:06 P.M. Charlie and Sue
Prayer and The Language of Light...

Ah, My Children, it is so **good** to see you! You **worry** so about your energy, and yet, you **waste** it. Why do you do that? You do not wait to replenish. You must take **care** of yourself and you must take care of your energy levels. How? Sleep properly; spend your time with the right, proper people. Do not **waste** your time with people who are **energy-grabbers**. Yes, you are ready for change. You think that everything should be on **your** time limit, too, but it is not. For there are other things that need to take place, and you must always be **aware** and be wise about that. For, there are other people that are to enter on your path, that you will meet, that will be a great part of your lives, and maybe **they** are not quite ready to meet **you**. So please, My Dears, be **patient**, for there is much that will happen. You are **such** impatient children!

I hear you speak as though you think that you will **not** be taken care of. I don't believe you **really** believe that, for you know you shall. For you both have **great** faith and yet, it is not happening on the time frame that you **want** it to happen and so, therefore, something's wrong! But no, nothing is wrong. Be **patient**, My Dears, for **patience** is one of those things that you are learning this lifetime. And you must keep in mind that it is **not** just the two of you. There is **more** involved than that, and not **everyone** is ready to gather, yet. Please be aware and be wise about that, and you will **recognize** those people as they enter into your lives, and you will recognize those that will not **stay**.

Take **care** of yourselves and take care of each other. For, yes, you wear yourselves thin. And you go to a place that you **think** gives you more energy, when in fact you sometimes use your energy unwisely. Stay in a place where you are continuously being **regenerated**, and your energy is not drained.

Yes, Sue, your energy is being **drained** at work, and, yes, it is almost **over**, it's true. Be patient, My Dear, for it will happen in the right way. **Allow** it to be. You were given great advice today, and the advice you were given is, " There **is** no decision to make," and that is true. Information comes to you in different ways. It comes to you with private, quiet meditation, it comes to you when you are together, and it comes to you by outside sources. What **that** means is, you must pay **attention** and you must **listen**. Listen to **all**, for you will hear right and you will hear wrong, and you will **learn** by both. Be gentle, and just be Loving. If you are gentle and Loving, no wrong **can** be done.

You are both so worried about idle time, and yet, there is **no** such thing as idle time. You are just so familiar with **fast** pace. Because we want to slow you down so that you will **take** the time to concentrate, to meditate, to think, to take care of yourselves, you become impatient for **you** want it to go **faster**, for that is what you are **familiar** with. You are familiar with the fast pace. Slow yourself **down** so your energy will stay regenerating and you will not deplete, as you tend to deplete yourselves. Try very hard **not** to deplete yourselves. Take **care** of yourselves; rest, meditate. You will get **much** answered when you ask the questions; you just forget to **ask**.

When you are outside, (as seems to be your **preference** these days), and you choose to sit and meditate in the open woods, it is **so** lovely there. You find **such** beauty there, do not forget; just as you protect **your** energy from anyone **taking** it from you, the trees and the Earth are happy to **share**. You have such a positive energy, as do they. You can ask their permission and they will **help** you regenerate your energy. It is a very, very **fine** place to sit and meditate. It is a **fine** place to rejuvenate, and it is a **wise** choice. For then you not only

43

will regenerate **your** energy, you will gather the positive fine energy **around** you and it will help you in your meditation. It will help you stay **stronger** and more alive, and it will help you to hear more clearly, and it will help you to listen with finer ears, for your **senses** will be **sharpened**.

Now, if I were to give you a lesson today, the lesson would be "**Listen**. Simply **listen**." It is time, right now, that you **speak less** and **listen more**. You will gather much information by doing so. Some of it, you will learn, is coming from a place that you do **not** want to be. That is OK, for you see, **balance** is in all of our Universe, all of our world, and it crosses through **all** of our dimensions.

So, for you to hear all of the **positive** and wonderful, you must hear and learn a little bit about the **darkness**, and that makes the Light much **brighter**. But you will use your fine intuition and your fine discernment. That is where you will learn **where** to place your energy, your trust, and your loyalties. **That** is where you will learn your many friendships and relationships. You will find that the opposites will come into reality; that which you **thought** was good will be bad. That which you **thought** was sweet will be sour. That which you **thought** was kind, will be mean. So just simply, pay attention and pass **no judgment**, and don't form an opinion before you have the facts; gather the **facts**.

Now it is time for you to rest, so have a wonderful, quiet, quiet evening. Take **care** of yourselves, rejuvenate, meditate, pray. Remember, **you must ask** questions **before we can** give an answer. And you must **ask** for your pleasures before we **can** give them to you. And now, may Love be with you, peace be your life forever, and Love will continue to **surround** you, as does the Light of God. We Love you. As the Star of God is **upon** you and it shall remain for the rest of your lives on this planet. And the Guides will be with you, at your sides at **all** times and you shall **never** be alone. You, My Dears, are protected. The Light of God is **upon** you and it shall remain

44

there. Continue to **ask** for the gifts, as they will be bestowed upon you as you are ready. Continue your prayers, your meditations, your Love and your Light. Keep it shining, keep it glowing! We shall be with you forever!

Thank You. Thank you.

6

Back to the Basics...LOVE

July 12, 2000, 11:05 A.M. Denis, Charlie and Sue

Denis, Charlie and I are together, and we call in our Guides, our Angels, and our Spirits, to ask for any information that we are needing today and any lessons that we are to learn today. We ask God to be with us, and for our best and highest good. We ask all of the Angels of the Highest Realm; Raphael, specifically, to help us and guide us as we ask for your assistance in our learning process. We thank you. I will begin by speaking the Language of Light, and ask for assistance and guidance.

Sue spoke the Language of Light and then began speaking in English:

Ah, **welcome** My Children, and so it begins...you are now **three**. You have **much** to listen to, and much to learn today. We will, again, begin in very simplistic ways. In many ways, we will go back to **basics**, for it **is** basics that have the most learning and teaching for you. Sometimes you try to get too **deep and involved** in something that is very **simple**. It is **very** simple, and truly, the things that you need to learn are very, very simple, and if you apply the simplistic **elements**, you are there.

As we've talked about before, we are going back into the heart, for the **heart** is the **center**. This is where your **learning** and your **emotions** are...with the Love in your heart, and with Love being the **number one lesson** for you (all you really need is Love). You Love with your whole heart, and **through** your Love, you learn. With the Love that you put out into the Universe....

Sue: I'm sorry, but it feels like there is something here...a block...or something here!

Charlie prays: Please remove any blockage and please protect us from anything dark or negative that is possibly trying to interfere. Please remove anything that might be interfering with this communication. It is our intention and our desire to communicate with the Holy Spirit, and with the highest vibration. Please remove anything that may be blocking this or interfering with it at this time.

Sue-: And so, we will envision, at this time, the Light of God, coming down from Heaven, encircling the three of us, protecting us with the Light and with the Violet Flame. We will have a very light and open communication with the Light of God.

Ah, **very** good! As the lesson has been **learned**! For you **recognized** something that you did not feel **comfortable** with and you took care of it! Lesson well taken! Lesson well done! And you will **continue** to do this by using the **discernment** within your heart as you come across not just people, but Spirits. You will have a feeling when it is best to **leave** a room, when it is time to go somewhere else, when it is time to **exit** from a place you are... because it doesn't **feel** right. You can **always** put up your protection. **Remember** to do so, for sometimes you forget. I do not want to frighten you, but there are **many** entities that do not want you to succeed at what you are doing. We will **always** be here to protect and help. And you **heard** that whisper in your ear, and you **cleared** what needed to be cleared. Continue to **do** that when you are alone and when you are together. You all **recognized** this, and it will be a **continuous** effort for you to do. Do not let **anyone** interfere with all the positive work that you are doing now and will continue to do. For...you are Creators.

All **three** of you are Creators, for you have **been** created by our Creator in His own image. You are also **here** to create, and you do. Never lose your **confidence** in your ability, for you can do **anything** you can imagine! If you can imagine it, you can **do** it. Always remember that **as** you **do**... you are **doing** it for the best and the highest good. Do not get wrapped up in the world. Do not get wrapped up in the **things** that are in the world, for **things** are not what are important to you. Gifts are important to you, and you will be getting **many** gifts from God as you continue, as you learn, as you educate, as you progress.

You have to **practice**... to progress. **Practice** the Language of Light. Practice with each other. **Clarify** what has been told, with each other. As you let the Love in **your heart** radiate to **all**, this is the example. You must understand, there is no **effort** here. It is simply by **being** and **doing**. Just **be** the Creators that you are, radiating the Love of God in your heart, and all will **see** and **feel**. They will **feel** that Love, that exuberance, that is coming from you. In turn **you** will become very sensitive to **others**. And that is where we say, use your discernment, for **not all** will radiate the Love that you radiate. You will become more and more **uncomfortable** with those that radiate something **other** than Love. You, actually, have **always** been uncomfortable.

You have come a very long way, but you still have quite a road in front of you. It is a **smooth** road, and you each have your **own**. We have cleared all the rocks away, and there are lovely flowers along your path...so this is a lovely, easy walk in the park. Do not complicate it. You can only **complicate** it by going off your path, so stay on your path. It is a very, very sweet, comfortable, loving walk. Stay **focused**. If you stay **focused** you will have no problem.

When we say to you, "Do not get wrapped up in the world", we mean, do not get wrapped up, not just in **things**, but in small **incidences** that turn you inside out! They are unimportant! We have discussed this. Work? Do you think that is really what you are put here to **do**? To do what...type a deed? I don't think so. That is **not** your purpose. Your purpose, very often, is being put in a specific job not because of the job itself, but because of the **people** you are to meet and to influence. You will influence them; they will influence you. That is why you are, all three, in sales. It is not Real Estate you are selling. You are really selling nothing. You are really **teaching**, and you are, really, **learning**. Everyone who is put in front of you is teaching **you** something, or you are teaching **them**. You are either the teacher or the student.

Remember **which** hat you have on, for sometimes you need to be quiet and **listen**. Listen to whatever the lesson is, rather than trying to **teach** what you **think** you are here to teach. Sometimes **you** are here to listen. Listening is as great a thing as teaching. Remember **you** are also here to **learn**, so take in what you need to take in. **Listen** when it is time to listen. **Leave** when it is time to leave. And **Love** at **all** times. Know that the only thing that you need to **do** is to Love with your whole heart. That is all! If you Love with your whole heart, you can do **nothing** wrong. There truly is **no** wrong in this world. For something **you** might recognize as wrong, might be someone else's lesson...and it might be **your** lesson.

Do not pass **judgment**. Never pass judgment! Trust me, you never know the **whole** situation. You never know the **whole** picture, unless it is revolved around **you**...then you might know the whole picture. That is why we say **never** pass judgment on someone else. For you **might** form an opinion without knowing all of the facts, and that is not fair. So pride yourself on **not** doing that. It is very **important**. It is one of the most **important** lessons for you to learn. This also means, do not pass judgment on the **churches** that are here on this planet. For through those churches, **other** people are learning and other people are teaching. It is not about **you**, that is why you are not in the center of it. If you speak with the Love of God in your voice, and the Love in your heart, you will say nothing wrong...even about churches.

Now, you **each** are going to have homework. You will each spend time by yourselves. You will each search your own hearts for **any pain** that is there, that **you** have caused, or that has been caused **to** you, and you will remedy any situation to purify your own hearts. Have you **hurt** someone? Have you **been** hurt? Identify it in a Loving way. Write it down. If you need to speak words to someone, **do** so. You will **know** what you need to do to rectify the situation, but you need to **do** it. **Purify** yourselves. For how can you **have** a full, pure, Loving heart if that is not what you **feel** in your heart? So **take care** of anything that needs to be taken away. If you **need** to be prayed over, pray over each other. Release **anything** that should not be there, and purify yourselves.

And **this** will be something you will do again. You will **do** it to each other and you will do it to **other** people as they come in to your circle...helping to **release** anything that is a blockage. For blockages do **not** help you...they will harm you. You need to **clear** all blockages to have a straight line to Heaven; straight-open communication. You will **recognize** other people who will come in your path who have blockages. Use discernment in what you say to those people, for sometimes **they** need to recognize things before **you** can recognize it for them. It is not **your** job. You will **know** when it **is** your job. You will be **asked** for help. For, you cannot **force** the Love of God on a person. You cannot **force** the Healing Power of God on a person. You cannot **force** Love on a person. You have to wait.

It is no different from the Angelic realm that is just **waiting to be asked** to help you. You are in that position now, where **you** must wait to be **asked**. It is not a **forceful** job you have. Just as we said, you will be radiating the Love. And **through** that you will attract people who need that Love. It is not a **forceful** thing that you do. It is a Loving, Loving. Be **yourself**, that's all. There is no **job** here; it is just being who you **are**. And you will be **perfecting** who you are and you will be helping each other do so.

As you grow, more gifts **will** be bestowed upon you, but like a child, you need to just take a **little** at a time. Take your baby steps, take your long walks, then take your runs...but not yet. It will all be shown to you as it is **time** and you will progress as you have learned. You will learn one thing at a time, you will **perfect** it and you will move on. You have to **practice**. You have to practice radiating Love to **all**. You have to practice. Look at the children. Watch the children. Watch the **purity** of the child, having fun and laughing and joy. That is what you are; Joy! Love! Purity! See everything through the eyes of God. You are **well** taken care of. You are very Loved.

You have a lot of work to do. It will **not** be work, it will be fun, but you have a **lot** to accomplish, and you shall. You have the will, you have the way, and now you are **learning**. Do not **forget** to call on your Angels and your Spirit Guides, for you have much help available to you. You do not even tap **into** all the help you have available. You **think** you are here by yourself... you are **not** here by yourself. You have many, many, many Angels that are just **waiting** to help and guide you, and whispering to you! That's when we tell you to **listen**. Please listen more. You have many Guides, with **many** ways of helping you. Just ask, just ASK and then follow your hearts...because your hearts do not lie.

When you have doubt, **write** it out! When you have questions, say the questions out loud, or write them down. You **will** get answers. You will get them in your **dreams**, you will get them through **meditation** and you will get them by doing what we **are** doing right now. You have to **put** it in the Universe, and you will ALWAYS have an answer. Now, I am not saying you will have the answer you **want**, I am saying you will have an **answer**. Sometimes when you have a question, you do not **clarify** yourself, and **we** do not understand what you are asking. Sometimes **you** do not understand what you are asking. Sometimes, you are not **ready** for the answers... so do not be **frustrated** if you do not hear **exactly** what you are expecting.

Sometimes, it is absolutely a matter of maturity, and you are simply not **ready** yet. So please have faith that everything will be answered in the time that it **should** be answered and everything will be answered properly. Also, look for answers in **all** ways, for sometimes they will come from people you do not **expect** or from **ways** that you do not expect; simple things, such as reading a book. Take a look at what is in **front** of you, for you will get answers in **different** ways. It is not **always** through a prayer. It is not **always** by asking a question to a friend and having her answer it. You can get your questions answered in different ways.

Never stop saying your prayers! Every **word** is heard. Every **tear** is felt. Every **fear** is felt. Every **wish** is heard, and if it is for your best and highest good it will be granted...but it will not be on **your** time frame. You are not **ready** for what you **think** you are ready for, and when you **are** ready it will occur. Everything is already done. Your **paths** are wide open. All you have to **do** is walk down them, and everything will happen as it should. Do not get impatient, for **that** is not a part of Love. When you have a doubt, ask yourself "Is **this** Love? Is **this** generated from Love?" If it is not, **ask for help** and it will be gone. You **can** discard it on your own, or **ask for the help** that is there, and it will be discarded. Remember there is balance in this world, so not **all** is Love, but **you are Love**.

Love attracts two things. Love will attract those that need help in attaining the Love. They will want to be shone **how** to feel and **be** Love. And there will be those who **hate** Love. And **that** is the balance. You know it as Lightness and Darkness. So, as we protect you...as you have been protected always but now **more** so, **remember** to call on your strength, your Angels, your Guides, and Your Creator. For you have **all** at your feet. Just **ask**. And you will be **teaching** the Love of God by **being** the Love of God. You see...you will be teaching by **being**. You have already received the greatest gift of all, and **that** is the gift of Love...for **you** are pure Love.

What you need to do now, is take **away** the layers that you have built up to **protect** the heart and the Love in the heart. Not only have you thought you were protecting it, but you have **prevented** it from **radiating out**. Because you have built these walls, and these walls you have cemented in, and **now** they need to be torn down. So you need to **visualize** the mountain; the mountain that will come **tumbling** down to **free** the Heart of Love.

This is your **own** meditation. This is a meditation that you will do, each on your own:

You will visualize the mountain. The mountain is cement; it is rocks. You will take each rock away from the mountain as you discard the pain that you have used to build up the wall around the heart, preventing the Love from radiating out. Do it as often as you need to, until the mountain is gone! And the mountain will be gone!

This is a meditation you will teach **others** also to help break away the walls that you, **yourself** have put up. And you have **help** if you need it. You have **much** help. You have **Spiritual** help, you have **Angelic** help, you have your **Guides** and you have **physical** help, for you will help each other. And once you take the pain out of the **heart**, you take the pain out of the **body** and you take the pain out of the **mind** and it becomes pure. And the third eye will be **opened**. And you will visualize and you will see, with your eyes **and** with your heart, the many Angels that surround you and guide you and Love you. For you have **more** help than you even know! There are **armies** waiting to help you. If there were a fight to fight, it is not **your** fight, for you have an **army** that will take care of it for you. So, not to **worry** and not to fear.

When your comfort-zone becomes **pain**, it is hard to **release**, for you **know not** what it **is** to have pure Love. For you, alone, have not **allowed** it. It was **there** for you to have, but it was **not** allowed, because you associated that with additional pain and you could **not take** more. Instead of the opposite, which was true... through Love, you **release** pain. We talked about opposites. We talked about reverses; that what you think with your **brain** is not true. The **opposite** of that is true, or the **reverse** of that is true. That is why you need to think with your **heart**. Let your **heart** now be your lead, not your brain...for your heart **knows** truth. Your brain does not. Your **heart** knows truth. Your heart knows **real** Love, your brain does not...but your **heart** does!

It is time now for you to get back to your daily routines. Remember what we have said. We have given you some **work** to do on yourselves. Take **care** of yourselves, for you have great **power** and you are very, very **needed** on this Earth right now. Take care of **yourselves**. Take care of each other, but do **your** homework. Release what **needs** to be released from yourselves, and visualize your beautiful path that is in front of you. You **are** on the right path. You keep **doubting** yourselves, but you **are** on the path you are to be on. Remember, you each have your **own** path and **different** lessons that you will each learn. Share with each other. And now have a wonderful, Loving day. **Know** we are with you. Know that we will Love you throughout the rest of Eternity! God is **smiling** upon you, Loving you. You will **never** be short of Love, never! And you have all the help, for God has given you **everything**. It is at your fingertips, you just need to **ask**. Learn happily along the way, for there is still much to **learn**, and there is much to **teach** and you will be doing both. With that we say, have a lovely, Loving day, and we Love you.

Thank you, thank you.

7

Dreams, Visions and Protecting Yourself

August 1, 2000 at 12:07 P.M. Charlie and Sue
Prayer for protection and the Language of Light spoken.

Now you know the importance of feeling good and good health. Good health is **essential** in getting proper information and understanding the information you receive. Feeling good is **essential**, for your energy must be at its highest level. **Keep** your energy high by doing the proper things that keep your **body** in good shape and your **mind** in good shape. By saying this to you, we mean taking **care** of yourselves, getting the proper nutrition, not drinking too much alcohol. Alcohol and drugs will dull your senses and you **want** your senses to be "in-tuned" at **all** times. With your "in-tuned" senses, you will have the ability to **decipher** what you **need** to decipher with everything that is going to be put in front of you. Information will be given to you in many different ways and different forms.

Your **dreams** are essential. Write them down. It is important that you take a look at them for they have **much** information for you. Yes, we have told you over and over and over, that you will be given bits, as you are ready; bits of food as you are ready. The **food** you are given to digest, is the **information** you will use to grow. Just as food helps a body grow, information helps your Spirit and your mind grow. And so, we **relate** it to you through the use of food in your dreams. You are in a **hurry** to eat too much. You cannot **do** that. You cannot consume that much at one time. Just as when you give a baby a steak, they cannot **digest** it. We are giving you the amounts **you** can take and tolerate and digest. It is not on **your** time schedule, and it **never** will be on your time schedule. What we ask of you is **patience**, **perseverance**, and to **pay attention**. For paying attention is very important at this time for your growth. There are many people and many instances, and many things, and many circumstances that are going to be put in front of you. You've used **good** judgment, and you are trying **so** hard not to place judgment. Different things we are talking about here, all very, very important. For you know that **everyone** that is put in your path is an important **growth-instrument**. As we have said before, sometimes you are the teacher, sometimes you are the student, and sometimes you need to pay attention to **which** it is you are. Do not pass judgment on people around you, for they are growing at their **own** pace. Everyone will grow at their **own** speed. Everyone has their own path to walk down. Please stop putting everyone on **your** path, for they do not belong there. You each have your **own** path. They may be parallel, they may be close, and there will be jogs in the road where you are **not close** at all. You must stay on your own path for you all have your own **specific** growth area.

Let everything be **seen** with the eyes of Love, and **think** about what is being said to you. **Think** about what is being shown to you. **Think** about what you are to **learn** from any situation or person. For **that** is what the **goal** is now, to learn the lessons gently. You are learning the lessons gently, and you are both listening very well. Continue meditating, together and apart. Just because you're not together physically, does not mean you can't do this at all times. Do this whenever possible. You can still **meditate** separately, and you can still **record** separately. And, when you can get together, get together. For the power of two **is** greater than the power of one. You have many Angels and Spirit Guides around you at all times. **Listen** to what they have to say. It's **easier** to listen when you are in a meditative state, but sometimes when you are in the car and you daydream, **think** about what is being said to you and what is passing through your mind. For very **often** you are given **messages**. As we said, you are given messages in many, many ways, for you both have a different accuracy in receiving information. Pay attention to **all**, and when possible, write it down or record it. If you are speaking out loud, please **record.** If you are dreaming and you wake up, please try to write down that which is coming to your mind. For it **will** be relevant later if it is not relevant today.

Soon you will be having **visions**. These visions are very **important**. Pay attention. The Angels surround you; all Angels... of every realm of every level. They are there for your constant assistance, Loving and helping. You have so much help and you can't **possibly** get off track because everybody is there keeping you on track! And when you start roaming a bit, you are, literally, **pushed** to the right or **pushed** to the left to stay in the middle of your road. That is where you will stay without any effort, so **stop** your worries. Stop your fear, for fear is **not** a part of God's Kingdom and **you are** a part of God's Kingdom. Yes, you have a job, and you have **help**, and you are going to do a fabulous, fabulous job in the name of God.

It is an important time right now to take **care** of yourselves very carefully, energetically. You **do** need sunshine. There is much talk about the ozone, but sunshine is good! You are taken care of. You have sunshine in your heart. It's OK to go outside. Stay **away** from any **negative** energy that you can. Do not **let** it zap you, as it does happen without your knowledge. So **protect** yourselves as you go outside. Cover yourselves with White Light or the Purple Flame. Allow yourselves to be **in** the public, but do take **care** of yourself. It is very, very **important** right now, for your energy is **sacred** and everyone will want it. Learn, now, to protect yourself, for later it will get **harder** for you. Light Energy attracts ALL. **Send that away**, which is **not** of Light. Send it away with Love...into the Light. Not **your** Light...send it to the Light of God, and **away** from **your** energy force. You will get to a point where you will not have to send it away as **quickly** and you will be able to **embrace** it and Love it and send it away with Love and Light...but you are not there yet. You see, that is one of the **goals**. Imagine what you will attract if you have the capability of **doing** that, for it is the Love of Jesus. It is **Jesus** that is sending you the energy and the knowledge that

He had, while He walked on Earth, to do what He did. Just say "Thank you."

You are oh so silly! Sometimes you think you are all by yourself...you have no idea the **crowd** that is around you! Not only are you **never** alone, but you have so **much** Love and energy; Angelic Love, the Elohim, and the Love of Jesus sent to you absolutely constantly. You are the **focus point** right now; you as well as the other Light Workers that are on this Earth right now, that are waking up to who **they** are...which is what is happening today. As you paint your pictures and you write your poetry and you sing your songs and you Love with your heart, **you** are waking up. And you **keep** waking as you paint; the **more** you paint the **more** you wake. Do you think **anything** is done that is not of perfect timing? Absolutely not! So, you have not yet pursued a place to sell your paintings? Has it occurred to you that your paintings have not taught you, yet, all that they need to **teach** you, and therefore, they need to be **here**? When the time is right, it will be. For with each painting you paint, the healing begins and as you name your painting, the healing is there. For each has special **meaning** for **you**, and once you release it, it will have meaning for **others**...but you are not ready. We are not talking about money; we are talking about **pain**. We are talking about **passion**. We are talking about who you **are**. We are talking about **feelings**.

You have done well. You have **listened** well. Continue. Know we are **here** with you. Know we are Loving you. Know everything you **do** is perfect, for **you** are perfect. You are where you should be, at the right time, at the right place, on the right day. It is perfect! You are right where you should be. You are **with whom** you should be.

And now, it's time for you to go about your day. Continue. Love with **all** your heart. Pass the Love to **all** with a smile or a gesture. Smile at people you don't know. Smile in your car. Be happy, because you were **born** to be happy. Listen. Pay attention, and know God **Loves** you! We **thank** you for doing what you're doing, and you **will** succeed. And, now, we will say good-bye to you, and we will continue talking to you through the day. And we are **always** with you, always Loving you. Have a marvelous, marvelous day and we will talk to you later. We Love you.

Thank you, thank you.

8

The Archangels & The Value of Silence

August 16, 2000 at 3:55 P.M. Sue and Charlie
Prayer for protection. The Language of Light is spoken.

Welcome! We **do** have a message for you. We want you to go to the bookstore and we want you to buy a book on all of The Archangels for there is **much** for you to learn. You are familiar with four. You learned about another, **Metatron**, today. There are **many** and we are all very excited about the work that you are beginning to do and the work that you will **continue** to do until it is complete. You have many, many blessings; as all are watching, helping, waiting, Loving, learning and teaching. You need to **continue** learning for you do have many who want to help. We are here to guide...to Love. We are here to teach. You are there to **learn** and to continue on with **teaching**. For you have a special gift to tap into the Realm of the Archangels who have been waiting and wanting to help. You just need to **ask**, and we are here to give all the help you need. You have many Spirit Guides surrounding you, helping you constantly, and they will **stay** there with you. They will be by your sides, as well as the Angels, for your entire time remaining on this Earth. For you walk in a crowd, but not **everyone** can see the crowd that surrounds you. Continuously **visualize** the crowd that surrounds you. You have Angels walking by your side, in front of you, behind you and over your head, for you have much work ahead of you. It is very **important** work and you will continuously be protected.

Do not be **frustrated** with the things that come in front of you on your path, for these **must** happen, for, you see, it teaches you to **stand up for yourself** and **be who you are**. So in your frustration, sit and look and meditate and realize the **lessons** that you are to **learn** from this; or realize the teachings that you are gathering to **teach** others. For there is much here for you to take with you. It is **not** a face value that you are looking at. You know that you go **beyond** face value to see **true** meaning and it is that meaning, behind the face value, that you are to gather and to **learn** from. You are learning **much** about being who you are. You are not done. You are **far more** than appears on the face itself right now. You still have **much** learning and **remembering** to do. You will have more frustrations put in front of you...more learning, more gathering, more discernment, before you reach your destiny.

When I say your **destiny**, I mean before you come into **our** purpose, for you are smack dab in the **middle** of the path that you are to walk on. You are not too far to the right; you are not too far to the left. You are right where you **should** be at this time. It is not just **you** that is being taught, but others, who think **they** are in control. They are not. You **know** they are not, for they are being taught, also, and **you** will be completing the teaching to them. You must remember **not** to concern yourself with other people's paths. You will be instructed at times to teach and to guide, but you must remember that this is **not about you**, and people must be on the path **they** are on for **their** reasons and you don't need to **know** all those reasons. It is **not** about you. So if other people come across your path, they are there for a reason; to teach or to learn. **You** do not have to figure out **their** direction. You just stay on your **own** path; follow your own direction. If they **need** directions, then you will be instructed on **how** to help. If you are not instructed, be silent.

Negative energy and anger and fear do not **serve** you. They serve no one. Fill your heart with Light and Love. You will be meeting some new people. They can help you and they can hurt you; use your **discernment**, for you have a marvelous ability with discerning. So be cautious; hear with your heart and your ears. See with your eyes and your heart. But, again, the caution; protect yourself, and we will be there Loving and protecting you. Don't **give** your energy away. Continue meditation. Continue listening to your Guides and your Angels.

Sometimes you have not the **faith** to listen and believe. Have the faith. **Believe** what you hear. Don't forget to be thankful for the help you receive, for there are many helping, Loving, protecting you. Remember to be **thankful**. You just don't understand... **you can't do it wrong**.

You will learn about the **value** of silence in the next few weeks. You are beginning to learn it now. When you want to stay away from answering in a negative manner, and you cannot **think** of an alternative, just be silent. Do **not** put negativity into the Universe. We need **no** more negativity in our Universe! **Speak positively or be silent.** You will have people who **want** you to partake in negative behavior and negative verbalization, negative talk; negative gossip. Do **not** partake; nothing can be **gained** by this. So when you look at an overall picture, look at it from both sides and front and back and up and down. What will be gained by my partaking? If you see **nothing** positive, stay away. Just **send** Light and Love to the people partaking in something you don't want to be a part of. Do **not** be righteous. Do **not** pass judgment. Send the Light and Love of God and smile and be true to yourself, but be Loving and gentle and good. That is who **you** are.

It is **okay** to want to be alone. It is **okay** to spend time by yourself to hear your own inner voice and to hear your own Spirit Guides. For you see, every person on this Earth has the **ability** to hear their own Guides and their own Angels, but you must **take the time** to do so. You **cannot hear** if you have a T.V. blaring, or radio going in your car. Turn it off and **take a quiet moment**; be it in your car, be it in your room, be it in your kitchen. Take a quiet moment and hear the **silence**. For in the silence, you will hear The Voice. For it is hard work to **hear** through dimensions. It is hard work to **speak** through dimensions. If you throw in a radio or a T.V. it's **not** going to happen! Now it is time for you to spend time to think and to meditate and to **hear** what is being said to you.

You must do some self-meditation, and self-realization, and self-acknowledgement to discover what your own **personal needs** are. It is time for deep meditation, and journaling and writing down feelings and thoughts and desires. Once you put them on paper, you put them in the Universe. When you let your free-will fly, you cannot put it on paper. You cannot put it in the box so you can look at it and **see** your heart's desire. So **write down** your heart's desire and you will then be organizing what **you want** and what **you need** to be your true self. This is **important**, and this is your current lesson. You have done fine work. You have been working hard and concentrating on your heart's desire. First, information that can be shared with **all**: tell them to **write down their heart's desires; they need to put them on paper.** This is something that can help... **only help**, everybody.

Now it is time to **go inside** yourselves. Listen with your hearts. Share with each other the messages you get. Continue sharing. Continue speaking the Language of Light. Continue being the Lights that you are, as you light up those around you. Continue to be cautious about passing judgment, for **that** is not serving anyone. Continue to realize that **everyone** has their own road to walk. Do not pass judgment for **you** know not that road. For as it has been said to you before, sometimes the greatest words are **silent**. For in silence, you **do not acknowledge** negative words that are said to you. In silence, you **do not acknowledge** the words that you do not feel are the truth. For in silence, much is understood by others. Sometimes your **silence can be the greatest words spoken**, as certain people will not be willing to hear your **words**, however, they pay close attention to your **actions**. So just simply, Love. And any negativity that comes in your path, send away with Light and Love, and wish the best for **all** whose paths you cross. There will be no more **argument** in your lives, for you will be silent if the opportunity arises.

Listen to your hearts. Listen to yourselves. **Pay attention.** Right now, the lesson is **pay attention**, for there are many messages in front of you both. So pay attention to them, **listen** to them, and **clarify** the messages. For, at times I watch you, literally, driving around in circles, instead of paying attention. Had you been paying attention that would not have happened. So you drive yourself around in **circles** emotionally as well as physically, from not paying attention. **Listen**. For you have asked to hear with your **heart** as well as your ears, so, that has been granted. Pay attention.

Your **feelings** are important, they are **relevant**, and they are to be adhered to. Sometimes you feel you don't **deserve** happiness. That is the goal; of course you should be **happy** at all times! Yet you get in your own way regarding your own happiness. Even though you are here on Earth, and you are here in human form, you still have every **opportunity** to be happy at all times. It is **choice**! For you have many choices that you can and should make. Sometimes you learn by the process of trial and error, but **make** the choices. Don't stand on the fence. Go to the right; go to the left, but jump off the fence! For you can do **nothing** wrong. If the choice is not your preference, you can **change** it.

Remember to **protect yourself** well. Remember to cover yourselves with White Light. You have much protection around you, but without **asking** for it, sometimes it's hard to **give** it to you for you give your energy so freely. Protect yourselves. Protect your energy; don't be **so** free with it, for all that **want** your energy are not always looking for **your** highest and best good. Even on a phone...negativity **can** be on a phone. Protect yourselves at all times. Any time that you are breathing and speaking and in **front** of other people, it is important that you protect **everything**. For your energy is expended when you speak, so if you are speaking in person or you are speaking on a phone, energy is coming from your body and is being **taken** from you. Sometimes it is returned because of the people you are talking to... in fact it is **doubled**... however, it also can be **taken** from you in the same fashion. Be **cautious**, especially when speaking to people you don't know.

Things are changing. Times are changing, and they will now be changing rapidly. Don't be **frightened** of change, for change is good! For with change comes growth; and with growth, you only **improve** yourselves. Just have the right Spirit. Just have the right thoughts. Just have the right **heart** and all will happen in the **finest** way. Think of it as an adventure! Things will be changing rapidly, and it will now continue to change rapidly. Stay centered. Stay happy. Have faith. Have Love. Whenever you have a doubt, call on your Guides, call on your Angels for you are heavily protected but **we cannot help you without your permission**. We need to know what **you** want. Tell us. Meditate more in private time. Talk to your Angels. Talk to your Guides. Talk to God. Talk! Let us **know** what you are thinking. Tell us **how** we can help you. Do this by speaking and by writing. Don't forget your heart's desires. Keep them going, keep them flowing, **keep** them in the Universe, and **speak** them out loud, for that is verbalization that travels through dimensions. Repeat them. Once you write them down, **say** them. Say them every day! Put them **out** there!

When you sit down to do your personal, individual meditations, ask for guidance and help. Ask for **clarification** on the things the Guides are trying to tell you, if you have doubts, or if you need further information. Do **not** doubt yourself. You are full of self-doubt at times and that is **not existent**, for you are **on** your perfect path. Go **within** yourself and ask your Guides concerning what you have written down. Ask them to **clarify** things and how it should look. They will help you with it through visions, through dreams, and through actual **words** if you take the quiet moment to hear them and write them down. You must **take the time**, in the silence, **asking** for help...and it will be before you and it **will** be made clear. For there should be no guesswork; and there **is** no guesswork, for whatever you want, you can have. Just **ask**!

But you must take a look at what lessons have been put in front of you for **you** to learn. Make sure that you **have** learned those lessons, or they will continuously be put in front of you to re-learn and they will be stronger and stronger and stronger to get your attention...if we have **not** gotten your attention. Every morning, **ask**, and it will be shown to you, for **everything** you need will be in front of you. **Discernment** will be one of your lessons now, as it has been, and you will get better and better and better at it.

And now, My Darlings, it is time to say have a wonderful evening, for you are learning well, and you are **listening** terrific! Let it continue, and may your minds expand to their greatest capacity to **hear** what is being said, to **learn** what is being taught, to gather all information as it is being **given** to you, and **absorbed** by you to be **held** in your heart. Love is surrounding you. Protection is surrounding you. We Love you and we thank you. God Loves you.

Thank you. Thank you.

9

Trust, Truth & Forgiveness

October 6, 2000 at 3:00 Sue and Charlie
Prayer for protection and thanksgiving.
The Language of Light is spoken.

You talk of **trust**. You know what trust is, and you are finally, **finally** trusting yourself! It is **good** to have you here, trusting yourself. That is where you needed to be first. Once you trust yourself and have faith in yourself, you begin to **understand**...and you are. You are beginning to understand and you are not **liking** your answers and **that** is what the problem is. The adjustment is **hard** for you. Be kind to yourself. Be kind, and be patient with yourself, for you are learning much and you are **doing** what you are to do, and you are trusting your heart, and you are trusting your feelings. And you are **not** liking your answers, but you are right. It has been a very long **time** for you to reach the place that you are at. You are expecting so **much** from yourself! Be kind to you.

Truth. It is about **truth**. Have faith in **yourself** for the truth is all right there! You remember to take care of you, and let others take care of **themselves**, for you are not finished. You are not finished taking care of **you**. You speak the truth. You know **you** are trustworthy. You know **you** have faith. You know **you** are Love; that is your essence. It is not for **you** to worry about another, for each, as you know, has their own lessons, their own learning, their own path, and each must walk his path to learn his lessons. You **must** let that be! For what is to be, **will** be.

Forgiveness? Identify what it **is** you need to forgive so that you can properly forgive. Be clear to yourself, for you have your own veil that you use to **hide** what it is you choose **not** to see. Only **you** can remove your veil. You have it on your eyes, you have it on your ears, and you have it on your heart;

but it is getting thinner and thinner, and it is, finally, almost transparent. You are working hard at the removal, and you are doing well. Please, please have **patience** with you, for it must be **gone** to see clearly. You must remove all obstacles. And when others ask us for help we can help, but we **must be asked**. You may not ask on their behalf; on his behalf, on her behalf, you are **so busy** worrying about others. Keep your concentration on **you**!

All the **answers** are in front of you. Continue your journaling, for the answers are given to you daily. Maybe you should do some re-reading of the information already given. You are surrounded with the help you have asked for. You are surrounded with the Love you **deserve**. You are surrounded by your Angels, by your Guides, and by God. You feel like you are moving like a snail, when in fact, you have gone **lightening speed** this lifetime! Look where you were five years ago. Look where you were ten years ago. Look where you were twenty years ago. Look where you are today! A hundred years ago, it would have been **lifetimes** of accomplishment! So **please** be patient with you, be **fair** with you, be Loving with you. Why are you afraid to have fun and rejoice in the **joy** that is in your life? Look at it, analyze it, and **discard** that which does not give you joy. Why do you hang onto that which is hurtful to your heart?

Because you do not like something or someone does **not** mean you pass judgment. There is **balance** in this universe, and that includes like, dislike, light, dark, happy, sad; there is balance. If something is uncomfortable to be around, **stop** it! You have control of **you**! No one else does, unless you **give** it. Stop allowing certain things to control you, when in fact, you **dislike** it so. Stop passing judgment on **you**! Why do you think you are wrong if you have a glass of wine? That is not so! Stop passing judgment on **you**!

Do you think it is passing judgment if you do not **like** someone? It's not. It simply means, "I choose not to be

around you because I don't care for the way you **behave**."
That's okay, you can still **Love** them. You can still send them
Light and Love, even if their **behavior** is not compatible with
yours. Some situations, you cannot control. You need to be
certain places at certain times. Certain people will be there,
and **they** might not be your choice, but you chose to be around
others that are there. That is good. You can send Light and
Love to all. **Protect** yourself with a Bubble of Light. Protect
yourself with the Purple Flame. Protect yourself by asking
your Angels for help. You can be around people that are **not**
compatible with your Spirit. You just simply **protect** yourself
so that you do not allow your energy to leave you, or be
zapped from you by another. So you see, you can still do **all**
that needs to be done, but not to worry!

Forgive and forget. **Forgiveness** is important. **Forgiveness**
comes from your heart and true **forgiveness** is a part of Love.
Forgiveness is a compatibility with Love. Yes, forgiveness is
a part of your very Spirit. Forgiveness is a **gift** you've been
given. Forgiveness is **important**, for without forgiveness, we
do hold on to things that do **not** benefit us. We hold on to
anger. We hold on to fear. We hold on to those things that are
not compatible with Love if we do not have forgiveness.
Yes, forgiveness is important. Yes, forgiveness must be
worked on; **concentrated** on. It is a part of the heart that
must open up because it is so important to free you. For you
see, forgiveness is a gift to you! For it **frees** your heart to be
Light and Love again!

Forget? Well, some **automatically** forget. Some
automatically forget once they forgive for it is not a grudge
being held in your heart and it is then easy to forget. It is not a
conscious effort. It is an ease. It falls into place with
forgiveness. Yes, your **mind** is a creative computer. **It**
forgets nothing. It is your **heart** that forgives, and your **heart**
will help your **mind** forget. It stays, though, for your mind is
the computer of the body. It is the mind that will not **totally**
allow you to forget, and it is the **ego** that will **want** you to

continuously **remember**. Try to let go. Once forgiveness takes place, forgetting happens. Don't push it. Be kind to yourself. If you have problems with forgiveness, then audibly say," I forgive you." Say it in your prayers. Tell your Angels you need help. Ask your Heavenly Father for help. Ask Jesus how He did it, for He **did forgive**! He is the **Master** of Forgiveness, as He is the Master of Love! He can help you and guide you. Just **ask**. Forgiveness and forgetting are compatible, but do not be so **harsh** upon yourself. For your heart is the window, and the window shows these lovely, lovely Loves and gifts, and happiness and forgiveness, and happiness and joy, and Love and Light; all the things you really **want** in life.

If you are choosing to try and help another, do it through **prayer**. For individuals **must** want to help **themselves**. You cannot intercede. For each person has his own lessons, as you know, as we've discussed. **Allow** them to learn them. They may **not** be your lessons and they may **not** be taught to you the same way they are being taught to another. It is because each person needs to learn in **his** way. Allow that. You must **allow** the learning to take place. Remember, at times you are the teacher, at times you are the student, and at times the **best** words spoken are silent. Be silent. When questions are asked to you, the best answer, at times, is **silence**.

In your asking for help with forgiveness, ask for **discernment**. It, too, is a gift. You have utilized it, but you could use polishing. So ask for additional help, and you will have it. Before you speak to people that are **hard** to speak to, ask for help, say a prayer, and send Light and Love before you speak your words. That will **help** you speak Lovingly, and that will help you speak with discernment, and that will help you with judgment. That will help you **release** your fear. That will help you with everything!

What are you afraid of? You must work on your **fear** some more. You have recognized that you must work on forgiveness, and it is true, but you have much help. Have you re-read your journal on your feelings? Have you been properly journaling on your feelings? If you had been properly journaling on your feelings, you would recognize who gives you **pleasure** and who gives you **pain**. And you would be concentrating on the pleasure and not the pain. Have you socialized? Where have you **gone** lately? What have you **done** lately? Who have you been with lately? How much **fun** are you having lately? It is time to make new choices. It is time to remember that **life** is a choice. It is time to remember that **joys** in life are **choices**. It is time to remember that your **choice** is Love and joy and happiness.

If **you** cannot properly Love you, how can someone else? It starts with **you**. Properly Love **you**. Properly take care of **you**. Properly give **yourselves** the joys of Love and Life. We need to know what you **want** to properly help. You need to be more clear with **you**. Have you re-read your Heart's Desires? Is it clear? Have you changed it? Re-read it every day, and **believe** it. If you can **believe** it we can help you. If you read it we can help you. If you **chose** it, we can help you. **Believe** in you. Step out of your shell, let yourself bloom, and **be** the flower you are. Release yourself, for you are the **fruit**, not the shell. Let the shell go. You are the fruit. It is like the coconut. You are the sweet, sweet coconut milk, and you are the sweet meat of the coconut. Let **go** of the hard shell so that you can be your true self. Let it all go; let it fall off of you. Let the **fear** fall off of you, for as that is released, you will be you. You will **be** the flower you are. For you are the flamboyant flower. You are the fuchsia color. You are **beauty**, and you are the talent! You are the brains! You have it all, and you are afraid to be **you**! Stop worrying about **another's** talent or success. Get off of that rock, and get on with **your** life. Stop. It is time to let it go. It is time to let **you** be you. It is time for the artist to be free!

It is time for you to listen to the **positive** influence that has been around you, and yet, you cannot **hear** it. You **hear** the criticisms. You **hear** the negativity of another. Let it go. Let him go. Let him get on **his** path of creativity. You get on **your** path of creativity; if they should meet again, hooray. If they should not, be who you are to **be**. We are waiting for you to be **you**. We are waiting for your flower garden to bloom. For the butterfly is meant to be happy, and you are holding the cocoon shut. **Let it go**. It's time to let the butterfly go!

When you make bread, when you have kneaded it enough, you stop and then you bake it, and it is delicious. If you take that bread dough, and you knead it, and knead it, and knead it, and you over prepare it, you ruin it. For when you bake it, it is tough, it is flat, and it is not flavorful. It is time to stop. It is time to stop kneading the bread, for the bread dough has turned to rubber. It is time to **let it go**. It can no longer be baked. You have heard the saying, "You cannot kick a dead horse." The horse is dead! But before it died, you led it to water, but it died of **thirst**! So let the dead, thirsty horse go!

For you have been so busy trying to **revive** the dead, thirsty horse, that you have not gone on with **your** life, and it is **your** life that needs to explode right now. Be prepared for jealousy… but Love and Light. Send Love and Light, for as you succeed, some will be jealous. You will have guilt, if you choose to. If you can pre-prepare yourself for it, it doesn't **have** to happen. Send Love and Light. Release. Move on to be who you are to be.

Stop the sabotage! You sabotage your own **you**, and who you are to **be**; who you **are**! Be the success, you are to be, for you are truly to be successful. Let it go! Let him go! We are waiting! **You** are waiting! Your Spirit is **desperate**! For you have **such** creativity. You have **such** exuberance. You have **such** color. You have so much! And instead of bringing out the rainbow of color that you **are**, you choose to color you gray. And you are a rainbow! Do you understand?

You have sabotaged your own success, and it is time. Please, we want it. We want it for you, for around you, your Angels are creative and they **get to help** you create. So please open up and **let** it be! Those that Love you will be so, so happy for you! They will be **joyous** with you! They will **celebrate** with you! And you will know your **true** friends, and you will know your **true** Loves. For true Love, and those that Love you, will **rejoice** in your success! And you can feel and see your Angels rejoicing in your success! And you will feel and physically **see** your friends rejoice in your success. And you will physically see **some** of your family rejoice in your success.... and you will be **surprised** at those that rejoice...and the few that don't.

Please prepare yourself, so you are not **hurt** by this. For one of your big lessons this lifetime was to **be you**. You will be you. You will be **you** and you will be sorry that you didn't allow it sooner. For it will bring you such joy and Love and peace. You will be so happy to find and fully understand the **real** you. You will rejoice!

Don't ever think you have **ever** been alone. Don't ever think you have **not** had Angelic help, Spiritual Guides at your side, your Heavenly Father looking over you, Loving you. And now with all that lovely energy around you, **ask them** to **join** you on a new adventure, for they are **waiting** for the request. You just need to accept it, and **start** it, for they are already at the door. They are waiting for you! Through this transition, you will meet new friends; artistic friends, Spiritual friends, and you will find joy. Begin your adventure, and **know** that Love **surrounds** you.

And with that, we will say have the most **wonderful** day, and begin your new plan. For Love is yours, and joy is yours, and happiness is yours. You just forgot to join it. It is time to **join** the fun! It is time to be **you**. Remember who you **are**, not who someone **wants** you to be. Be who **you** want to be! Now, continue your day. Have a lovely day, as we watch as you **create**, as we watch as you **continue**, as we watch as you **begin anew**, for it is time. And it will be **so** fun! And we are all excited! Have a wonderful rest of the day, as you begin to plan your new life. We Love you. We are here for you. We thank you.

Thank you, thank you.

-10-
Denis' Channeling

October 9, 2000 at 10 A.M. Denis alone.
Private Channeling, included the following wonderful message from God,
The Creator:

Oh, My Child! You are making this so hard and it is not meant to be hard!

You are meant to be who you are, which is Love. You are Love and Light. And you must know that I have unconditional Love for you. Do you know, whatever you do, I will Love you? I always have. I always will. You can do NOTHING to make me stop! You can do NOTHING that will ever change that! You could pull a gun out at this very moment. You could flatten this entire sub-division and I will look down upon you and I will say to you, "My child, I still Love you!" You can do nothing that will make me stop. You can try to protect yourself, but I will Love you forever. You are a part of me, and you are Love at it's greatest! Be who you are for you, My Dear, are Love and I will Love you unconditionally forever and ever and ever! Do you see? There is no end. Do you see? There is truly, nothing you can do to change that. You can try, but I will be here, and I will be casting my Light upon you! And I will be here sending Angels to rescue you! And I will be here sending you Guides, as you need them.

You have it all, My Son, and you always will. Why do you doubt? That will be part of the release. The doubt will leave; the Love will remain. The fear will leave; the Love will remain. The despair will leave; the Love will remain. You will be what you are, which is pure and simple Love. You can do what you want to sabotage it, but you will remain the Love that you are. And I will remain The Creator, The Giver, The Love, The Light, The Essence, and I will be here always, helping, Loving, protecting, giving. I AM the Alpha and the Omega. I AM the Beginning and the End.

And this is part of what you will do, for I need to be back. I need to be back on Earth, in hearts. I need to be back with you, for it is not just you, who has put a wall around his heart, it is many. And so it begins. You will help Me with this, and we will end the walls; we will break the walls down. For no one knows Me anymore, and I need to be known. I need to be brought back, and it is through you that I will do this. It is through all of you, as you begin to spread The Word, the REAL Word, The Word of Love.

Jesus was wonderful! Let Him guide you; He will help you. Let Him be the Master that He is. Call on Him, for He knows His way around your Earth! For the Love must be returned to the Earth, to the people. They know not who I am anymore. They know religion, and religion has harmed Me. They have harmed who I am. I am not fear. I am not despair. I am not anger. I am Unconditional Love; a Love you truly, in your mind, cannot comprehend. It can be comprehended only through your heart, which is why we must soften the hearts and remove the walls that have been put up. For it is only in the heart, it can be conceived, and it is only in the heart that you can feel. For I AM The ONE. I AM The Creator. I AM the Love Essence. I AM your lifeline, and I LOVE YOU UNCONDITIONALLY! I ALWAYS have! I ALWAYS will! It is done! For this is just the beginning, for it must come to be!

Your Angels have been so wonderful! I send you all the help you need. I give you all you want. I am here to absolutely fill your every want, and yet, it is you that sabotage yourselves! As the Archangels look over you, they shake their heads and say "What? What is it that you want?" For you talk out of both sides of your mouths! " I want this; but I want it my way...I want this, but I don't want that...I want this, but I want the answer to be that!" You see, you put conditions on yourselves. It must stop. Stop with the conditions, stop with the judgment; judgment is not a part of Me.

Oh, yes, the religions love to say, "And Judgment Day will pass"...IT IS NOT SO! You are the ones that put judgment on yourselves, for I have unconditional Love for you all! And with unconditional Love, there can be no judgment! Do you see? There is no such thing! For it is strictly Love, and with Love there is no judgment! That is not compatible with Love!

As you know, you each have chosen different paths. You have chosen these paths to learn. For when you are with Me, you know nothing but Love, and there is no balance outside of Love, for there is just Love. You must leave that dimension to know your essence. For you cannot feel compassion when you are in a state of Love, for Love is all there is. So you see, that is why you chose to incarnate, for it is here that you can feel the differences. You do it by choice. You chose this to learn. It is by choice, you see? So you cannot do it wrong!

Do you know, there is no Hell? Who made this up? You create your own! Do you know that beyond this Earth, beyond the other planets, beyond the other

77

dimensions, when you are simply with Me...you are simply Love? You LEARN in the other dimensions, and you choose your learning as you go. Now, listen to the helpers that are sent to you, for they give you much good advice, and it is time for you to listen to them.

Always remember: You are Love, and you are, truly, Unconditionally Loved! Regardless of what you do, you are Unconditionally Loved! And you have all you need to be what you choose. And you have all you need to complete this life's purpose. And you will be successful at all you do. Now, My Child, continue to listen.

Thank you. Thank you.

-11-
God's Friendship & Be "Mindless"!

October 17, 2000 at 1:20 P.M. Sue and Charlie
Prayer for protection and thankfulness and The Language of Light is spoken.

It is good! It is good to **see** you! You have listened well this morning. It is time to be in the "I AM", not the I **will**, not the **can do**, not the **tomorrow** but the **present**, the **today**, the **now**. It is time to be the I AM. You are human **beings**. It is time to **be**. Be who you are. Be what you are. Be all you want to **be**. It is time to **expand** your relationship with God. It is time to develop the **friendship** with The Creator that it **never occurred** to you to have. **He** is your **best friend. She** Loves you forever. **He** has unending Love, energy, truthfulness, Light, protection, truth, wisdom; all you want, all you need, all you can endure. It is **time** for your **friendship**. It is time your best friend be **allowed** to be just that! We are **all** messengers. We, in the Angelic realm, are **messengers** to you, and you are **messengers** to others. You are Light and Love. You are **Bringers of the Light**, you are **Distributors of the Love**.

Do you remember, we mentioned to you, the finest words you can say, very often, are the words that are **unspoken**? Let them **ask** the questions. Do not be pushy. Do not **push** someone onto your path; do not push someone off his own. Answer the questions as they are **asked** to you. Be helpful in the gifts you have been given that can help another. There is nothing you need to **do** to spread the Light other than **let it shine**! It shines **through** you by what you do and what you say and who you **are**. You are in the perfect place at the perfect time with the perfect people. If it doesn't feel good, let your Light shine! Protect yourself. Let your Light shine! It will repel those that cannot endure it and attract those that need it.

Use your discernment to **stay away** from those that do **not** help you grow. Be aware of the fact that you might be the teacher, and you can help **them** grow. So be conscious of the questions that are asked to you. For if you answer them properly, they will **know** they are the student... if they listen. But many do not know **how** to listen with their heart. They are still trained to listen only with their ears. You must listen with your heart. You must speak through your heart. And you step **outside** of yourself, outside of your mind, so that it is your **heart** that does the thinking and the feeling and the being and the seeing and the hearing. This cannot be **done** when the brain is in tact. You are very **wise** to pay attention to your feelings. You are very wise to understand, when you are in a place that feels good, **that** is the place you should be. When you are in a place that does **not** feel good, **leave**. It is simple. It is not hard. Pay attention. Listen with your heart.

So...the flower has **bloomed** and the seeds are being planted. There will be many more flowers, many more buds, many more seeds, and it will be your Light that shines upon them to help them grow. **Be** who you are! All will happen in the time and space that it is **supposed** to. Have faith…

It is I, Your Creator. Don't be afraid to be my friend! Throw away all that was taught to you. There is no vengeance. There is no judgment. There is no Hell. There is Love! Know Me. Love Me. Embrace Me. Trust Me. Have faith in Me. It is not I who has failed you; for you have gotten everything that you have wanted. You sabotage yourselves so often; step outside of yourself. Know Me. For I have given you all you need to remember who you are! Now it is time for you to go inside of yourself to see that flame that is ignited within you. And by seeing that flame, you will know Me, and you will know you! For you are a part of Me, and I am a part of you! We are One! All you have to do is ask and believe for I will be here for you always; I always have, I always will! It is Eternity that we have known one another and will, always!

I have sent you many, many special Masters and teachers. There are Masters among you. There are Masters that are walking your planet now. Listen, listen, listen; listen with your heart! And you will learn so much! Your school is not completed; your teachings are not over. You are still a student, and yes, you are a teacher, but you are still a student. Don't take your student's hat off. Don't be so impatient! You <u>do know</u> that you are perfect. You <u>do know</u> you can do nothing wrong. You <u>do know</u> that you have Eternal Love and Life forever! You DO KNOW that! You DO KNOW it all; it is all within! You simply need to RE-MEM-BER! For the flame within you is growing and getting bigger. As you remember, a little at a time, it is coming back! Your third eye is opening! Keep utilizing the gifts you have been given. They will be used to help so many, for you are Bringers of the Light! You will bring the Light to so many! Remember who you are!

You have been given many, many Angels and Guides and Spiritual helpers. They are surrounding you now, and they are among you. The Archangels look after you and Love you, protect you, guide you and teach you. Listen! That does not mean you cannot talk to Me! You can talk to Me. I am here. I hear your every word. I see your every tear. I hear your thoughts before you think them. I know! I am the KNOW ALL!

Re-learn; <u>remember</u> who I am. Throw away what has been taught to you about who I am! For it is <u>you</u> who will show others the Love and the Light of God! For it *is you that will teach that God is Love, that God is truth, that God is wisdom. There is no fear in My name. They have ruined My name by teaching wrong teachings. Correct them, but please, do it gently, for I am a gentle God and I Love you all! People are afraid to Love Me, for they think I am a God of vengeance. They think I am a God of judgment. I am not. For I Love each one perfectly and completely. For each one of you are perfect! I Love you for where you are today, yesterday and tomorrow. I always have; I always will! I am not a God of punishment. I don't need to punish you for anything for I simply am Love! I see no wrongdoing. I simply see Love! I simply AM Love! I only know Love! There is no need for punishment when you punish yourselves so severely! For in the name of God, you kill! For in the name of God, you maim! For in the name of God, you have wars! In the Name of God, I want you simply to LOVE!*

It is I, Michael. I am here to share information with you, from the Angelic Realm. Please understand and know the teaching **never** stops, and the learning **never** stops. We are **all** teachers and we are **all** students. It is how **we** grow. It is how **you** grow. It is how your **Spirit** grows. It is how we **all** grow. It is very difficult, at times, to bring to you an understanding from the Realm of God, when we are so limited in our language. For it is only **here**, on this planet, that you have the concept of time and space as you know it. So please understand, at times we are limited in explaining things to you, as we are trying to **teach** you, too. At the same time, **we** are learning.

As no judgment is passed upon you, try with your **hardest**, with your heart, **not** to pass judgment on others. Just as the Angel card said to you today, "**What would Love do?**" Say **that** when you are confused. **What would Love do**? How would Love take care of this? Love is not angry. Love is not greedy. Love is not mean. Love is not fear. Love is good. Love is embracing. Help yourself by saying that question... **answer** it with your **heart**. All that come in front of you and cross your path are not on the same Spiritual road. Use **discernment** in how you speak. Have discernment in how you listen, for very often the tool you need is the **listening** tool, not the speaking tool. Listen with your **heart** as well as your ears.

You do not have to take **any** abuse from anyone, but those that are abusive are, very often, simply **hurting**. Their hearts are hurting. Their Spirits are hurting. Send them Light and Love frequently, for that is what they need. They cannot hear words, but their Soul can **feel** the Light and Love you send. The Light and Love you send can often, **soften** a heart so that is what you need to do. In your discernment you will see many people, where words **cannot possibly** help them. For to **hear** the words you say, they must listen with their heart. They do not know how, for the heart must be **softened** to hear. So Light and Love is the answer there. When you feel negative energy around you, send Light and Love. Draw on additional Light and Love by asking The Creator to **shed** it upon you and others.

For those that are hurting, ask The Creator to send **additional** Light and Love. And ask for special Healing Angels for that person, for He **listens** to you. He listens to **all**. He hears all, but those that **need** it the most don't **know** who to **go** to, for they do **not** have the Love, the trust or the faith. They do **not** have the wisdom. They do **not** have the knowledge. They do not understand! They simply do not **know**. But they will not listen to **you**, either, not yet, and that is why Light and Love is needed. Send them Light and Love **automatically**. Start it as a **habit**. Ask your Creator and ask your Angels, for there are many, many thousands and thousands and thousands of Angels that are here for that purpose. We just need to be **asked**.

And so your path widens! The path in front of you is lighter and brighter and **wider** and there are flowers along your path, and the rocky road is gone. It is smooth. It is hilly, but it is beautiful! It's a beautiful path ahead of you! It is bright. It is shiny. It is perfect! And as your path is widened, it is so **easy** for you to stay on it. There is no effort any longer; **no** effort! You can't walk off it; it's so wide. And so all you need to do is **be**. For now you have developed the skills to listen. For now you have **developed** the gifts.

Did you know your creativity, alone, is healing? For did you know the creativity, that is within **you**, helps **heal others**? Did you know Light and laughter is healing? Did you know that your **artwork** is healing? Not only does it heal you, it brings pleasure to others. And it is **through** that pleasure, that the healing begins. Be creative! Step outside of your mind, or as they say, **be mindless**! For it is your **heart** that is hearing and seeing and breathing and **knowing**! All you need to do is listen to your heart!

And if it is said, "You are out of our mind"; say, "Yes, it's true! Thank you! Thank you, I **am** for it is through **that** that I am creative! It is through **that** that I'm outside of the box and it is through **that** that I **know** my Creator!" And so it is. And so, be **mindless**! Being mindless is **not** being **brainless**. You have the **knowledge** and you have the **wisdom**. It is **through** the knowledge and the wisdom that you step outside of your mind. And by doing so you will see **different** options and remember different ways to be creative. And you shall.

We have given you much to do, so we will let you do it. We will guide you, we will Love you, we will be **here** for you and your Heavenly Creator is watching over you. His Light and His Love are upon you. Have no fear. Start each day with joy and Love and laughter, for the joy is now **here**, and the laughter is now **here** for you. Laugh more. Enjoy more. Have fun more.

There are still some things to learn, but there **always** are. We are still learning and it is unending and it is **fun**! We are here for you guiding you, too, as is your Creator. And now begin. We will talk to you soon. We talk to you every day; will you please **write** it down? Begin by writing it down and share with one another. Yes, you are the I AM, not the I WILL. You are the I CAN, and I DO and I AM, not the **may** I; for your Creator has given you **all**. It already is done! And now it is up to you to bring it out from within, for **you know** it all. So now **do it**! We end with Light and Love. We shed our Light and Love upon you and we **protect** you. Your Guides are with you always, as are we. We Love you.

Thank you, thank you.

-12-
Denis' Automatic Writing

10/24/2000
Automatic Writing from Denis:

Dear Angels,
How am I doing with my writing? Am I doing this right? Am I making any progress? I am having trouble remembering... Is there more that I should be doing?
Thank you.

Love,
Denis

10/24/2000
Dearest Denis,

You are such a **wonderful** student! You have been working so hard. We are very **proud** of you and we are very **pleased** with your progress. Yes, the wall is crumbling and cracking. Soon it will be gone. You will be so much Lighter without all of that pain and fear and despair.

You are correct...your pain and fear all started at the time of your **birth**. You **could** feel it for awhile but it was too difficult for you, so you gradually began building your wall to protect yourself. It did not happen overnight; it took a long time. You can see from your writing that even at seven or eight years of age, you could still **feel** this pain and despair and fear. Most of that feeling was absent as you became a teenager. You were still building your wall up until a very short time ago.

You are correct. You have been living your life at "Point Zero". Life is so much more **meaningful** if you allow yourself to feel the pain, sadness and anger, as well as the joy, happiness and elation! Don't be a "Zero" any longer. It is your choice. We are helping you each day and night. Your dreams are very active. Write them down as they are lessons. You are making **great** progress! You are doing all that you can do and you are doing it very well!

We Love you!
Your Loving Angels

-13-
Be Who You Are & Be In The Now

November 7, 2000 at 10:45 A.M. Charlie and Sue
Prayer for protection and thanksgiving. The Language of Light was spoken.

Good morning, and Love be with you both! It is good to **see** you; it is good to **talk** to you. It is important for you to know, that **now** is a time where changes are happening very fast, and you must take **care** of yourselves and be in the **now**. It is important that you **be**. It is important that you **be who you are to be** by behaving as you are shown to, and as you feel. Feelings are important! Things are happening **very fast** now, and you may be tired. Things are happening very fast, and you are being **re-wired**, as you are aware; you and many, many others. It is important. When you are tired, please rest. It is a time when you should be gaining your strength. It is a time when you should be in **your know**. It is a time when you are to **listen to yourself** and go inside of yourself to hear properly. It is necessary for you both to know you do **not** need each other to hear what is inside of yourself; to hear us, to hear The Creator, to hear your Guides. It is not important for you to be **together** to do that. Learn to do it separately as well as together.

When you are together you have a greater energy level, and it is very, very wonderful when you are helping **someone else** into this new energy level. It is **especially** helpful when you are bringing someone **else** into the know. But do it alone, also. It is important for you to learn to **go inside**. Hear your own Guides. Hear your own Angels. Hear your Creator speak to you, individually. You will be needing to **do** this more and more. You will be given information separately, to share with each other and many others. It is important that you listen, and so now is a time when **going inside** and hearing is important. It would be wise for you to keep your recorders in your cars and with you when you are alone, so you can **record** that which is being told to you. You started to do this, and then you stopped. Start again, and keep doing it; it **is** important for you will be getting more and more messages separately, that will be shared.

Just as you were told to **be in the now**, it is very, very important...for you both get so **impatient**. Part of it is frustration. Part of it is anxiousness, as things are happening very fast and the **vibration** is changing, and **you** can keep up. And you are **aware**, and it makes you anxious because **you** want to know quickly. Instead of being in the **now**, you want to be in the tomorrow. Be in the NOW! It is important for you to be in the NOW! For you **must** know, your Heavenly Creator has taken care of all. Be in the NOW, and be in the KNOW! For it is done! Accept that! Accept the **fact** that it is done! And you can simply **enjoy the now**, for it is already accomplished. It is already taken care of. You are on the perfect path. You are doing the perfect things. You are following **exactly** as you are instructed. For everything happens as it should. There are **no** accidents.

It is I, your Creator. It is I, the Beginning and the End. It is I, the Alpha the Omega. It is I, the up and down, the right and left, the North, South, East, and West.

You are so protected! You are so engulfed in Love! You are following the path in front of you in a perfect way, and I am proud of you! For put your head high; hold your chin high! Smile at Me as I smile at you, for I Love you so! I am with you always. Hear Me when I speak, for I am here, and I listen to you and it is done! All that you ask for will be; all that is for your highest and best good will be taken care of. For you are a part of Me, and I am a part of you. I want the best at all times for you, and it will be!

We have been given strict instructions, from The Creator, to protect **everything** about you. And it **is** done! You have **no** reason to have a fear. You have **no** reason to be anxious. Just feel the Love and joy that is bestowed upon you, for it is **taken care** of and done. And you listen well, and you follow the path as you are instructed. You follow the path that you, **yourselves**, have set in front of you. As we help guide, it is so easy to guide you, for you are already in the middle of the path. For you are the **messengers**, and your time is near. And it is beginning. And it is **now**. **Be in the now**.

Do what you **Love**. It **is** taken care of and all **will** be done. You don't have to **go** anywhere, it will be **brought to you**. It will be laid at your feet, and you will take **care** of it, as **you** know how. For you will teach many. For you see, you teach by simply **being**, which is why we ask you to simply **BE**. For it is in your very Spirit, in your very Soul that you are who you are. You don't **have** to try. You don't have to do anything but **be who you are**! And you **see** and **feel** the Angels around you, as we Love and guide and protect. Do you **feel** us? Do you **see** us? Do you **hear** us? We don't even **need** to instruct you for **you** already know!

You are **remembering** more and more daily, as you simply smile and **be who you are**! For you are **teaching** with the children in front of you. For you are **teaching** with the people that you are put in the presence of, or they in your presence. For you **teach** as you smile in the grocery store, and you smile in the car, and you smile on your front door, and you smile wherever you are. And through this smile, and through opening your eyes and looking at people, they see the Love of God and feel it, for it is **so easy** to see and feel for it **surrounds** you.

That does **not** mean you should not **protect yourselves**. As we have told you many times before, you also will attract an entity that is not **of** your like, but it is **so** attracted **to** your Light. It wants to **overpower** your Light with its dark, but it cannot be, for **you don't know how to allow it**. It can **never** be! Send it **away** with Light and Love. And it will come in different **disguises**, so prepare yourself by asking God for the gift of discernment, which is already bestowed upon you. It has already been done, so **know** it's been done, and **use** it!

Many teachers and many messengers have been in your presence. They have learned from you and you from them. And it is like the lights of stars that will now go in different directions to **spread** the Light. Wish those Star Sisters and Brothers Love. **Love** them. Send them off with blessings! For you must **help** one another. Be the Master you are, and understand, that these Light Brothers and Sisters are messengers, as are you. They are **not** deserting you; they are spreading the Love and Light of God by being who **they are**. For that is the **intent**, and **that** is what you have **come** to do. And they may call on you once and again, and they will ask you for **help**; and sit with them and help them. Help them **regain** their energy that is depleted. Help them **regain** their Light that is dim. Help them by Loving them, and **pray** for them. And continue Loving, Loving, Loving, for that is the answer to **all**. As you hold a new born baby in your arms, can this child be Loved too much? Nor can you or any other with the Love of God.
No one can Love too much!

Learn the lessons that are put in front of you, for you have much to do. Please, when you are tired, rest. Please take a time-out when you need to. Please speak to Me when you want to. Please remember I Love you. Talk to Me. I am your friend. I have always been your friend, and I am Your Creator. I am the Love that first existed in your life, and I will be the Love for your whole life, and your life is without end! Your essence is Love!

Now go, BE WHO YOU ARE! Talk to Me! Love Me! Embrace Me! Know Me! May Love be with you, always! Know, just as I spread My Light upon you, give it away! Give the Love back! Not to Me, for I know you Love Me, give it to others. For not only do they not know Me, they don't understand Love. Teach them! Teach Love! Teach Light! Do it by being who you are. When asked, tell them who I am. It is not fair to be pushy; you don't need to be.

Understand that being who you are is what I need. For being who you are, all by itself, shows what God's Love does; shows what Loving God does to your very Soul and being. Do you understand what I'm saying? For it is so simple, it is so simple.

There is absolutely nothing for you to do but be who you are! For you are the Essence of Love. Just go and be that every day! And when you are laying in your bed, and when that anxiety tries to touch you, reach for Me! I am always there! You have never been alone for a moment! You never can be. You never will be. You both actually walk around in quite a crowd! Know it! Feel it! Love it! For it is I who give you these gifts! You can have anything! Do you know that?   It is through Love without end, amen.   Remember! Remember! You are a Member of Me; I of you. Re-Member who you are! You will! You shall! It is done! I Love you so!

It is I, Michael. We have been given special instructions, and you are **well** taken care of. Your Heavenly Creator will **never say good-bye to you**, as I often do when I send you on your way to complete your day's journey. I do it, **knowing** that I am **here**; knowing that **you know** I am here. Your Creator will **never say** it, as He never **feels** it, for He is **never** in a place to say good-bye, as He is **always** there.   He is **surrounding** you. He is a **part** of you. He is **within** you; and you within Him.

There are **many** Angels that are now here protecting, and you will be doing more and more **verbalizations**, but do remember... **listen**! For people will come to you and speak. Listen to them. Don't jump in too quickly, as that **will** be what you **want** to do. Instead, listen. It may not be **true**, but listen and smile. Smile and send Love. Smile and **ask for guidance** from God above, and He will give it, and we will be there. For it will be a visualization that your Love and your smile and the Light of God through your eyes...when people ask questions to you, that **you** are in the know.

You do **not** want followers; you want to **teach the teachers**, and let them teach, too.   Proper words **will** come to you. It **will** be known that this is true. Not to fear; not to have anxiety, for your path is clear, smooth and full of sunshine and flowers.   You have more protection than you **can even** imagine! There is more Love surrounding you than you **can possibly** conceive! For if you **could** conceive it, you would **melt** in the **awesomeness of the whole**, for it is **huge**!

It's the **vibration** changing upon your Earth. The vibrations are **changing** in you and in others. Some will not be able to **endure** this increase of vibration on your Earth and they will leave. Again, do **not** pass judgment on them. Do **not** have pain about this, for **you know** there is **no death**. You know there is **only** Eternal life. There is much work left to do, but the **secret** of it all is that it does not feel like **work** to you, for it is **joy and Love**. And yet, you will be **so** happy doing what it is you have come to do to fulfill your purpose. **Thank you** for being who you are, and **choosing** to do what you chose, and **agreeing** to listen as we speak and guide you and help you and Love you through it. Always know we are there. And when you cry we will **comfort** you. It is all a part of the big picture.

Remember one thing; if something is **forced**, then maybe it should not be. If it's not clicking together, it's **not supposed** to be so. If you force a round peg in a square hole, you will eventually get it through, but you will have chipped off a lot of wood! **If the wood begins to chip, leave it alone**. **Let** it be what it **is** to be. Don't make the square peg a round one. Let it be square. Do not make the round hole a square fitting. It is meant to be round. So if you **feel** that shape of the chipping wood, lay it down and **let it be**. If it fits together perfectly, it **is** the way it **should** be.

As you know there are **no accidents** and there are **no coincidences**. You may use those words occasionally, and you will hit your own forehead, and say, "Oh my goodness! There **are** no coincidences, there **are** no accidents!" And you will laugh at your own joke! And you will smile at God above, and say, "Thank You!" For you will know He is smiling down upon you as you recognize His lovely handiwork!

You will find it impossible **not** to **speak your truth**. You no longer **know how** to hide behind false statements, or pretend walls. You simply don't know how anymore. Isn't it good? It is really **wonderful**! There are still too **many** who know how to, but **you** don't. You will speak nothing but **truth**. And you will speak it with **Love and Light**. You are learning well. Jesus has guided you. Ask upon Him when you need **help**, for He is really, really present on this Earth now. He is helping **many,** for there are many Masters, and He is guiding them. He is guiding them to use Light and Love to **change the world**, to raise the vibration, to change the reality from what **was** to what **is**.

Just as you see in the **corporate world**, mergers and takeovers and buyouts and changes everywhere, you will begin to see it in the churches. You, yourself, said, "**My** new church is Joy!" That is **so** perfect! Let your church be Joy! And if someone asks what church you are going to, answer, "I am going to God's Church of Joy!" That is **perfect**, for that is what you are! When the two of you get together, it **is** church, for you **speak** to God yourselves, and you have **listened** so carefully!

Now you will be doing it, individually, at **all** times. Listen **carefully**. Keep the radio off. **Listen to the silence** and you will hear many great things. For it is in the **silence of your Soul** that you will be told the next step. You don't need to be told; your Soul is the one **leading** the way. By **letting** your Soul be the leader, you have eliminated many, many steps. Continue as you are, for you are perfect.

Now, it is time for you to continue on with your daily routines. It is time for you to complete the tasks at hand. It is time for you to say good-bye to us, for the moment. We will talk later. Our Love and our Light is sent upon you. We are here with you. We are **protecting** you. We are **absolutely engulfing** you! Now, have a lovely, lovely day. Love be **with** you always.

Thank you. Thank you.

14

Stay Centered & Stay In The Moment...the Now

November 20, 2000 at 10:00 A.M. Sue and Charlie
Prayer of thankfulness and for protection, and The Language of Light was spoken.

It is I, Michael. I am here with you today, and I am here with many other Angels. We are all **surrounding** you, for we Love you very much as we giggle and we laugh at you. For we have given you **all the information you need**, and yet, you are afraid to **believe** or **apply** it.

For, as we have told you before, just as the flower blossoms, it takes time. The flower does **not** grow from a seedling into a full, mature, blossoming flower in a moment. It happens over a series of moments. Now, in this moment as **you** are blooming, you want to **rush** into the mature flower. Why? We have told you over and over, it is the **moment**, it is the **now**, it is the **second**. Enjoy it! Enjoy this **very intimate moment**! For as you are well aware, as you have been taught and as you know and believe, all is as it **should** be. All is **exactly** as it should be in the moment, in the second, in the minute, in the hour, in the day. Why can't you **enjoy** it? Now, because of the **know** that you **are**, because of the absolute certainty that you **know**, because you have **given all back** to The Creator and it is done, **what** are you asking? For you see, everything that **should** be, **is**. And everything that **is**, should **be**, and it should be **now** in the perfect time and moment.

If it is **not** in the perfect time and moment, then it should **not** be. If you are afraid to enjoy this moment, and want only to **worry** about tomorrow, you will **forget to exist**. Now, let's come back to the **now**, for it is **in the now** that you are. For it is **in the now,** that things happen. For it is **in the now** that things exist and will be. Live in the **now**, not in the yesterday, and not in the tomorrow. For tomorrow shall **be** what it **shall** be.

Now, listen. You look up at the sky and you see a beautiful, beautiful blue sky, and it is perfect. And in the **shift of a second**, the wind blows and the snow starts, or a hurricane hits the town, or a tornado goes through the city. It happens in a second, and **all changes**. Now that is what will be. But **your** world is perfect. **Your** world is exactly as it **should be**. Now do you hear what I say? I say **your** world, not **the** world. For in **the** world, things will happen in a moment, but you will look at each other and giggle and know, for **you know** it is to be and it is perfect. For **you know** that it is the way it should be. For you are **in the know**, because you live **in the NOW**. Please understand what I say, for it **is** the right thing. And sometimes that is why we say we tell you **too much**, for in doing so, you expect more, instead of living in the now! You want to know the tomorrow, but tomorrow **doesn't exist**, yet, nor does it **matter**. It has already been, it already **is**, and it is taken care of, and yet, it **isn't** yet. So, do you **see** the turmoil we have? Do you **see** the misunderstanding that has taken place? Do you **see** the inability we have in communicating?

It is the **now** that is important to you. It is the **now** that is important to **us**. It is the **now** that is important to your Creator. For it is in the **now** that people cross your path. It is in the **now** that you Love with all your heart. It is in the **now** that you exist and you **are**, and you **will always be**. For it is only **here** that time exists, and it exists differently than other places, and therefore, it is difficult. So **please** live in this moment! So please **Love** the moment you are in! So please understand that **in a moment** it changes. So please understand that as it **changes**, it is **perfect**. So please understand that it is **taken care of** and it is **done**, for **all** is done as it **should** be. Do you **understand** what I say to you?

Do you know that we are surrounding you with Love, and with protection and with Light shone upon you? It is huge!

97

We want, very much for you to gain the understanding of the **now**. We want very much for you to live in this moment **in the now**. For it is in the **now** that it must **happen**, please. Please. You are such little impatient beings! You **do know** that you came to **learn** patience! You **do know** that is one of the items and purposes of your return. And this is a perfect opportunity for you to complete that task! For you see, there **are no** accidents in things that happen, and you **know** that. For you see, it is **perfect** and it is being done. For you see, as your purpose is absolutely being **fulfilled** in the moment, you want it to be over. **Enjoy the moment!** Enjoy the **now** and know that the now is so perfect; that **you** are so perfect, and that you are doing **all** that you wanted to do, and you are doing **so** well!

Things will unfold, as they **are** to unfold. Be patient. This is not something you want to rush through, for it is **in the patience**, that the learning is complete. For it is **in the patience of the moment**, that you continue your learning and your teaching. You need to take the time to **allow** those to come in your presence. You need to **slow down**, for you are rushing so fast as you **feel** the urgency in the vibration. Please try to concentrate on slowing down and **enjoying** the very moment. Enjoy who you are **with**. Enjoy your **moments alone**. **Utilize** them. Sometimes you waste them. **Utilize** them with your writing and your reading. **Utilize** them with your meditation and your prayer. **Utilize** them with your thankfulness. **Utilize** them with your intelligence. **Utilize** them with the Love in your heart.

Look up and see the **beauty in all**, for you are recognizing beauty that you had not **recognized** before, and that is the beauty of the **now**. For you are seeing snow and you are saying it is beautiful, but you **have seen** it all your life. You are looking at the clouds and you say, "Oh my goodness, see the color!" but you **have seen** this all your life. You are looking at the flowers with a new vibrant color, yet you **have seen** this all your life. So you see the **importance** of the **now**?

You see the importance of the moment, for you are taking the time to **appreciate** God's beauty. And you need to **fill your heart** with that beauty, for it is that beauty, and it is that **Love** that will maintain you, as the vibration increases even more so.

Now you find it **so important** to know the future. Yes, you are a great **part** of the future. Let me share this tidbit with you. I want you to enjoy the now, in the moment. The future has much ahead if it, but it is **all** in control, as you know, so what matter? What is the **matter**? Why is it you need to **know**, for it is all done and it is all right and it is all perfect? Now, if you **must** have an inkling, I will share with you. There will be many, many, **many changes** and they will be rapid. You must remain in the **now** and **you must stay centered**. That is important. That is essential!

It is in your **centeredness** that more will be attracted to you, for all else will be chaotic. **Stay** in the **now**. **Stay** in the **know**. Things will happen **quickly** in a moment's change, and they will happen **all over** the world, as such. And **you** will stay centered, and **you** will stay honored. And **you** will stay in Love, and **you** will stay in **know**. And you will be **surrounded by protection** and you **know** that all is perfect. And **that** is what makes you so powerful; is that **you know** it is perfect! And **you know** you are taken care of! Because **you know** you always have been, and you always will be! And it is unfolding before you as you **watch** in wonder and you watch and you giggle and you think it is so wonderful. **You know**! **You always have known**! **This** is the way it will be. So protect yourself by staying in the **know** and in the **now** and **stay centered**. Protect yourself by covering yourself with the **Bubble of Light**, and know the Angels are surrounding you at all times.

The vibration will increase after the first of the year. Things will happen rapidly, but don't let that frighten you. It will frighten others, but don't **let** it frighten you, for you **know** it is right, you **know** it is fine, and you **know** you are protected. So that is why I say to you, "All in YOUR world is perfect! All in YOUR world is protected. All in YOUR world is **exactly** as it should be, and you may laugh and giggle and enjoy!" That is not the same as in the world around you, for not all have your knowing, and not all have the **know** and very few are living in the **now**. Live in the **now**. Live in the moment. Enjoy and Love with all your heart. **That** is what you need to do!

You are becoming more **verbal**. You are **speaking** your truth. It is good. Again, you are being taught discernment. Pay attention. We will be with you to help you. A Loving heart has a hard time discerning against that which is **not** always Loving. For you **want** with your heart, to believe the **best** in all, for there is good in everyone. When there **is** a decision to make, simply say, " What would Love do?" When there is a decision to make that you find **difficult**, ask Jesus for His help, for He is **there** to guide and help you at all times. He is the Master that **knew** how to handle those situations on this Earth, as no one else has done since, to the **degree** that He did. You can **learn** from Him. You are doing well. Not to say there are not other Masters who have done well, too. There are, but Jesus seems to come into **your heart** first, so you ask Him and He is there to help at all times. He is guiding you, watching you, Loving you. As are **all** the Masters, as are **all** the Angels, as is The Creator. And **know** you are **following** and it **is** okay. And it is through the **help** that you will find the discernment that is needed to read the hearts of others. Yes, you **want** to believe the best. Yes, it is hard **not** to believe the best, so simply use your Love in your own heart and the discernment will come, and you will do well, as you do all with Love and Light.

Wear your protection and wear it **daily** now. You will have **much** come up over this holiday season for you both. For you will be **tested**, although you won't see it as a test, but the **others** will see it as a test. You will pass with flying colors because **you** have no judgment, and that is why you pass. For you see, you are doing very **well** in discerning, even though you are impatient. Try very hard to simply **concentrate** on what you have learned already, for you are doing well, and you are moving fast. You are moving faster than you have **ever** moved in your Spirit. And it is good and you are good at what you are doing. So just remember, as others **ask** you questions, and they will this holiday season, many questions will be asked of you... speak with your **heart** not with your head. Ask for guidance, ask for protection and speak with Love. And all will be perfect as it always has been.

Well, we hope that helped you a bit. The true message to you today, please, is to **live in the now**, to **see** with Love, to **speak** with Love. Many will be crossing your path. It will be **across**, it will not be parallel, it will be perpendicular. In that short passing, much will be learned and much will be taught. You need discernment and you need to live in the moment. For **that** is your job now, especially in the next six weeks. You know we **want** to talk to you daily, we Love you so. We will help keep you where you should be. Never be afraid to **ask**. We are always here for you, and we Love you and we guide you and we protect you. There is **no** fear, not in your lives, not in your heart. For you are full of Love and you are absolutely covered with it! You have **more** protection than you can see with your mind or with your heart. You are perfect and all that you **do** will be perfect. It is **exactly** what you are to do. Yes, you are impatient because you are still lively, little children, and **that is** what children do. You have very, very joyful, adventurous Spirits! And they want to go quickly! Calm them. **Stay** calm. Stay centered. It is so important in this moment. It is **so** important. Help each other stay centered. There is **nothing** to fear. You have **nothing** to fear. Only joy and Love is ahead of you... and adventure! You have **much** adventure ahead of you. And as things happen, they will happen **around** you, not **about** you. And as things happen around you, keep yourself centered, as others will come to you. And it is due to your **centeredness** that they will be attracted to you. It is due to your very **knowingness**! It is due to the Love you exude! It is due to the Light that you shine! It is due to who you **are**! It is who your Spirit is; it is **how** your Spirit shows itself to the world. It is in your eyes. It is in your heart. It is in your mind. It is in your Soul. It is in you! It **is** you! It is every **cell** in your being! It is **who** and **what** you are! And you will be glowing with Love and Knowingness!

Now, we send you off to be in the **now**. We send you off to have a joyous, happy day! We send you off to smile and send Love through the world. We send you off, knowing we are **here** with you and we are going to help you stay in the **now**! Do you have questions for me?

Charlene: Yes. I am concerned about my financial situation.

I am so sorry! We will help you. Your faith is huge! Your faith is gigantic! It is done, it is taken care of. Don't have fear; fear is **not** a part of you. It will unfold a little at a time but you are well taken care of, and will be **better** taken care of soon after the first. And as it unfolds, it will unfold in a beautiful way and you will be very, very satisfied, please know. Do you have another question for me?

Charlene: Yes. I still have confusion about my relationship with Denis.

At **this** very time you need to be by yourself and he needs to be by himself. Let him be who **he** needs to be. It might not be on **your** plan, but you need to know, that it is in **God's** plan. Let him be who **he** needs to be. Let him learn what **he** needs to learn. As we said before, paths will cross, but not run parallel. His path will cross, and not run parallel. That does **not** mean in the future it could not run parallel again. You must let him be who **he** needs to be, and it is imperative that **you** be who you are! He is **learning**, and you are **taught**. As he asks you questions, answer them as you would answer anyone.

Sometimes, letting go, is the **hardest** thing that Love does; letting go of **yourself** and giving yourself to God and letting Him run the show; and letting go of **another** and letting you be who **you** are, and letting him be who **he** is. Sometimes you need to be by yourself to **find out** who that person is. Again, ask yourself, "What would Love do?" For as the old cliché says, " If you let it go and it flies away, it is meant to fly away. And if it is **meant** to be with you it will fly back home." Let it go. Sometimes lessons must be learned **singularly**. Even you and Sue learn lessons singularly. Do you Love each other less? No. Do you have to see each other daily to know that you Love each other? No. And if you don't see or speak to each other for days, you know that you still Love one another. You see, Love is a Universal feeling that travels from dimension to dimension and world to world. In this dimension and in this now, you **must** let go, for Love does not bind! He will learn to let go when **you** let go. And it will be **then** that he will **really learn**. As we have said before, each has his **own** path to walk and lessons to learn. We cannot stifle the lessons of others, and you know this to be true. Did I answer your question?

Charlene: Yes, thank you.

It is time to say good –bye. I want you to know you are **covered** in Love. I want you to know we are Loving you. We are giving you special Angels right now to **comfort** you and Love you and give you courage and peace, for you are having heartache. We don't like seeing you in pain. You will have special help. We will send Denis special help. You see, Love does **not** go away. It stays, and it will **always** stay. And you are covered in Light, My Dear. But what **must** be will **need** to be, please know. We are shedding Love, protection and comfort upon you. And now we are sending you to your **now**, and to your **know**. We want you to have a lovely, lovely day. Enjoy the day.

Thank you. Thank you.

15

Denis's Automatic Writing

11/22/2000
Automatic Writing from Denis:

Dear Angels,
I noticed the eagle. What is the message you have for me?
Thank you.
Love,
Denis

11/22/2000
Dearest Denis,

It is I, Michael. Before you were introduced to this Earth, you were Love. Love **so** powerful that you were **awesome**! Love that was so huge with God's Light and so very bright! You were totally **incomprehensible**! You were in constant touch with God and with the Archangels and with Jesus. You were, and are, very, very special.

You came to Earth to learn **compassion**. You came to Earth to experience the Human Experience. You were **unable** to tolerate the pain and fear and sadness as a child and, therefore, you built a wall around your heart to protect you from it. This wall has been reinforced, with more and more density, over many years. You have forgotten **how to feel**. You are easily capable of dealing with these feelings now, as an adult, **especially** since you are in the "know" and living in the "now". You are ready, now, to allow the wall to come down.
We are with you and we will **help** you to understand your emotions. Please do not be afraid. There is nothing to fear. You must frequently release all of your pent-up fear, anger, despair and heart-ache. You do not **need** this anymore for you are completely safe. We are here protecting you.

The memories of "Who you are" are now beginning to appear. You are awesome! You are ALL possibilities. You are Love so huge that you cannot even imagine, yet. You are ALL these things. You are <u>Grace</u>. Your Light is so bright that humans cannot comprehend it! Your **very presence** is so badly needed on Earth. You are an inspiration to ALL. You must peel back your fear, anger, pain and despair like a banana peel so your Light will be exposed and allowed to shine forth! You do not **need** these peelings any longer. It is time! It is done!

Love to you,

Michael

Can't You See My Light?
by Denis Hill

I am the small boy whose sadness lingers
Because the glass slipped through my fingers.
Being made to feel like I'm not alright...
Why can't you see my Light?

I am the small boy who lies in my bed
With feelings of fear filling my head,
While hearing your fighting throughout the night.
Why can't you see my Light?

Hello, it's me, your very small son,
Who wonders how long until you'll be done,
And give your loud anger a little respite.
Why can't you see my Light?

I can't stand the sounds of your angry projection,
Your absence, withdrawal, or your rejection.
When will you love me and kiss me good-night?
Why can't you see my Light?

If I were good and my siblings the same,
If Dad hadn't faltered, so no one's to blame,
I'd feel your love strongly if <u>conditions</u> were right.
Maybe you **can** see my Light?

But then once again the sky would grow dark.
A big, ugly storm caused by one tiny spark
Destroyed any peace or loving in sight.
Why can't you see my Light?

So I toughen-up and refuse to feel...
My fear, confusion and pain were unreal!
So I must pretend that I am alright.
I guess I'll **hide** my Light.

I can survive on this planet called Earth,
By building a wall around my heart's girth
To protect me from fear, pain, and my plight.
No one will know I am Light.

This wall works perfectly, keeping out pain,
But somehow I feel it was all in vain.
It also blocks happiness, love and delight...
Do I even know that I have a Light?

Remember me? Your boy, now a man?
Now eating alone...my food from a can?
Whose life-companion has since taken flight?
She could not live in my absence of Light.

My mission here is to tear down my wall,
To allow me to feel, every strong brick must fall.
Then by clearing away all the clutter in sight,
I can begin to rekindle my Light.

This process is hard; to remember my pain
Is like living it twice, though **this** time for gain.
I'll forgive and release it, to do it right.
I think I'm beginning to **remember** my Light.

When through with this process, my hopes are just this:
To FEEL once again, the pain **and** the bliss.
That my essence, again, is allowed to shine bright,
And everyone will then see my Light!

The Angels have shown me a sight to behold!
They showed me **myself**, just like they foretold.
I am awesome! I'm a wonderful, powerful sight!
Creativity, exuberance and Love that's so bright!

It took my breath away when I, actually, saw
My Own Light!

-16-
Patience, Relationship With God, Light & Love

Sunday, December 3, 2000 at 1:55 P.M. Sue, Charlie and Denis
Prayer for protection and giving thanks for our relationship with God. The Language of Light was spoken.

It is so **lovely** to see you on this fine Sunday! It is such a lovely day and it is so lovely to see the **three** of you together! There are many here with you today, as we send you Love and Light and our encouragement and faith. As we look down upon you and we feel that you are so **impatient**.! As we have told you before, **patience** is one of the lessons you are learning. Patience is something that will help you in your teaching and your learning. For you are now, **fine-tuning** your learning, and you will begin to do more teaching. It is very, very important that you have the **patience** that you need.

For rather than rushing forward, you must take the time to **be** who you are, in the **moment**, to make the impression you are to make, with the **people** who are put in front of you. Your paths are widening. That, of course, means that you **cannot** do anything wrong, for your path is so wide, you cannot fall off of it. Not only is your path widening, it is smoother. The rocks are less frequent, the mountains have disappeared, and the hills are now made of sand. It is **smoother**; it is a smoother ride for you now. As your path is widening, it is making room for **more** people to be put in front of you and beside you. As we have discussed before, it is imperative that you **not ask** someone to walk **your** path with you. If it is walked with you, it is walked with you out of **choice**. Life is about **choice**.

You are now **sharing** the Light, to give choices that people did not **know** they had. It is about choice. It is about knowledge. It is about Spiritualism. It is about **knowing** The Creator. It is about knowing that The Creator has given you help; so **much** help; help no one knew they had. For they had **heard** of Angels, for they had **heard** of Guardian Angels, for they had **heard** of The Archangels, but they did not know the **personal relationship** that **that** entailed or meant. They did **not** know that **that** meant that they could have a **personal** relationship, and that God The Creator Himself has given all that He can give to you; to give you all that you **want**, and **all** that your hearts desire. One of the things that you will help others realize is the fact that they **have** been given **all**, and that the **choices** that they have made have been of their **own** accord. They **cannot blame** The Creator, for The Creator has given them the **opportunity** to make the choices that have been made. It is now time to **be accountable** for those choices each have made.

It has been said that **if** we had a God of Love, things that have happened on this Earth would not have taken place. Oh! This is **such** a fallacy! And it will be **you** who will show that **that** is not true. It will be you who show the others that those choices have been made **by them** alone. That God has given them all they wanted, and **they** have made those choices.

For wars have been created in the name of **God**, because **they** will not be **responsible** for the wars that they **themselves** have created. Your Holy Creator looks down upon you and says to all, "*I Love you! I have so much Love for you! If this is what you choose, then you will have it.*" So you see He will give you all, even that which is not good for you, because you believe it **is** good for you. He knows. He knows it **all**. The Creator knows **all**, and Loves you all in spite of the **poor choices** you have made. And it will be **you** that will show those, the choices have been **theirs** alone. And **that** is what your lessons will be.

You will be silent and you will be listening, and when it is **asked** upon you, you will state the truth! For the **truth** is all you **know**! For you have now created yourselves; you have now **re-created** yourselves to **see truth** above all. For you have been **purifying** yourselves. You have been working on judgment, and you have been doing a fine job. You are recognizing in yourselves, **when** you pass judgment, and catch yourself at it. You recognize in others when t**hey** pass judgment, and it is an affront to you. You are **recognizing** more and more and you are learning about discernment and this is good. There will be many, many, many, many changes in the near future. You will **recognize** these changes; they are all man-made, but some will **try to blame** your Heavenly Creator, and you **will not allow** it. And that is where your work begins.

There will be many that are put in front of you soon. Do use discernment, and do use Love and kindness. For you know that you will have some **difficult conversations** with **difficult people**. And they will be very insistent on things that **you** will know **are not true**. So when you have a difficult time responding, first say to yourself, "What would Love do? What would Love do?" and then speak with your **heart**. You will have much help. Your own personal Angels and Guides will help you in the **language** that you use, and in the words that are formed. And your Heavenly Creator, of course, is beside you at **all** times helping you. For He is Loving that **you** are trying to spread the Love that He **wants** spread on this Earth. For **all** on this Earth have the **capacity** of great Love, they just simply **forgot**. Some still remember, and **some** have totally forgotten. There are the Enlightened Ones, as you are, who **remember**; who remember the Love. That is what you are. You are Love. So you must **also** remember that **each** person is created with Love. And when you have a difficult time seeing the Love in another person, ask to see **through** The Creator's eyes, and you will **see** the Love that exists. And it will be **easier** for you. It will be **easier** for you to respond in those times when you are not treated with Love in return.

It is time for you to utilize your own **personal power**. You **all** have it. It is time for you to **utilize** the help that you have through your Angels, through your Guides, through the

Archangels, through The Creator. It is time for you to be who you **are**. It is time for you to **continuously reflect** the Light from within. You do it with your smile and you do it with your eyes and you do it with your kind acts and you do it by just being your sweet selves.

It is I, The Creator. I am here to remind you how deeply Loved you are! I am here to remind you that you are well, well taken care of. I send you so much help. I send you more help than you can comprehend. I am here to remind you that, all the Love I bestow upon you, I bestow upon all! I need your help to remind others who I am. It is a Spiritual time right now. It is a Spiritual time in the Christian community. It is a Spiritual time in the Jewish community. Remember who I am. With your whole heart, try not to judge the churches, for they have also done good. And they believe they are doing good. They believe they are doing good. They do not know that they are harming Me. Know that! Know that, as you spread the Love. Know that!

I want you to know Me as your friend.

For I see the friendships that you have, and you must know that I am there! I am there in the Center! I am there surrounding the Love you have! I am there shedding Love and Light and joy upon you! I am there, wanting you to know I am your friend, too! I am there wanting you to know, you are My Friend! For "friend" is a word that seems very important to you. I want to be a part of that importance.

For I know you Love Me; I know you, and I Love you so! But it is beyond Love! For you see Me as The

Creator. For you see Me as above; for you see Me as "Bigger." You see Me <u>over</u> you; I am not <u>over</u> you, I am a <u>part</u> of you! I Love you. I thank you for the Love that you give each other. I thank you for the Love that you are spreading in this land, in this world, on this Earth. For as you know, Love never ends, and it goes on and on! Love IS! Love IS the I AM! Love IS the EVERYTHING! It is the ALL! It encompasses ALL! It will be forever! It is the beginning and the end. It is everlasting!

Continue your learning and your trying. You are doing so fine! I am so proud of you! Be patient with your teachers. I am here. I am guiding. I am Loving. You will have all that you want, you always have. And you will have all that you need. I am here for you and I HEAR you! I hear your words before you speak them. I see your tears before they are shed. I see your Loving, giving hearts. I see your heartbreak. And I see your Love!   Continue on your fine journey and remember...this is a grain of sand on the beach of Life!

It is I, Michael. It is nice to **see** you here. I see you have questions. Do you know the importance of verbalization? When you **verbalize**, you put things out into the world. It is **good** to verbalize. It is **good** to ask questions. It is good, even, to doubt. For if you doubt, you are **thinking**! That is good! We are here to guide and to help and to provide you the answers that you are asking. For it does not **seem** short, but your life on this Earth is short. It is a breath in the sentence that you are speaking today and tomorrow. It is nothing. But it is **important** in this moment, and that is why we ask you to live in this moment and to **be** in this moment. All three of you like to **escape** now and then, and you want to go into the tomorrow, and you want to go outside of this Earth. It is important that you **be here now**, for you have **chosen** to be here, and we are proud of you for that choice. For you are **needed**!

For the Light that you shed to others is **so very** important, for it is **raising** the vibration, and it is teaching others. It is, actually, **re-teaching** others. It is helping others remember that which has been forgotten. It is **shedding the veil** that has been put upon this Earth. It is **weakening** that veil until it is gone, and that is what we must remove. It is spreading the fog, so you can **see**! It is important you be here, and we are thankful, **so thankful,** that you are! We are here to help, to guide and to give you information as needed. But we try to remind you to **be in the now**, please. For it is in the **now** that things are happening. It is in the **now** that things continue to change, and that remembering takes place, and the vibration changes. And you have questions, so please ask them.

Charlene: I have a question. We are often reminded to be who we are, and yet, it seems like it is not enough for us to be doing...

You are Light and Love! You **know** you are Light and Love. Maybe I am not understanding your question. You are Light and Love. Let me clarify. You are Light and Love. That is your **creation**; Light and Love. Through the incarnations, through the many, many, many incarnations, you have **forgotten** the Light and the Love. You have been **reconditioned** in many ways, and cellularly, you are remembering the wrong things, in many ways. It is the **Light** in your Soul and the **Love** in your heart that needs to shine forth **to change the vibration** of this Earth. To save this Earth. There will be **no** Souls lost, so don't be concerned. There will be **no** Souls lost because our Creator Loves them **all** that are here upon this Earth. Some, however, will **not** be able to maintain the vibration needed to remain. Did that help?

Charlene: Yes, thank you.

You have other questions, and many of those questions that you have are very **Earthly**. Let me tell you this; you are **taken care** of. You **each** have a path, as does everyone that exists on this Earth at this time. Many paths will cross. They will cross your path to teach you. They will cross your path for you to teach them.

You have been given a gift. It is the gift of **discernment**. You will **know** what is **needed** with each person that passes your way. You will help each other. You will help many. You will help thousands. You may not be **recognized** as the helper. Do not be concerned with this, for **that** is not what is important. You did not care about that from the beginning and you will not care about that tomorrow. The important thing is to **be who you are**! When we say **be who you are**, we are saying shed your Light, shed your Love, and smile your smile. And with your eyes, the Light of God will come through, and **you** will be recognized.

So you see, it is **you** who needs to be recognized by others, and you **will** be. Others will know they can **come** to you, by the Light they see, by the aura, by the feeling, by the glow. That is **why** we say **be who you are** so others can see you! For in being that lovely, lovely Loving person, others will want to **be in your glow** for it feels good! For **you** are Love and Light! And you are **not afraid** to **be** Love and Light!

Others will be **attracted** to you for they find happiness, consolation and they feel good! When you are around Spiritually, the Light of God, when you have **left** your body and been in God's presence, you **know** the Loving glow that is felt. That is how **others** will feel around you. For the three of you can be **together** and Love one another and bask in each other's Love and Light. It has become a familiar territory to you now. It is not odd, it does not feel different. It feels very normal. It will **not** be normal to others. They will want to be around you just to **bask** in **your** Light. You **might** attract those that you may **not want** to attract. Send them Light;

that's what they are after. They are after the Light. They are after the Love. This is where the gift of discernment will help you, for you will know who to **send away** with Light and Love, and who to shed **additional** Light and Love on, to help them know God. They will ask the right questions and you will know. You don't have to have **any fear** about anything! All you have to do is **be who you are**! So now **that's** all you need to do.

As you see the tornado around you, it will twirl and twirl and twirl, but it is not about **you**, for you are totally content as you bask in **your own** Light and Love! For **you know** you are taken care of. For **you know** that The Creator is looking down upon you and that you are personally covered with Angels for total protection! And you know **nothing** can touch you. Nothing can touch your Soul. Nothing can touch your heart. Nothing can affect your Love and your Light. You are **who you are** and you will be that forever! And you are now helping others remember, just by **being** who you are. So now does that help you? Do you understand?

All you have to do is **be** who you are, and **don't rush** into tomorrow, but **be in the today**! If you rush into tomorrow, others don't have **time** to even **be in** your Light, for you are rushing away. So you see the importance of being in the **now**. That is your job now, just BE! All will **happen** as it should happen, in the perfect time, in the perfect way, and the perfect space. You'll be directed and guided by God, Himself. And you'll be protected by all The Archangels and all the personal Angels that you have. There are many **armies** waiting to help and protect. All you have to do is **be** who you are and you will be taken care of. All will happen in the way it should, in the **very perfect** time and the **very perfect** way, for **you** are becoming **very perfect** in everything you do.

Release all fear, for there should be **no fear** left in your heart. For you **know** all is taken care of, and all that remains is Light and Love. And when you feel fear, you know it is **ego**; let it all **go**, send it **all** to the Light. Even though you are Light and Love (that is what you are Spiritually), you are still human beings, being here now. There is **no getting away** from that, for the time being. You will be here for just a short while longer. As you know, time and space is **so different** here on Earth! It is very different. So you will be here for a moment, you will be here for a hundred years; you will be here for a day and a half. Time **only** exists here. You will be here for as long as you are needed. Again, that is not something to be concerned with or to worry about.

There will be many others that will be leaving this Earth before you, for **you** are **needed**. For we will bring Light to this Earth and it will **stay**. There will be **no more darkness** when it is over. And **that** is what we are releasing. And **that** is what **you** are doing, as we **remove** the veil that surrounds this planet Earth. There are many other things that will be unfolded at a later time. It is not time, now, to discuss it. It is time for you to live in the NOW and be in the KNOW. It is time for you to BE. It is not time to reveal.

Do you have other questions? You will. You will have other questions. As you do, know that **you each** have the power, the knowledge, and the ability to get these answers, just as you are doing in this moment. You **all three** have the ability to **channel** and to hear what is being said to you from other dimensions, from your personal Angels, from The Archangels, and from The Creator. If you have doubt on the things you hear, **write it down**. For sometimes it is **easier** for you to write than to verbalize. Do what is easiest for you and share with one another, the information as you receive it, with the questions that you ask, and the answers that you are given. For it is **important** that you share. You are all doing a very, very fine job and you are wonderful in all that is happening in your lives. We are proud of you. We thank you. We thank you **so much** for all that you are doing! Continue your good work. We are here guiding and Loving you as you do. Know that you are **never alone**, and know that we are protecting you at all times. Do not let fear enter your heart, for it does **not belong** there!

And now we will say good-bye to you, even though we are **with** you at all times. **Reflect** on the things that you need to know. **Reflect** on the things that you heard today. We will help every way we can. We will clarify if you need clarification. But the important thing is... today right now, to **be who you are**. Reflect the Light of God through **your** eyes and through **your** mouth and through **your** heart and through **your** mind in **all** that you do, for it is **shone**. It, actually, is **visible** for all to see. It is important now, and we thank you for being who you are, and we Love you.

Thank you. Thank you.

Love
By Denis Hill

When your feeling for someone is maximum appreciation,
When you cherish and adore them with passionate anticipation,
When you are enchanted by them with deep feelings of respect,
When you are devoted to them with strong desire to protect,
When you honor and encourage for their successful deployment,
When you can't wait to be with them for your ultimate enjoyment...
You are in LOVE.

The Spectator
By Denis Hill

The spectator watches as others have fun.
He sits and observes as they play...as they run.
He chooses not to join in, nor give it a try.
He would rather allow the world to pass by.

The spectator watches as others now cry,
Not even affected by their reasons why.
He doesn't allow himself to feel pain...
He just sits in the bleachers, all full of distain.

The spectator can't feel his own highs or lows
So he watches as others put on the shows.
Their emotions are theirs and not his concern,
Like a foolish investment without much return.

Being a spectator is a pretty good deal,
That way there's no need to actually feel.
You watch as everyone else takes their turn
At laughing and crying...it's not your concern.

But wait...am I missing out on all of Life's zest?
Should a bird live his life without leaving his nest?
Would you order ice cream and say, "Please hold the flavor"?
Of course not! All of Life has something to savor.

The decision is made...I will get in the game!
The people around me just won't be the same
When they see me living Life to the fullest extent!
I will now be Life's greatest participant!

17

Speak Your Truth

December 12, 2000 at 3:05 P.M. Charlie and Sue
Prayer and the Language of Light spoken.

Hello, it is I, Michael. I am here today with you, and there are **many** with me. Joining us today, are many Archangels, many Angels and Guides, and your Holy Creator. We are here, and we will give you some information.

We want to **thank** you. We are **thanking** you for listening. We are **thanking** you for paying attention. We are **thanking** you for being who you are. For it is through **you**, that the Light and the Love is spread. You do not realize the impact on other people by your very **presence**, which is why it is so important. Just **be you**. Just **be who you are**, and be who you are **now**. Be in the today, and be as **centered** as you are. There are others that will be put in your path. It is important for you to **stay** as centered, as you are being.

It is important that you **speak your truth**. You can speak your truth **kindly**. You can speak your truth with Love and Light. If you have doubt, or if you are worried about how your **words** will be interpreted by others, ask for our help. For we are **always willing**, we are **always waiting**, and we are **always wanting** to be at your side to guide and assist. Have no fear! For all you say and do will be perfect. If it is "**too much information**", it will not be understood and it will be forgotten. If the heart is **ready** it will be heard and it will be understood and it will be accepted.

Now is a time that **many** in your path will be working on judgment. They will be learning. Do not worry about what **others** think of you, for **that** is not important. Just stay who you are, and stay centered. Other people's thoughts are **not** important, for they cannot **affect** you. They are working on their **own** judgment, and it is not about **you** to enter their path and show them they are being judgmental. They must learn **that** on their own. For now is a time when everyone's "stuff" is being put in **front** of their face; whether it be money matters, judgmental matters, church matters, relationship matters, friendship matters, or business matters.

There are many roles a person has. You will be **eliminating** some and you will be concentrating on **who** you are and not **what** you are. And how **lovely** when you can help one another! That is one of the keys to the Love that is presently missed on this Earth. But it is coming back, and you are **bringing** it back. Many are bringing it back; teaching it, showing it, Loving each other. Many are **helping** each other by opening a door, **helping** each other by picking up something dropped, helping and Loving each other just because; not because of a **reward**, not because of what you get by doing so, but just because **you** are Love! And **that** is what you are spreading. And **that** is so, so important! It is **urgent** now! For you see, the positive spreads **positive** and the Love spreads **Love**! The negative spreads the negative.

You with your positive...the positive attitude, the positive behavior, the positive environment, the positive thoughts, the positive **everything**... you are **eliminating** the negative. As you know, **without** the Love that surrounds all, the negative can easily take over. Which is why, at this current time, the veil on this Earth, the fog as you call it, is being **lifted** and eliminated. For it is only Love and Light that **can do** that. And it is through you, and it is through others who are discovering again and **remembering who they are**, that it is lifting that veil and spreading that Love and eliminating the negativity.

Your creativity is exploding! You can teach and you can profit by **much** that you are doing now. Not just your paintings and your glass, Charlie, you have much **more** to give. Yes, you have **that** and it will be profitable but you have more. You don't have to think about it. You don't have to respond to it, for it is already there, it exists, and it is created. You continue to **create**, and the profit will come.

You are wise to concentrate on discernment. That is **huge** right now! You are both learning, and as we **said** you would, you chuckle as you learn. For you know **you** are taken care of and you are! Listen. Try hard **not** to pass judgment, for **that** is not what you are. Love all through their learning. Not **all** are at your level of enlightenment. You are very blessed! Continue practicing and continue learning. Continue discerning. Continue asking for help. Continue Loving. Continue **being**. Continue to **stay centered,** for it has begun. The chaos has begun. Do not worry what **others** think, for that is not important and is **so** meaningless! See the best you can in others. Recognize their goodness. Recognize goodness when others cannot, and point it out, for that will make you shine even brighter. But, **believe** it; as you say it, believe it. Ask to **see** the Love in everyone's heart. Ask to **see** the goodness in everyone's lives; by doing so you will help them bring that goodness to the surface. For that positive energy will grow and expand and lighten their life, as it **needs** to be enlightened.

You will be put to tests. Not by us! **Not** by Your Creator! You will be put to tests by those you **think** are friends and by those you **think** you Love and trust. You **do** Love them, you **do** trust them, but you will be put to tests that might hurt your feelings. Do not **let** your feelings get hurt. Know that they don't know **how** to **ask**. They don't **know** the questions. They don't **know** the answers. They don't understand why **you** are happy. They don't understand why **you** glow. They don't understand why **you** have changed. They don't understand **what** makes you different, for you **look** the same. Be careful with the **words** you speak, for **they** will be judged. By knowing this, **speak with Love** in your words and Love in your hearts.

And if, when asked a question, you don't know how to respond in a Loving way, call your Angels in, call your Guides, call in ALL of your help, for we are here. And we will assist you in **showing** you what Love would do and what Love would say and how Love would respond. You have grown to such a point that we do **not expect** you to need our help. We will be here Loving you, but at times, you **may be caught off-guard**. It will be specific people that will catch you off-guard, and you will know it. It will be a **shock** down your spine; it will be a tingle down your spine and you will know, "Oh-oh, I need to call my **help** in!" You will **recognize** it as it is said to you.

Family doesn't **mean** to hurt, but they do. They don't mean to. It is not intentional. Know that... for they do Love you. They are **confused.** As we spoke before about the chaos, as we spoke before about the tornadoes that were **around** you but not **about** you, it still has **an effect** on you, for they will come to you with questions. For **you** are not **disturbed** by any of the chaos and they don't get it! So they will come to you for answers, and that's okay. You will not do **anything** wrong, for you are perfect in **all** you say and do. But prepare yourselves and each day **protect** yourselves. Each day, say a prayer for each other. We are here. We are Loving you. We are guiding you. Help each other, as you are here to help many. You don't realize the lives you touch, but you do touch others...everyday!

You have both become very **wise** about your own children. You are recognizing what they are here to learn, and what you are here to teach, and what you are to be silent about. For they, too, must learn **their** lessons and they cannot learn the lessons if you **take over** for them and solve their very problems that they must learn from! See how you've grown? You have grown **lifetimes** in just a few, short months! In two years, you have grown more, Spiritually, both of you, than you have in **several lifetimes** combined! You are trusting. You are learning. You are Loving! You are being who you are! The Universe is grateful!

One reason the two of you are not as holiday oriented as you normally are, is due to the fact that you **are in tune** to what is happening in the Universe, as opposed to what is happening on a day many years ago. It has **new** meaning for you now. For you feel the blessing **every** day! You feel God **every** day! You have no need to take **one** specific day and thank Jesus for bringing it to all people's attention that He was born and He spread great Light and Love; that He brought new meaning to the Earth, because they had such a hard time listening. It is **no wonder** that it has lost the luster it once had for you. For you see, you have grown **beyond** it. Do you see? You celebrate **every** day! It is funny! For the gifts you have purchased for each other were not purchased last week, but through the year. And you have given each other gifts through the year, for **that** is how you celebrate now. It is not one day a year; it is **every** day of the year! And **that** is good! And **that** is the way it should be!

Now you will **recognize**, in some of the organized religions, **where** certain things came from. There are some religions that do not celebrate birthdays and Christmas and the other spiritual holidays and other holidays throughout the year. For they celebrate **every** day. You are learning to celebrate from your **heart**, not the calendar. You are learning to do that without the help of a specific organization, you simply **do**. And you do so **without** putting down others for celebrating or not celebrating, for calling it Christmas, for calling it Hanukah, for now **you** understand the **true** meaning of celebrating life! **Every** day is a holiday!

Different churches have brought **different** goodness to mankind. Which is why we say be gentle. For as much as they have brought some goodness, they have done some harm in other ways. Harm is a harsh word. They have, blindly, **miscommunicated the original intent**. What happens is

123

humans **forget** who they are and they become **Earth**lings, attached to the Earth, instead of the **BE-**ings that they are. They are **forgetting** where they came from and are only considering where they are currently **existing** in the physical sense. Hence, they have lost the **intent**. They have **lost** the true meaning, and have become Earth-ly. When you are of the Earth, without the consideration of the Heavens, you are **not** whole and complete. And when you are **not** whole and complete you can see only a **portion** and not focus on the full picture. You can only see **a very small** side; the darker side, **not** the lighter side.

With the work you do, you will **remove** the darkness. For the shadows will not exist, for the Sun is directly above you in the sky; in the bright blue sky! And when the Sun is directly above you, look…there is **no** shadow, for the Sun is centered **directly** over you. And it is through the work you do, the Light Work you do, that **all** shadow will be removed! For the Light will be directly overhead! And the film and the fog **will be gone**, and the air will be clean and bright and there will be no smog! And the **Light** will remain! And the world will **become anew**, for the vibration will be where it **should** be, and it will be raised to the degree that it **needs** to be, to transcend the Earth to the place it will be.

This will be done by your Light Work, for it is **through** the Light that you bring, for it is the Light that you share, for Light **creates** Light in the hearts of others. So as you **spark a heart**, it will become a blaze and it will spark another. And the Earth will be as it **should** be. And the Heaven will be as it **should** be. And the Universe will be as it **should** be. And all the Souls will **recognize** each other again. And the **Love will be back** the way it was, and it will **stay** the way it should! And lessons will have been learned, and **all will be well** in God's Kingdom!

And I will be here **assisting** you, between God's Kingdom and Earth. I will assist **all**. Do not worry. Do not **worry** about your children. Do not **worry** about your families. They are all where they **need** to be right now. Remember to **let** them remain on their path. Remember to Love them through whatever it is **they** are learning. Remember to Love **all** through what they are learning. You will meet others that are on your path or parallel with your path. You are yet unaware of how **many** lives you are touching and how many Souls you are touching. You are not finished. Do not allow time to be an **issue** for you, for it is not.

The more you stay **out** of your mind and **into** your heart, the more lives you will touch, because that is **not** where you are…you are simply being **who** you are. And **that** is the way it will happen. You will continuously touch those by being who you are. It is something that you cannot stop, something you cannot change, something you didn't create. It is something that simply **is**. All you have to do is **be you**! And by **being** you, you are fulfilling our purpose. For you are Light and Love! Your roads ahead of you are very smooth and paved, and **flowered** along the way. We are so very **proud** of you for, finally, taking the time to smell the roses. Don't stop! You are seeing beauty in things that have always been there, because you DO hear God, you DO feel His touch, you DO hear His voice, and you DO see His beauty! You do know, when we say His, it also means **Hers**. Your language, your language, your language…it is so limiting! Speak the Language of Light to us, for **that**, we hear perfectly. For it is the Language of Light, that **we** hear and see your heart.

It is I, your Creator. I must tell you! I must share with you! I so Love you both! I Love you ALL! Thank you for hearing Me and Loving Me and seeing Me and knowing Me! Thank you for your friendship with Me! Thank you, for I have always Loved you, and I LOVE that you Love Me back! You never KNEW Me the way you Love Me now, and the way you know Me now. Thank you! I am always here. I have always been here, and as all want to talk to you because you so listen! We thank you for that.

They ALL want to talk to you. They all have the same things to say to you, and I will always be here to talk to you, to listen to you and to know you and to be with you. Know that I am proud of you! You know that you give Me Great Joy! Don't ever have fear. Know that your lives are full of Joy and Love. Know that you have more help than you ever needed or wanted. Know that you are taken care of, and know that I Love you! Obviously I have more to say to you; know I am here, but I will let others say good-bye to you, as I will talk to you soon.

It is I, Michael. I will now say good-bye to you both. You are **covered** in Light and Love! Merry Christmas! Happy New Year! Happy **Tuesday**! Happy December! Happy day! Happy night! Happy hour! Happy minute! Happy times! Now, go **spread** your smile, **spread** your Love and **spread** your joy and **spread** your Light! Learn the **lessons** that are in front of you. Spread the words as they are given to you, and BE. Just BE! And with Love we say good-bye.

Thank you. Thank you.

Spark A Heart
by Charlene Hill

"Spark a Heart", the angels said,
"And watch the flame ignite.
That is how you spread God's Word,
That's how you spread the Light."

For when you are kind and loving,
You spark other people's hearts.
God's Flame of Love ignites in them,
And a chain-reaction starts.

Each kind deed, each ray of Light
That shines through one enlightened,
Eliminates darkness from the Earth
And heals the lost and frightened.

"Have no fear, we're here with you.
We never leave your side.
Just ask yourself: What would Love do?
Take judgment in your stride.

Don't be concerned if others think
That you're out of your mind.
Stay in your heart, BE who you are,
Light and Love, forever kind.

The time has come...the time is now,
To wake-up and remember.
It's time to spark each person's heart,
And fan each tiny ember.

Bring back to Earth the Love of God
Within the hearts of men.
God loves each one and wants so much
To be known by them again!

God is not fear or vengeance,
Not judgment, wrath or war.
God does not think that you have sinned,
Or love your neighbor, more.

God does not cause catastrophes,
Wars and death and woe.
God wants you to love and be His friend,
Because He loves you so!

God is Love...that's all God is,
And Love is never mean.
God does not judge or punish,
Yet every act is seen.

Yes, every act, both large and small
That happens on this Earth,
Is seen by God...He knows you well,
And loved you before birth.

You were not born of sin, you know.
You are, from God, a thought.
God is part of you, and you, of Him.
You were incorrectly taught.

God wants so much to be your friend,
For He sees your friendships here.
He wants you to know Him and His Love.
That you, to Him, are dear.

The way to get this message out,
Is through the hearts of men.
When each is burning bright with Love,
God will be known...again!"

18

Denis' Automatic Writing @ Feeling

12/17/2000
Automatic Writing from Denis:

Dear Angels,

I am now beginning to feel again. It is not as scary as I thought it would be. I, very much, appreciate your help and your Love. I Love you back! I surrender my control to God's control. I surrender my will to God's will.

I am excited about a new beginning. This next year will be great! I am living in the "now". I am appreciating where I am, who I am with and what I am doing. I am even appreciating how I am FEELING! My heart is open! My Soul is excited and exuberant! I'm filled with Love and Light. I have so much to give and teach and yet I have much to learn.

I am beginning to Love myself! Please teach me how I can reach my highest potential.

Thank you. Love,
Denis

12/17/2000

Dearest Denis,
We are so **proud** of you! You are such a sweet student! Your Light, now, is bright for ALL to see. Those who **need** your special Light and Love and encouragement will be attracted to you. You do have so much to give! Be creative. Be humorous. Be Light and of course be Love for that is **who you are**. We Love you so!

Yes, Next year will be **very** exciting, full of activity. You are needed. We will instruct you. You will experience Great Joy as you simply enjoy being "you". The word you used, "**Exuberance**" describes you perfectly. You are an inspiration to everyone. They say,"How can he be so happy and energetic and loving ALL the time?"

You will **reach** people through your talents. These talents are very special gifts. The Creator has given you these gifts so that **you** can help make this world a more enjoyable place. These gifts are inspiring to others. Please use them and Love them and find joy in them. You are learning how to see the best in people. You are **beginning** to be able to see their hearts. Please continue to notice. We are ALL connected to The Creator. We are part of Him...He is part of us. Look past the exterior and notice the **essence** of each person. You will make a connection, instantly, with their Soul. There will be an instant Homecoming as you do, for both of you.

Now you wear the Halo of Light. This halo glows bright for all to see. No one can mistake your Light and Love. Your **exuberance** is irresistible to others. Your positive encouragement is appreciated and needed. Be you!

We Love you and are with you always.

Your Angels

-19-
Creativity

December 19, 2000 at 1:55 P.M. Denis, Sue and Charlie

We thank The Creator for being with us today. We ask for any information that You might have for us, to share with us, through The Archangels, all of our Angels and Guides, and through The Creator, Himself. We are very, very grateful to You for coming and joining us, being with us, helping us, and giving us clarity in our path. We are very thankful. We ask that any and all information be given to us for our highest and best good. We ask The Archangels to be here with us today, and help clarify any information that is passed to us; may it pass through you. As you come in, would it be possible to identify yourselves so that we can get to know you on a more personal basis? Thank you.
The Language of Light was spoken...

Well hello, everybody! It is I, Michael. It is nice to **see** you all together. It is nice to have such a beautiful day for you to enjoy, and it is nice to see your smiling faces. It is nice to see your happy Spirits. It is nice to see your joy. It is nice to **see you**. I would like to **share** something with you today. I would like you to think about your own **creativity**. I would like to talk about your **ability**. You see, being creative means to use your **imagination**. You **all** are creative. **All** are given the gift of creativity. It is **not** just drawing a picture. It is **not** just writing a book. It is **not** just singing. It is **not** just music. It is **more** than that. For you to reach your full **potential** is to use your imagination. You see, you **limit** yourself. You get in your own way. **Think outside the box**! It is limitless. You can do **anything**! You have not **allowed** yourselves to expand by using the imagination you have, for you are afraid to truly **believe** that you **can** have anything you choose. You see, if you can **imagine** it, if you can **think** it, you can **do** it, and you can **have** it.

You have **old tapes** playing in your head; tapes from your childhood, tapes from many, many years ago. You rewind them and play them occasionally, and rather than it showing you that **it is limitless**, you tell yourself what limits **you have**, when in fact there **are** none! There are **no limits** to what you can **do** and what you can imagine! Just think outside the box! You have been told your whole life, of what you **can't** do and of what you **are not**. You have allowed those things to take over your mind, instead of what you CAN do, and what you ARE! And what you **are** is Light and Love! **How** do you put Light and Love in a box? How do you put boundaries on Light and Love? Do you see? There are **NO BOUNDARIES**! Whatever you can **imagine**, you can do! Whatever you can imagine, you can **be**! For what you are, Light and Love, there are **no boundaries** and there are **no limits**. So let yourselves **go**! Be who you are and let yourselves **go**! It is **not** what you are not, for you are **all**! Do **not play** those tapes any more! Do **not listen** to the words that have been spoken to you many years ago. Put them outside of your mind. They **do not** belong to you. Do **not** own them. They are **not yours**!

Now, let's talk about creativity. For in creativity, and **all** are creative, all create differently. And all create differently with different **things**; whether it is a pencil and paper, whether it is musical instruments, whether it is ink, whether it is clay, whether it is chalk, whether it is metal; whatever choice may be, **anything** can be created. You can **use** your creativity with whatever you have at hand. **All** are creative. Every human being on this Earth is **creative**, for you have creativity in your very Soul! Part of who you **are** is being creative and creating. Now, since **everyone** is creative, and everyone creates **differently**, many, because it is so personal, create and they **hide**... for it is **so** personal it belongs to just you. And it is **hard to share** for it is a part of **your** very heart and your Soul. It is a part of **your** experience. Therefore, it's **hard** to share and **if** shared, there is an element of **fear** for it might be judged. Learn this lesson. Judge **not** someone else's creativity, for someone **has created** something. It is a **masterpiece**, for it is a **part** of them. Whether it is made of paper, whether it is made on canvas, or whether it is made from metal or whether it is made from concrete does not matter, for it is an **expression of self**. It is artistic in the artist's eyes.

It is **perception**. You know art is perception. It is perceived in many, many different ways. As you all are creative, as you **all** create, as you all use a **different** means of creating, you compliment each other. You give each other encouragement. You see, **that** is what you need to do for **all**. You give encouragement. You **help** others bring out, from within **themselves**, their own creativity by the means they choose to express it. All **express** creativity in a different way. If it is **not harmful** to someone, then it is good. It is **not** to be judged because it **is a part** of that artist or that creator. Are we understanding my point? Are we understanding what I am saying? For it is **another** lesson in judgment, but it is also a lesson in bringing out the creativity and imagination in other people. Everyone needs to learn the way **they** need to learn and they are on their **own** path. Just as you have your own path to walk, you have your own path to learn. You also have **your own path** to **create**. Allow each to create in **his** way.

You spread the Light and Love throughout the Universe by being who you are. You realize you do it just by **that**; by smiling, by offering a hand when someone needs it, by picking up an item someone drops, by smiling at a stranger or by holding a door open for someone you don't know. All these little, little things help your Light shine brighter. Here is what that **does**; that Light that you shine, you shine through your eyes, you shine through your very Soul. As others see it, it sparks **their own** Soul. So you see, it is you that **ignite** the Light, and you do so by just **being**!

Here are three bright Lights in a room, and you all three leave and you go to three **separate** dark rooms, and now you bring Light into that room. And if one other person walks **into** that room you are in, you ignite **their own** Light by being who you are. By **being** who you are, they ask you questions and you answer. You do **not ever** be pushy. You do **not ever** insist on

133

anything other than simple, simple, simple. Don't **make** it hard. It's **not** hard, it's just simple. You see, all you have to do is **be**. As the dim sparks ignite, they become **brighter**, then **they** leave that room and they go to another; because **they** now have a Light that shines, they then shine it on another and **you see**, you are playing a game of dominos. You simply add to the **chain**; the chain of Life, and you do so by just simply **being**!

Others will come to **you** because all around you is chaos. All around you there are tornadoes. There are volcanoes erupting. Storms are swirling all over the world, but not in **your** world. **You** are centered. **You** are happy. **You** spread joy. **You** spread Light. Through all the chaos, **you** have an inner peace of quiet, for **you** know all is well. You **know** it from the very bottom of your heart, and **you** are fine with it. That is when they will come to you and they will say, "**Share** with me **your** happiness and **your** peace. Share with me **how** you can stay so joyful."

And you will share. And you will all teach. You will teach them what they **really** are. You will teach them that **they** are Light and Love. You will teach them that The Heavenly Creator is **their friend** and Loves them very much. You will teach them, no... you will **re-teach** them. For you need to **erase** the old tapes that have been in the lives of too many people. It is a **re-teaching**, and it will start immediately.

Archangel Metatron is here today, too. Metatron would like to tell you a few things for himself:

Hello. It is so **nice** to see you again. I know you **know** me. It is I, Metatron, and I am with you daily, too. I have been with you in your meditations and I am the one that talks to you frequently and forgets to tell you who I am. I just forget. I **know** you **know** me, and I **forget** to say my name. I want you to know that I am **always** here for you, too, for I am here to help you. I am here to help **bridge the gap** between Heaven

134

and Earth. So if you are feeling that you need to **center** yourself, it is I who will help you. Your Heavenly Creator, of course, is here, too, and He is **always** here for your help, but I am right here to help you, too. I have **always** been here to **help** you bridge that gap.

I have **always** been here to help you when you got yourself into such an Earthly situation that you **needed** to be touched by one outside of Earth, by one outside of **your** world and into mine. And I have always been here to help, and I always will. It may happen. Do not **ever** have fear. As the world around you is **changing**, and as your government is changing, and as the world itself changes leadership, do **not** have fear and do not worry. As I have said to you before, just chuckle, for you **know** you are taken care of. For you know all is well in **your** world. For **you know** all is as it should be!

Good afternoon! It is lovely to see the three of you! It is I, your Creator. I have one thing to add to that. I would like to let you know that fear is not only not a part of your life, it should never touch your hearts, it should never touch your Soul, for you have more help than you realize! Now, I have a simple statement to tell you. When you feel the world around you, so chaotic, and you become shaken, think of Me and visualize this:

Visualize My outstretched hand touching you, and through My hand is the Light that enlightens you. That IS you. That is Me, and it is coming down to you, into your crown chakra. Visualize this. And it goes through you and it goes out your feet into Mother Earth and you are centered and you are perfect and you are happy and you are well and all is well in your world. Do not get shaken, for I am here. I am here with you. But know that that which is to come to be must be. And know that it is a part of the ultimate plan. And know that you are *perfect and you are well and <u>all</u> in your world is well. Just remember that what must be, must be. And it is going to happen at the perfect time in the perfect way. And <u>know</u> that Love surrounds you. And <u>know</u> that I am here. And <u>know</u> that I send you much help. And all the Angels in Heaven Love you. And they are so grateful! They Love talking to you, as do I. They have more to say to you and I will let them. Know I Love you.*

It is I, Michael. I **do** have some more to share with you today. It is more about the people who will come in your path, for you really have a **mission** here and I think you all realize that. For **not only** does your Light shine, it needs to shine amongst those that **need** it most. For you see, here are the three of you, with three beautiful Shining Lights. You have ignited each other and **you are ignited** and now you need to help those that have darkness. That does not mean you can't be together, but it means you have **separate** paths to go on now. It means that you have **different** people to be in front of for different reasons. It means that many will ask you and do not be afraid to ask **us** for our help, and do not be afraid to ask each **other** for each other's help.

Your job will be **setting each Soul** into the Light. You will not be **teaching** them how to do this, because you will help them **re-member**. They **know** how; they **forgot**. So it is not **from scratch** that you go. You are helping them **re-member**. And it is through the Light they see in **your** eyes, and it is **through** your soft-spoken words, and it is **through** your kindness, and it is through the simple acts that are every day. There will be many miracles, but it will **not** be going into the middle of the street and healing everybody from a car accident. It will be the **simple acts** every day. You see **that** is what makes the difference. Yes, there will be miracles, but do you **see** what I am saying to you? It is in your **everyday being**; that is why we say **be who you are**. For in being who

136

you are, your Light just shines! And it is being who **you** are that helps others remember. Through this you may be doing workshops, you may be doing meditations, you may be having private meditations, you may be doing many things, and will, but it is in the **every** day that you need to concentrate.

When the Master that you know, the Master Jesus, walked on this Earth, do you think He only "hung out" with those that were the holiest; with those that **knew** God in their hearts? He did **not**, for you see, preaching to the choir is redundant. It is those who have never **heard** the choir. Do you know those that Jesus "hung out" with were not the most liked? They were not the popular people. They were not the **respected** group in society. Now I am **not** telling you to go to shelters, I am telling you to pass **no** judgment. I am telling you to just be aware. I am telling you that those that are in your path are there for a **reason**, every one. They may be teaching you, and you may be teaching them, but it is **important** that you listen.

Sue, you listened to us well. For you **so** wanted to speak and we kept telling you to stay quiet, and you did, and we were **proud** of you! But you see, you went far **further** by being quiet. You have no idea, but your husband jumped a football field, where he would have taken a step **backwards** had you spoken. Instead he leapt forward. For you not only allowed **him** to speak, you **validated** his very feelings. You **helped** him grow, and he is not finished yet, and he is stuck, but only **he** can get unstuck.

No pushing! Do **not** push! Do **not** pull! Do **not** yank! He has to move on his **own** accord, but now he **knows** he can speak to you. And you were very wise, for you set your limits in that yes, he was allowed to speak, and yes, he was allowed to speak respectfully, but **only respectful** speaking was allowed. You in **no** way, any of you, should **ever** take abuse, however, when abuse is in front of you, remember to send Light and Love. For it is the heart that **has fear** that brings out abuse. Fear brings it out, for **they** are hand in hand. You see they are best friends. And **that** is fear's favorite playmate; abuse. You may be ridiculed... remember that means **fear**. It is not **your** fear. Remember don't own what is not **yours**, and **that** is **not** yours. It is another's. And when that happens again...Light and Love. Remember to be silent.

Others will come into your paths, especially this holiday season. Remember you will knock them backwards if you preach. Do **not** preach! **Validate**. Make sure **respect** is a part of the combination. If someone has an opinion other than yours, and is forceful, send them Light and Love and smile. Arguing serves **no** purpose. So you respectfully say that you respect **their** opinion and you respect the fact that **you** are allowed to differ from it.

Be respectful in your differential of opinions. You may say, "**I, respectfully, have a difference of opinion and that's okay**." Or you may say, "**I hear what you are saying, and I respectfully disagree**." You see, you **must** handle it with respect**,** so you want to validate anything they say; that you have **heard** it, **not** that you agree, but that you have **heard** what they are saying and that you **respectfully disagree**. When these things happen, as your Creator instructed, as your Creator suggested, He gave you a simple, **simple vision** that will be most helpful to you during those times of frustration. Stay centered with the Light of God.

Do you have questions for me? If not, then I tell you to have a lovely day! I have **so enjoyed** seeing you today! I have **so enjoyed** hearing what you have to say today! I have **so enjoyed** sharing with you today! We are **always here** for you. Please continue writing. Write every day. Write your feelings, write your thoughts, write your dreams, and use your **imagination**. There are **no boundaries**, so you can't color outside the lines! There **aren't** any! Put color in your life! Keep joy there! Every day, wake up with a passion for life, with a joy for the day to begin, with a knowing that it is perfect; with a thankfulness, and with Love. You are **covered** in Love! You are **surrounded** by Love and protection. All is **well** in your world. And now go spread the Light and Love that you are! We **thank** you. We thank you for **all** you do. We are so very, very grateful that you are who you are and you are **being** who you are! **Stay centered** in this lovely day! Good-bye now.

Thank you. Thank you.

20

Denis' Automatic Writing…"Why?"

12/30/2000
Automatic Writing from Denis:

Dear Angels,

Thank you for these conversations. I love talking to you and your help, advice and instructions are so much appreciated.

Would you, please, explain the instructions that were given to Charlene, that she should "move away from me emotionally"? We both want to understand what you mean by this and do what is right. I love her and she loves me and we want to be together. We want to Love together. Please clarify this and help us both to know what we are to do.

Also, please help me understand why I have lost everything. Where did I go wrong? Why is this happening to me? What must I learn from this? When will the struggle end?
Thank you.
Love,
Denis

12/30/2000
Dearest Denis,
Good morning! We are glad that you are back from your trip. We showed you many things while you were in Salt Lake City. We were with you always.

We will try to explain the instructions we gave to Charlene. We know that when Charlene focuses on you and your needs and wants, she is not focusing on **her** and **her** needs and wants. It is very important, at this time, that she pays attention to **herself**. She must listen to her heart. She must go inside. She must think outside the box without distractions. We are **not** telling her not to Love you...we **are** telling her to Love herself first and realize what she needs and wants from within herself. She has devoted all of her attention in the past to you and not to her. You can be together if you want to, but

Charlene must know that it is not required and it will be a choice.

Denis, you have not lost everything! You have much more than you realize. You have been given much **knowledge** that few people have. You have been **shown** who you are! You have an open line directly to The Creator and to us. You have good health. You have the ability to center yourself between Heaven and Earth. You have the ability to imagine and create. You must use these gifts to produce the joy that you want. You must use these gifts to create the financial security that you deserve. In so many ways, you are starting over. You are being taught that at **no** time does any human have nothing. We have never forsaken anyone and we never will. You will enjoy how well your new gifts work for you. We are very pleased to give you these gifts. You will give these gifts to many others, for you will grow to appreciate them so much!

Remember we are helping you get back on your path. You are going to be leaving some things behind as you move on to your path. Please do not be afraid. You will like your new direction. You will like how much easier everything will be. You chose to make it hard. You chose to struggle and hurt. When you are on your right path, everything is effortless and joyous.

Please don't worry about Charlene. She is finding her perfect path as well. Your paths are different and you must follow your **own** path. They will take you in separate directions but don't worry. Your Love will never die. You will always Love her and she will always Love you. Perhaps your paths will cross again soon and you can renew your relationship. Both of you have some very important work to do and it must be done separately. We hope that helps you both understand. We Love you .

Your Angels

21

Bubble of Light, No Death & Dealing With Unenlightened

January 2, 2001 Sue and Charlie
Prayer and The Language of Light was spoken.

Happy Tuesday! It is nice to see you both today. It is nice to see you together, and it is nice to see you starting off with such a **bang** in the New Year. It has begun, as you have been told. You have been warned. You have been prepared for the **chaotic style** that will be present here on this Earth and it will be here for a long time. And it **has** begun.

It is I, Metatron. It is nice to **see** you. Stay focused. Stay centered. It is beginning. There will be many leaving this planet. They **need** to; for as the vibration rises and changes, many will **not** be able to withstand it. You see, the vibration is **hard** to hold. Those in Light-ness, those who are enlightened and **can** hold the Light, not only **can endure** the vibration, they **swim** in it! They **thrive** on it! They **Love** it! It is pleasant; it is happiness, it is good, for it is lightening. It is lightening up your load even more as **you** Lighten up the Earth! For it just **continues** to get lighter and lighter. And as the Bright Lights lighten the load, the **load** also Lightens, do you understand? For the Light will **raise** the vibration and you will Love it!

Now Light attracts Light and like attracts like, but sometimes it has the **opposite** effect. You **will** attract the opposite, too. You must protect yourselves at all times. Those that carry the Light will **recognize** the Light Souls. Those of darkness will also recognize **your** Light Souls and try to dim your Light, so protect yourselves at all times. Now we must share with you. You have **much protection** on the outside. You have many, many, many armies of Angels, as Michael has **battalions** that are constantly guarding and protecting **all** of the Light Workers that are working on this Earth. For that is our purpose, for **that** is why you are here! For you are spreading the Light and Love of God! You are **helping** those remember.

If darkness enters into your path, into your aura, into your comfort zone, **send it away** with Light and Love. Put a **protective bubble** around you. It will be guarded by many Angels. Just **remember**, you must remember. You are both sensitized to a point that **you feel** it quickly. That is good. You see, you are learning. You see, you are growing. You see, you have come a long way, for you now **sense** the darkness without the physical. It is all done with your heart and your Soul and your Spirit. You **know** now. You have **power**. Use it wisely. Use it well. It is the Light and Love that you spread that gives you more and more sensitized ability and the discernment. You are discerning well, and that is **so** good!

You are both doing **so** well. It will get harder, but we will be here to help. It **will** come closer and closer to your homes. It **will** come closer and closer to your hearts. Know that **you** are protected. Know that all is as it **should** be. Know that **all** that happens has **been agreed** upon and it is right and for the highest and best good of all. There will be times you **don't** understand and you will get confused and you will cry. But we will be there Loving you. We will be there comforting you. We will be there helping you understand. You know we are **always** here for you and we will always help. Know that this is what **must** take place.

Many changes will be taking place and they will be taking place very quickly. Do **not** have fear about that for you have been well warned and you have been well prepared. Do **not** have fear. This is the way it will be. This is the way it **should** be. This is the way it **must** be for it is the highest and best good of all. As these changes take place, **continuously protect** yourselves. Continuously comfort each other and help each other, for it is through **this** that you grow. You grow and grow and grow. You become Lighter and Lighter and Lighter.

It is not each other that you will be helping as much as it is **others** that will be crossing your path. You will stay **centered** and by your centeredness you will be very much in control. And you will stay and remain your happy selves. The chaos is not understood by others who are **not** of the same frequency that you are. They will have a hard time understanding you and **this** is where you will teach. This is where much will be learned, for you can verify these things, for **you knew** it would happen. You will **validate**. You will **know**.

You will have members of your own family that will be leaving this Earth. But because you have **no** fear of death, because there **is no death**, you will have no fear at all. We will **comfort** you through your losses. Don't worry and don't have fear. For if you think about it, you can pick those out that are **not** carrying the vibration that they need to. And you can pick those out that **reject** the Light and Love that you send them. It is not rejection; it is **fear**. For you see, fear has taken over the hearts of many. And it is with your Light and Love that you will help **reduce** that fear. But for some it **cannot** happen. For some it is **best** that they leave for it is **too** uncomfortable. For you see, it is **not** a bad thing for they are **already** at an uncomfortable level, so have **no** fear. And we will help them and we will help you.

Pray for your children. Pray for your grandchildren. All of your grandchildren are here for a reason. They **need** to be, for **children hold the Light**. Children hold the Light **better** than most. The children will be holding the Light for their parents. They have not been conditioned to a point that many adults have been conditioned. Now you are here, and you are staying centered, and you will help re-condition and help others remember who they are. And you will help them and guide them and **remind** them. You will **re-introduce** them to their Creator who is Light and Love at its finest and best! Many **do not know** The Creator the way you do. For you have thrown away the tapes, have stopped re-winding, and you have thrown them away. Therefore, you **know** The Creator. You **know**

144

the Love that He is! You **know** the Light and the unending, undying Love! It is **eternal**. It is **unconditional**. It is **forever**! And you **know** it! Not **enough** know it and they need to be reminded and **that** is what you will be doing. Through the validation of the things that will take place in the near future, you will be sharing information that you have been given and because your tapes are dated, the information will be believed.

Have no fear. Fear is **not** a part of your heart. Fear is **not** a part of you. Do not **allow** it in your mind. Do not **allow** it in your heart. Let Love abide there with Light and **you** are fine. Do not take on another's unhappiness or discomfort or learning or teaching if it does not belong to you. Each learns his or her own lessons in the way they have chosen. It is not up to you to **change** that which already **is**, for it is the way it **must** be. It is agreed upon. You forget. It is already done. **All** is already done. And so you see we are here to prepare you and help you understand. It is done and it is done for the **highest** and **best** good of all. Understand and know this. Comfort those that need comforting. Love those that need Loving. Have compassion for those that need compassion. Help those that need help. Send Love and Light to **all**.

Much is happening right now as we speak. Charlie, your friend will be fine, but she is hurting. She is **emotionally** hurting. Send Light and Love. She is trying very hard to have no fear, but she **has fear**. Send Light and Love to **take away** the fear that she is feeling in her heart and in her mind. She is letting her **mind** rule her heart at this time. And that is not good... for your mind cannot **comprehend** what has been agreed to. Only your heart and your Spirit know. If she asks or requests you to go and be with her, do so, but be prepared to put a halt on your trip. She may realize it is too much, for she has more on her plate than she has **ever** had. She will get help from a source that she does not expect. It is **part** of the growth and **part** of the learning and **part** of the teaching. She knows she can depend on you, and **that** is worth more than anything else. For she Loves you very much, and she trusts you very much. She is afraid that all that has been revealed **will** happen as it has been revealed, and she is afraid that it **will not**. She does **not** know which she fears more. Send her Light and Love for **clarity**, for she is having a hard time with clarity. She is doubting herself. Send her Light and Love for she should **not** doubt herself.

It is I, Michael. I am here to share with you and to tell you there are **battalions** of armies. They are in front of you, they are behind you, and they are above you. You have more protection than you have **ever** had, and you will **need** it. Not to have fear, but you will need it because you see you are becoming more and more **powerful** and coming into your **own** power. For you know **how** to use the creative power of Light and Love. You see **that's** what it is; that's what it is all about. Light and Love can do it all! And now you **know**, and with it, you are very, very powerful. We will be helping you. We will be protecting you. And we will be spreading out to protect others as you touch their lives and ignite the flame within. Continue to ignite! I have many **more** battalions of armies! We will **not ever** run out! Know you are very, very, very well protected! Remember, also, when to keep **silent**. That is still a very, very important lesson.

When you have headaches, Charlie, start writing. Very often it is an **energy** level that is rising because your Angels are talking to you, and they are not talking in the **correct** frequency, and you get headaches... when in fact they are trying to talk to you. Sometimes your Guides are talking to you and if they are saying something other than what you **want** to hear, you have trouble hearing it. Open yourself up more, and have no **expectations** about what you do or do not want to hear. If you have trouble, write, for it will come **out** in your writing and it will alleviate your headache. It is the **energy**. Also speaking the Language of Light will help relieve any pressure in your head. The Language of Light is actually **your heart speaking to God**. It is your **S**pirit speaking. It is not the English Language as you know it; it is the Language of the Soul. It is the Language of the Soul, understood by the Angels, by the Elohim, by God, by **all**, and by those on the other side. For it is your Spirit speaking... it is your Soul. So **words** get in your way. With The Language of Light words **cannot** get in the way, for it is a **frequency of feelings**. It is one more thing you can never do wrong! Are there any questions for me?

Charlene: I have a question about my conversation with my father. Did I do harm? Did he back up?

No, you can **never** do harm! You are dealing with a heart that is **hard**. You are dealing with **walls**. You are dealing with an **inability to hear**. You are dealing with a person who has an **inability to feel**. For you see, **he** has tapes that play in his mind, and only **his** tapes are right. That is what he was **taught** to believe. He was **taught** to believe a child could **never** be the teacher, only the parent. Therefore, as **you** are the child, he was **incapable** of hearing a lesson from his child. Do you understand? You were **perfect**. You could not win. You were wise in your recognition of that. You see, his lessons will **not** be learned this lifetime. He has his path.

You must understand that you are working with the human mind, and a human mind that has **not been enlightened**. With the **lack** of Light in certain Souls, they have made the **choice** not to be enlightened. Some have done so to help **you** learn. It is **through** those unenlightened Souls who ask you questions that you will learn and learn to listen to your Guides and Angels and God, in how to address them. So you see, **everything** is learning, even when it is out of your realm. With your human mind, **you** see an unenlightened Soul or an unenlightened person. Your Spirit sees an **opportunity** to help **teach** and even to **learn**! It is not about a **better** way or a different way. Each Soul hears things **differently**, and each Light is ignited in a different way. Those who have been enlightened, and were yesterday a drug addict and today are enlightened and Love The Creator, were enlightened in a **different way** than one who was in **denial** and was raised with no God in their home and has, literally, no tapes to replay. Everybody learns in a **different** way and so you **cannot** pass judgment about which way is **better**. You cannot **do** that. That's not the way that works.

You have to use your **discernment** with each individual person as they come across your path. You have **learned** discernment. You will **use** discernment in what to say and what not to say. If you say too much, they will not comprehend. Sometimes you will recognize the **blank look**, and you will go backwards and talk to them in a more elementary fashion; or realize that it is too much information and you need to jump backwards. But you will learn that **by doing**. It is **not** a right and wrong. There **is** no right and wrong. It is how well one **chooses** to listen and feel. Do you understand?

Charlene: Yes, thank you. I have another question...Denis shared with me, his vision that the essence of each human being on the planet makes up the energy of the Earth, herself. Would you please explain this to me?

Everything is from the **same** essence...**everything**. All of you; each individual and every tree and every planet, is all a **part** of the whole...with the **whole** being The Creator. Therefore, if you can understand, it is **correct**. He is correct, but you need to encompass the ALL. You see you are **all** part of the whole. At any time, you can **separate** yourselves, or you can join back. You are all one, and yet you are separate. The concept is not easily put into words in your English Language; again **words** get in the way. The **concept** is correct, for **all** is a **part** of the whole. You are **all** a part of the whole. You can come together. You can separate. I am not sure how to put it into words that you can comprehend, but the answer is, yes, he is correct. It is **true** but there is **more** and I am at a loss for the proper words in your language. I am sorry that I cannot give you more to help you comprehend. Did I help you?

Charlene: Yes. He was talking about the Circle of Life that he saw, that went up out of the Earth and went back down into the Earth. The supposition that, this essence is, in fact the Earth, and that what we are standing on and what we think is the Earth is nothing more than our essence.

Here is what I must **say** to you: You are everything and you are nothing. You are **all** and you are **one**. Everything is a **part** of the ALL, and yet there is nothing. There is **infinity** and there is **no time**. There is yesterday, today and tomorrow, and there is no space. There is no **time,** there is no **space**, there is no **gravity**, there is no nothing...and yet, there is **everything**! This is **beyond** the comprehension of the human mind! And it is actually **all** true and real and yet it is not... it is a lie. How do you hold air in your hand? How do you **do** that? You see?

It is not a **human** mind comprehension, and it is not something you will **have** the **ability** to properly understand while incarnated in this lifetime. It is real and it is not. It is here and it is gone. It is there and it is yesterday and it is tomorrow and it is tonight and it is...you see...it doesn't matter. **All** is a part of the **whole**. All that is created is created with Light and Love. How do you **measure** Light and Love? You see? I will **never** be able to explain time and space to you! I don't **need** to because it is not a relevant part of why **you** are here... time and space. Much of what you are talking about right now, many of the questions you are asking are real questions...it is hard to give you real answers that you can **comprehend**, and it will not affect the outcome of **why** you are here now. Does that make sense to you?

Charlene: Yes. Thank you.

It is now time to say good-bye to you   All is **well** in **your** world. You have much protection, much Love, and **all** is well. Be ready to help others, as this will be coming up quickly for you. You will be a teacher to many. Have no fear. Know you are protected and Loved, and continue on the straight path you are on. You are perfect in every way! You are doing **well** in everything you are doing, and all is well in **your** world. Remember do **not get caught up** in another's world, in another's chaos. We Love you. Call on us if you need us. We are here always. Good-bye for now.

Thank you. Thank you.

22

Prayer and Channeling for Our Friend
Charlene:

I have a dear friend that I was sharing some of our channeled information with. She asked me to tell her the names of the Angels and Archangels that we were speaking with, and I told her the name of Metatron, among others. She attempted to reach him, too, and instead, pulled in some dark energies. They told her that their names were the same, but they were very tricky, dark entities, and she had a horrible experience. I don't know if she protected herself or prayed prior to calling them in, but whatever the circumstance, it was a very scary, evil experience for her. She contacted me to warn me. She said that she could no longer trust God, and she was very angry. I found this to be most upsetting! After speaking with Denis and Sue about this, and praying about it, we decided to do a special Prayer Channeling for our friend to see if we could help her get back on her right path.

The following is that Prayer Channeling:

Jan. 5, 2001 A **Prayer for our friend**.
Sue, Denis and Charlene are present.

Our dear Father in Heaven, Almighty God, known by many names; Eljabel, Yahweh, Jehovah, the God Almighty, the most powerful God of all, we call upon You today to please hear our prayer for our friend. We feel Your presence among us, and we thank You. We also feel the presence of The Archangels and the battalions of Michael's protective Angels, and we thank you. And we are so grateful for the knowledge that You have given us, and the Light that you have given us and the information that You have shared with us. We are so grateful for the peace that is in our hearts at this time. And we ask that our throats be clear, and that our channel from God be clear, that we might impart the correct words that will bless our friend and that will help her understand You, God, as we understand You. That she will know that she is constantly protected, however there are times that we need to remember and we need to tune in. Like a radio station with the beam always on, it cannot be picked up if the radio channel is jarred, even the tiniest bit, there is static that comes in. And we know that Your Spirit is with us at all times, but there are times that we get distracted by the things of this Earth. We get distracted by the things around us. We get distracted by negativity we hear. This is a situation that we know the planet has a dual polarity and dual energy and sometimes we get distracted by the negative energy and by the things that are not of You. So therefore, by protecting ourselves, what we are doing is tuning back in to that which is always constantly with us. And as we protect ourselves, we are remembering and we are getting back on track and we are tuning back in to the correct signal. That's why it is so important for us to stay constantly with a prayer in our hearts, and Love in our hearts for You, so that we might hear and we might stay on the right radio station, so to speak, that we might hear the correct information coming through, that we will not be distracted and that static and negativity cannot and will not be allowed to come in, as we are tuned to only one station. At this time, we ask a special prayer on our friend, that she be given an enormous dose of the gift of discernment, an enormous dose of knowing and an enormous dose of listening through her heart. We ask that she might get out of her head, stop listening to what is coming through her head, and listen to what is coming through her heart. For only through your heart can you hear God. When sometimes we try too hard to understand through our minds, and to find logic in things that are illogical, we find confusion. And that again takes us off of the right radio station just a little bit and static has an opportunity to come in. So please allow her and please help her to stay on the correct signal at all times. We ask for enormous protection to be around her. We ask for her health, her strength, for her physical body as well as for her spiritual bodies, as well as for her emotional body...

My Dearest, Darling Children! I Love you so! I see you and I Love you so! You come with such glorious and Loving hearts! You do not know this affects all! You are so Loving and so good! The power amongst you is amazing! Now, My Darlings, please, please listen! I see your Love and I see your hearts and I see your intent and how I Love you for it! You have been taught well and I am so, so proud of you! You have been taught and you listened! Oh how good you are!

Now My Darlings, please! You are well aware that each, My Dears, are on their path. You are aware, My Darlings, that each have free will, as you do. You are aware that one cannot change another, for that would do away with free will, and we must not do that. What you have done, today, is you have, with the power of the Light, you have given your friend more Light than she has ever encompassed in her life. It is now her choice,

My Dears, to listen. She has all the information. She has all that is needed for her to be where she should be and will be in her time. It is not for YOU to choose when and where she should be. All is done, My Darlings. It is done. All your Loving prayers have been heard! All your wonderful protection is taken care of.

You are wise to start your days the way you do. You are wise to first, talk to Me upon your waking moment. For in doing so, you have ultimate protection. You have done this now because you listen well, and you are so well taught! The Universe is proud of you. The Angels sing praises to YOU! You are blessings on Earth! You are noticed. Your stars are bright! Now, what you have done is opened paths. You have opened walkways! You have opened walkways from Heaven to Earth and back again. You have cleared the path for others. And you are not finished. My Darlings, you are doing so well! I am so proud of you! I am proud of you for what you recognized. I am proud of you for how you are learning. I am proud of you for teaching each other. I am proud of you for listening. I Love you so!

Your work is just beginning. Do you see how you have progressed? Do you see how well you have learned and listened in the past few months? You have grown eons this year, this past year. You have grown eons this year, also! And it is just beginning, My Darlings. Now you have learned a lesson here and the lesson was do not get caught up in another's chaos. You immediately rejected it. You went right to the Source, which is Me, and you took care if it. I am so proud of you! You did it quickly. You did it efficiently. You are wonderful! That is what was needed! You identified what you needed to identify, and you all three, immediately knew this was not what you wanted! You immediately knew it did not resonate with the Light. You immediately knew, and yet, it was not even in your presence! Do you see how powerful you really are? I am proud of you!

Now, your dear sweet friend, do you think I Love her less than you? Oh My Dears, she is so Loved! She is unconditionally Loved! She will again remember and *know* this. She can do nothing that will change the Love that I have for her, as all on Earth are in that position. You see there is nothing that will change My Love for each of you! Some know how to listen more than others and you are now in a position to help teach. You will help teach them to listen. As you have been taught, you cannot say too much. For if it is too much it cannot be understood, and therefore it cannot be a part of their life, for it cannot be understood and therefore it cannot be demonstrated. She is growing now and she is becoming enlightened. You were wise not to call her as she needs to have time to process. You can offer her the best through the prayer that you have done.

All three of you tickled Me last night, for you ALL had a discomfort about what happened, but you came right to Me, and I comforted you. I am so proud of you! I am so proud of the way you handled this! You did exactly what you should! You were perfect in every way! And now, you will continue on with your jobs. You will continue on with your teaching and your learning. You will continue on helping one another. You will continue on helping those in your path. Be careful not to get caught up in another's chaos. It is most important that you stay centered. Stay true to yourselves! By doing so, My Darlings, you stay true to Me. You stay pure of heart. You stay encompassed in

Love and Light. You are totally protected. You are doing everything perfectly! I hear everything you say, and you have done a marvelous, marvelous job. I am very proud of you!

Your friend, right now, is totally encompassed in White Light. She is filled to the brim! She is not yet aware of what it is that she is feeling. Give her time to process. Give her time for the enlightenment. Give her time to write and give her time to sleep. For very often it is through the dreams, that the enlightenment comes. Each learn a different way. Do not judge how another learns. You know this already; I am simply reminding you. Even the three of you have a different way of learning. And the three of you have a different way of teaching. And the three of you are perfect and correct in every way. Do you see? And now, her road is ahead of her. She can take the high road, or she can take the low road, but you see it is her choice. Allow her to take and make her choices. My Love to you, My Dears!

Hello, My Dears, it is I. It is Michael. I am here to share with you, too. I am here with battalions and you are **so** protected! They were in force, and have been in force, and will **continue** to be in force and there for your ready need! Just say the word! Yes, you were heard. You were **heard** and there were **battalions** over you all night. You were **wise**, for immediately you called in help! How **proud** we all are of you! We sent your friend much help, but she needs to call in the help, herself. **She** is the one that needs to do it. You understand that. **She** is the one that must say, "Help, please **help** me. I need **additional** help from The Creator. Please send me **additional** help. Michael, The Archangel, please **send** me the battalions of armies to help me. Heavenly Creator, I trust and Love you. Michael, I know that you are there to **help** me and I trust that you will." **That** is what your

155

friend must say. We are there, too on **your** behalf; we hear you. But you know, free will is **free will** and we all abide by the **rule** of free will. It is a Universal law.

My Dears, I now say good-bye to you. I just wanted you to know there are many, many millions of Angels. There are many, many millions of **battalions** of Angels. You are NEVER alone! You have more help than you have **ever** had, or ever knew you needed! You have more help than you, truly, **do** need. For you see, the three of you have more **power** with your Light than **you** even are **aware** of! But we are here and we hear you and we always will! I just wanted you to know! The Realm of The Archangels is here and around you at this very time, and they will **stay** with you and they will **be** with you and they will **help** you in every way you need. Just **say the word** and it will be done.

It is I, Your Creator. I am here to tell you to have a lovely, joyous day. You are so full of joy in your hearts! You are so wonderful to watch! You are wonderful! I thank you, again. I Love you so! I hear you. Unless you have something to ask of Me, I will send you on your merry, Loving way.

Thank you. Thank you.

23

Denis' Automatic Writing @ Path

1/6/2001
Automatic Writing from Denis:

Dear God, The Creator,

Will You please tell me exactly where I got "off my path"?
I am very anxious to get back on my path. I am beginning to feel again. I am noticing a big difference in the way I am interpreting things. I am listening with my heart, not just my ears.

Thank You so much for Your Unconditional Love. I surrender my control and my will to Your Control and Your Will. I want to be YOUR best friend, just as YOU are mine.
Thank you.

Love always,
Denis

1/6/2002
Dear Denis,

You have been working so hard and I Love you so much! You are a perfect Beacon of Light. Everyone who sees you can recognize your Light and Love. I am very pleased that you want to spread this Light. You will have many challenges. Remember you have only to ASK for help and you will be given all you need.

As for which direction to choose for your income, please don't fear. All will be OK. You will know what decisions are correct for you. You will Love what is in store for you. Only YOU are perfectly suited for this. You are so very special. have you noticed that your interests are very diverse? This is part of the plan.

Denis, you are now on the correct path. I am so proud of you! You took a wrong turn when you decided to be what you thought others wanted you to be. You veered off course because you believed that other people's opinions were more valid than yours. You believed that other people's expectations of you were more important than your expectations of yourself. You believed that your feelings were evidence of weakness. You believed that you had to be tough, hard and strong at all times. You believed that in order for you to be "manly" you had to be unfeeling. You believed that you must attack first in order to avoid being attacked. Denis, you are beginning to understand, now, how untrue this all is.

Denis, you can, now, feel again. It is wonderful! You are, now, beginning to believe in yourself again and Love yourself again. Your opinion, of how things are, IS valid and correct. Trust! Trust in you! Trust in Me! Listen with your heart! It is never wrong. Your heart is the instrument, like a thermocouple, that senses everything and then communicates to your Soul. Learn to trust your heart!

Remember your heart attack? This was to teach you about the importance of the heart. If the heart is not working correctly, you will cease to exist on Earth. When your heart is open and clear and your senses are attuned, life is SO beautiful! Love is Possible! Light can shine! Your Light was dim! I needed to clear you out so it could shine bright. Denis, you are bright! You are Love! You are beginning to understand the Love that I have for you, which is UNCONDITIONAL! Thank you for listening. I Love you so!

Please keep on your path. You are leaving all of your old baggage behind. You are leaving all of your old mis-beliefs behind. You will open many others up to the Light and help them find their paths. It is Done!

Love,
God

24

Names & Archangel Michael's Centering Instructions

January 10, 2001 at 1:43 P.M Sue and Charlie*:*

Charlie and Sue are together, and together we ask The Heavenly Creator to join us and be with us and help us. We feel like we are really needing some help today. We come with loving hearts, full of gratitude and Love as we ask for Your help. We feel that we need some information. We ask The Archangels to be with us. We ask our personal Angels and Guides to join us. We specifically ask The Archangels of the highest Realm to talk to us and give us any information that can help us. Please share with us in any and every way that can help us grow. We ask all of this for the highest and best good of all. We are very thankful to Our Heavenly Creator for all You do for us, for all You've shown to us, for the growth that You have helped us through. Please shed Your Light on us and help us to have a greater understanding and give us clarity in all of the information that You share with us. Thank You very, very much.

The Language of Light was spoken.

Oh, My Darling Children, it is I, Your Creator. I do have information that I would like to share with you today, and I find it best that this come from Me. There are many here with Me that would like to talk to you, but I would like to be first. I am so happy to see you! I am so happy for your happy little ears, your happy little voices as you talk to Me all day; it is wonderful!

Now I would like to let you know that you may call Me God. You may call Me The Creator. You may call Me Yahweh. You may call Me Jehovah. You may call Me The Purple Flame. You may call Me ANYTHING you choose. It will not change who I am. It will not change how I am and who I am and what I am. You may choose to call Me anything you want!

And Now, as I talk to the two of you: Charlie, Momo, Mrs. Hill, Charlene; Susan, Aunt Susie, Grandma,

Susan Eagen, these are names that are meaningless. They are names you go by and I Love them, but do you think I know you by _name_? Do you think it is your _name_ that I recall and I say, " Oh, I must run down and say Hello to Charlie and Sue." Heavens no! It is not your name; it is your essence. It is the Light. It is your heart. It is your Love. It is the feel. It is the touch. You see? I have shared with you, the names that you have gone by in the last week or the last two weeks. You have many more names in _this_ lifetime. Now, should we go back other lifetimes? Do you know _how many_ names you have been known by? Do you know how unimportant it is to Me what you choose to call yourself? It is not important! All that is important is your lovely Light and your beautiful hearts.

You see, I know _you_! I know you by sight. I know you by feel. I know you by touch. My Darlings, I know YOU! Not because of the name you choose to call yourself. Your Soul is your Soul is your Soul. Your Spirit has been forever! It has not changed, My Dears. It is the same. I have known you _forever_. I have known your beautiful, beautiful, Loving, glowing Spirits forever! Your Spirits have been called...your Spirits have occupied _bodies_ that have been called many, many, many names! You have been different sexes. You have been different names. You have lived in different places. You have had different color hair and different color eyes. Do you think that's how I _know_ you? Oh My Darlings!

And if you called Me, well, let's say you chose to call Me "Oregano"; do you think I would _look_ different to you? Do you think I would _feel_ different to you? Do you think I would BE different to you? Oh My

161

Darlings, no! For you see, we know each other not by name. We know each other by the Love, by the feel, by the glow. We know each other by each other's essence. We know each other by each other's Love. And I so Love you, and I so Love your humanness at this time! For you see it is so human of you to need to have a name. Names are not important.

I bring this to you because I have to share with you, it was your choice, My Darlings, it was your choice. You asked, "Please, my dear darling Angels, please identify yourselves by name." Now, if you recall, it was Archangel Metatron who came to you and said, "It was I. It was I who would speak and not give you my name, because I know you know me as I know you." My Dears, you DO know Archangel Metatron. And you DO know Michael. And you DO know many, many, many other Angels! And you know them by feel, and you know them by Joy, and you know them by Love and you know them by Light. It is not by names that you know them. And that is why they did not choose to give you names; it was at your request.

Now I bring this to you because The Realm of The Archangels are so enjoying your humanness! For first you want, and then you don't, and then you just don't know what you need! And they are sitting and here with us now, and they are laughing at you because they so enjoy watching you learn and teach. They watch you grow out of your humanness and into your Spirituality, and they watch you stumble. And, My Dear Little Darlings, you tripped! This is a lesson, and the lesson is: NAME is not important. And… "words"… now you understand, "words" can get in the way! What is important is the FEEL and the LOVE and the LIGHT

162

and the TOUCH and the overall LOVING ESSENCE that is amongst all of those in the Angelic Realm, and all Light Beings; Angels, Spirit Guides, all of MY HEAVEN, all of MY Creation, that is enlightened and glowing with the Love of The Creator!

And now, My Darlings, many want to talk to you today, but I needed to share with you so that you would have an understanding of "words" and names. Go by the FEEL, not the way a name is pronounced, but the FEEL and the LOVE and the POSITIVE ENERGY and the KNOWING and the LIGHT and the LOVE, truly, the LOVE! You see it is a Lightening Being, that is enlightened, that glows with the Love that you know! When that Loving Glow is not able to be felt, that is when you know this might be an entity that YOU don't want to be around!

I DO want to share with you, that words <u>are</u> powerful. I am not taking away from that fact. For words can bring about negative energy, which is why you are in such control with your own choices. Words are important in that you want to speak in a positive fashion, not in a negative fashion. For negative words can bring negativity. But I do believe you understand what I am meaning with names. Names are not important for you are known by many, as am I. And I will <u>always</u> be on call for you as I am! For I hear you. I see you. I Love you, and it is not your name that I know, it is your Loving, darling, beautiful Spirits. And now, My Dears, I will sit and I will listen and I will be here as others choose now to speak, and I so Love you!

Well, good **afternoon**, you two! It is I, Metatron, and I **know** you know me and I know you and I am **so sorry** for any

163

misunderstanding that has been brought about to your friend, by **my own name**. It is **so** ironic, My Dears, for it was **my** name that caused the confusion, and it was **I** who wasn't giving a name. Do you see? It is quite **funny**! Your friend will be fine, for we all Love her so! And you are **wonderful** for you worry about her so!

Just as other messages have been given to you, you must stay, My Dears, on your **own** paths. And you must send Light and Love to those who need it. But you must remain on **your** path and allow **others** to remain on theirs. For there are lessons to be learned and you learn them from your **own** path and they learn them from their **own** path and you must **allow** that to take place. As much as you **want** to "save the world"... just as you wanted **names** (and that got us in trouble), you must **allow** those to be on their own path to learn their own lessons. You cannot take a lesson **away** from a body and if you do, it simply **delays** the learning process. So it is something to be cautious of, and we will help you. For you **try** very hard, and we see with your Loving hearts, **how** hard you try, and we will be here to help remind you. There are times we feel we remind you too **much**, and yet, you still have a **hard** time hearing. Please open your ears and open your hearts. Please step out of your mind but use your brain! Please, if it is **difficult**... if the **choices** are difficult, **make new choices**!

If you need our help, we are **always** here; talk to us, **write** to us. We see your Loving, wonderful hearts, and The Heavenly Creator has given **us** much guidance, too. We are **all** here to Love and protect, to help and to guide. As you know, we cannot make **decisions** for you. The decisions are **yours** alone, as you have free will and free choice. What you need to do, My Dears, is make a list of all of the things that you want answers for. Then take a look at that list, and make a list of the **answers** for each item you want. Then take a look at the choices **you** can make to get them. You see, it is a **process**, and you need to follow the process. You want to jump ahead and you cannot **do** that, for it is a process, and there are **lessons** to be learned along the way.

We Love you all. We will **help** you all and we will **protect** you all. You have grown leaps and bounds, My Dears, and you are much Loved and you are much protected. We are **proud** of you for listening as well as you do, for we **know** how hard it is. For in spite of the fact of your Spiritual growth, you are still human. Sometimes, **we** even forget you are human. I Love you very much and I will **always** help you, and I will **always** help your friend, even though **she** thinks I am not good. I **am** good and I Love her, as do **many** others Love her and help her! You are doing a fine job **there**, too! You listen well. We will help **clear** the cotton out of your ears so that you can hear more completely. For you see, it has **all** been set in front of you. It has **all**, already, **been said** to you. You need to go back and to listen with full, open hearts. You need to step out of yourselves and listen. It is all **there**, My Dears... it is **all there** for you.

Well, good **afternoon**, My Little Students! It is I, Michael. You just give us **such** a chuckle! For you see you are in such a **learning curve**! My goodness, how you jump leaps and bounds, and then all of a **sudden** you stumble and fall...you are too **funny**! Do you **know** how much we Love you? And do you know how much we just Love **watching** you? We do not mean to find joy at your expense, but you **do** make us chuckle! For it is the funniest, silliest things that you **choose** to get hung up on! When everything is **right there**, out in the open for you to take a look at and just jump through that hoop. But oh **no**, you would rather try to build a wall **around** that hoop so that you **can't** jump through it. Well, My Dears, I am going to work very hard at helping you unload that load of bricks to build that wall. So that your opening of the hoop that you are to **jump** through, is bigger and wider than **ever**. It is absolutely in **front** of you, and we've done **everything** but push you through it! For you see, we know you **so** well and we Love you **so** much and we see your Loving, wonderful hearts!

And by the way, you can call me Mike, you can call me Michael, you can **call** me **anything you want**! But I am still the **same**, and I am still the very same Spirit that you know and you Love! And you are the very same Spirits that I know and I Love! We all Love you so! You can call me The Warrior, if you want...for I am... and I am **fighting** for **you** all the time, and I will continue. And I will continue to put up any barriers, to protect you, that I can... and I shall. For My Darlings, you are **so** Loved! And the work you do is **so** great! Now, I know that I was **teasing** you, and I know that **you** know I was teasing you, and I Love you so much! And I Love that you **let** me tease you! For you **know** how much I Love you, and you **know** how much I will **fight** for you! And I shall. But it is those funny little quirks that we really **do** enjoy! I hope that's okay; I hope you **truly** don't mind. We aren't laughing at you, we're laughing **with** you. I know you have many thoughts and many questions. I will help you with anything I can. What can I help you with today?

Charlene: How can I stop sabotaging myself?

First of all, you must start **centering yourself**, and you are not centering yourself, My Dear. Concentrate **very** hard on centering yourself. What that means, also, is concentrating on YOU. You need to concentrate on **you**; your needs, your wants, your Loves. Center yourself. Take a look at **your** individual self-wants. Not what **anyone** else expects from you, but what **you** want. Think **only** of yourself. Do you know **you do not know how** to do that? You have additional Angelic help now to help you **learn** to do that. They will help you as you meditate, to center yourself **around yourself**, and **that** is what you need to do.

Now this is a **conscious choice** and decision that you must make, and you must tell yourself and all the Angelic help you have. Ask them to help you center yourself and then say:

" I hear consciously. I ask God the Creator to help me and assist me as I Center myself, as I concentrate on my self needs; as I concentrate on my self wants that are for the Highest and Best Good at all times.
And I ask for all fog to be removed from me, and I ask that all self- doubt be removed from me.
For I want to be the greatest at doing God's work.
For I know how GREAT His work is, and I know I am doing it with the Love and Protection of God.
And I know that Michael is protecting me at all times.
And I, hereby, Center myself in doing God's work.
And I open myself up to all that is available to me.
And I ask that God put everything carefully and easily on my path for me to see.
And I ask that clarity be given to me as it is put in my path and that as I see it, I recognize it.
And I take in all the Love and Light that God has given,
And I grow and I progress and I stay in the Center of my path for the Highest and Best Good of All.
For I know who I am and I know what I need and I know I have it because God promised and I believe Him."

Do this every morning, and do this every night...do this **at all times**. This is how you stay centered, and protected at all times. That is **truly** what you need to do.

Charlene: Thank you.

I am **always** here to help you, as are many, many others. I have always chosen, when I come and talk to you, to **tell** you who I am, and I have always done so. I would like to ask your permission to change your minds about asking **others** to do so. Do you understand why? What we want you to learn is not a **name**. We want you to learn a **feel**, a **touch**, an **aura**, a **Light**, a **healing**, a **Loving**; we want you to **feel** rather than **hear**. Hearing is important and when I say hearing, I mean a **name**…rather than **hearing** a name, we want you to **feel** it… **the <u>essence</u> of a Spirit**. That is what Your Heavenly Creator had intended. You see, it is through the **sensitivity** that you are learning, and you **have** learned, a positive Light being, versus a being of darkness. For your sensitivity is **very** in tune. Now we would like you to become even **more** in tuned.

Maybe it would work for you if **you** would choose to name those coming in. For you are named many names, for the different performances you do: Mom, Momo, Grandma, Auntie. For the different performances you do, you are different names and you understand them thoroughly and you **know** they are about you. Maybe you would choose to name them yourself, and by doing so, you would understand **feel**, versus **name**. The importance here is that you **know** a Spirit, as the Spirit knows you, by your Loving good Spirit. You see we all know **you**. We **don't care** about your name. We know you by your heart and your Spirit and your Love and your Light. And so **we** want to be known as the same to you. It is a learning process. Do you **see** how words and names got in the way of teaching? We don't want that to happen again, for I must share with you, the dark side is creative, but the Light side is **more** creative! Far more creative, so **use** that creativity! Do you have more questions?

Charlene: Yes. Will you please explain how to remove myself, emotionally and continue to do "what Love would do"? I am having a hard time with this one.

You need to be **centered on yourself**. What you have done in the past is, you have been trying to keep you and Denis emotionally pulled together, so that you are unable to center yourself. You are not giving yourself enough **space** and room to be **able** to center yourself around **yourself**. You are such an artist, My Dear, and you are **not** giving yourself enough space to create! You must **do** that, for that is what you **are**; an artist! We are not asking you to **stop Loving**, my goodness, **no**! Love **never** goes away! Love **never** goes away! **Love does not die**! Love is the one lasting, eternal, growing, wonderful, feeling, entity, being, state of being! **Love does not die**! Is there anything else?

Charlene: No, just thank you so much!

I am here at **all** times for you and I will answer any questions you have. As you know, I cannot make your decisions **for** you, but please call on me. **Ask** me. I can guide; I will guide. I will help you **every** way I am allowed! But I am **not** allowed anything that could alter your free will or free choice. You understand that much Love is surrounding you. Have faith in **yourself**. You are Loved, you are protected, you are guided, and Your Heavenly Creator is shining a **spotlight** upon you! He **so** Loves you! And He is always, **always** there to answer your questions, too.

Well I will let you have your day now, and I will be off with Light and Love, for it surrounds **me**, too. I will have the battalions waiting to protect you. They are here. They are **always** here. Charlie, you have been given **additional** protection. You have been given **additional** help. The Creator has sent additional Guardian Angels to protect you. They are very large! They are here helping you; they will help you as you want to **stay centered**. They will help you, guide you, and Love you. We are **all** here doing that. Now My

Dears, I will say good-bye, and I ask you to have a lovely, joyous day and we will talk soon! With all my Love I say good-bye!

Thank you! Thank you!

-25-
Walking Our Own Paths and Allowing Others to Walk Their Own

February 3, 2001 at the Cabin, at 2:25 P.M.

Sue and Charlie are here in joy and Love and happiness. We ask our Angels and Guides to join us as we ask for clarity and guidance in our life path. We especially, ask Our Heavenly Creator to help us with anything we need help with for our best and highest good, and the highest and best good of all. We are very grateful and very thankful and we come to You in Love and gratitude. Please protect us from anything that is not of the highest vibration. Thank you.

The Language of Light was spoken.

Ah, My Children! How lovely! How lovely to see and be with you again today! And what a glorious day it is! As I sit and I watch you enjoying all the nature around you, and getting the <u>thrill</u> of it! As you see the snow fall and you look at the beautiful sky and the tops of the trees and you take joy and pleasure in the beautiful sight!

Ah, My Children, I am so proud of you! You see, what you have done today is, you sat back and you talked and you took heed in the lessons that have been taught to you; the lessons that have been brought forth. You paid attention and you listened and you shared, and I am oh so proud of you! And it is that kind of a day...to sit back and have a quiet, peaceful day. Enjoy the nature around you. Enjoy it! Take heed in its beauty and know that I give you this day with Love. It is wise of you to go back and listen, for you see, you have been given all the answers. All the answers are in front of you, so now you are sorting out your questions and you are sorting out the answers given, and you are matching them together, as if a puzzle. And you see, My Dears, that IS what life IS! It is a game; it is a puzzle for you to unravel.

Much protection is given to you on a daily basis. You are starting to recognize your path from another's. You are starting to recognize, and are recognizing what belongs to you and what belongs to another. You see, you are learning well, and you are wise and you are both understanding discernment, and we are all so proud of you! I, Your Heavenly Creator, The Angelic Realm, your Guides, your personal Angels, and all the Loving Spirits around you, all applaud you! Yes, we are, oh, so proud of you!

Now My Darling Children, the lessons are not complete, for the listening has not stopped, and the lessons continue. They will continue on a daily basis, but there are times when it is a time to take a moment; to take a quiet moment and reflect back and share and talk and understand and learn from each other. For you see, you each are teachers to each other, and you each are students to each other. And all is right and all is the way it should be. And you are totally, totally, perfectly on your paths of learning and creating and teaching. Do not rush that which should not be rushed. Take it slow and take it quietly. Just as you were told before, the flower does not grow from the seedling in a moment. It takes several moments; several days, for that seedling to become a grown flower. Don't rush yourselves to be something you are not ready to be. Take the time. Listen to yourself. Listen to your heart. Keep yourselves centered. Listen carefully. Use the tools you have.

Believe what you hear, Charlene. Believe in yourself, for you are very, very precise in your listening skills, and yet you are afraid to believe what you hear. Have faith in you, My Dear; I do!

As always, there are others that want to speak to you, and I will let them. I just needed to share with you how proud I am. Thank you for listening. Thank you for hearing. Thank you for trying! Thank you for Loving. I so Love you!

Hello, Ladies! It is I, Michael. It is so **nice** to see you today having such a lovely time playing in the snow! Actually, I know you would like to play a little bit more than you **are** playing, but there is a time for everything and **now** it is a time for quiet time. Now it is a time for rest and relaxation. Now is a time for simple enjoyment. Sometimes you think if you are not traveling at a **fast** speed you are not having fun. You know better than that. Sometimes it is the quiet time that is the **most** fun. It is that silence. It is that lovely, beautiful nature! It is that time when you can sit and simply look out a window and watch... that you can have your highest fulfillment of joy! And now is **that** time and look at what is around you. You have the **glory** of a fire in a fireplace. You have the **beauty** of snow falling on the beautiful trees about you. What a lovely place to be in! And how wonderful that you **recognize** the beauty and the joy!

Now take that beauty and joy and **create** from it! For you are **both** very creative and it is time to take the beauty about you, around you, that surrounds you, that is a part of every breath you breathe; **take** that beauty, and what shall you do with it? There is much, My Dears, there is much. Not **only** do you have your photographs, but you have your paints and you have your poems. Think of **all you can do** with what is in your heart at this moment. For in your hearts and in your minds you are filled with a creative loveliness and a creative beauty

173

and a creative wonderment of the Glory of God! And the wonder of it all is that you **know** it! Ah! If **only** we could teach **others** to recognize the beauty that **you** see and recognize as a Creation of God! And you recognize it as beauty that God gives you because He **Loves** you so! And you recognize it, not just as a creation, but as an **inspiration**! An inspiration to you and to others to say and to do **more**! To create through the inspiration given you! Ah! I wonder if we have an idea now? Could there be poems coming up? Could there be photographs that will inspire? Could there be paintings that could be inspiration from a photograph, from a memory, from a day, from a beauty of the Creation of God? **Ah**! You never know!

We are very proud of you for the recognition that much of what needs to be done with another is **not** about you. Let him walk his own path and learn his lessons, please, please. For you see, you cannot teach and he cannot learn if he is not wanting to, and you **cannot** teach someone not willing to learn. It is the lesson that he must accomplish on his own. If you **enable** him, you will prolong the lesson from being learned. You will prolong the Light of Creation from going off in his **own** brain. He must be totally responsible for the end result. For if he is not, he will doubt himself forever! And he will **never** believe that it was he and **his** listening skills and his creation that got him out of the spot he is in now.

Remember, this is **so** not important. These are life lessons, yes, but you are all here for the experience. You chose this; it is an **experience**. This is **not** your **eternity**! For your **eternity** is living in Total Love! **This** is just an **experience**. For how can you **know** what Total **Love** is unless you know what it is **not**? How can you **know** what Total **Perfection** is unless you know what it is **not**? How can you **know** what being nonjudgmental, totally compassionate, eternally Loving, unconditionally Loving is, **unless** you know what it is **not**? So now you understand.

174

Stop worrying about what **others** think. Stop worrying about something **you** find beautiful. Stop **caring** if someone else doesn't. You see, it is not important. You see, it is **not** relevant. What is relevant is what **you** see and what **you** feel and what **you** think. Everyone is responsible for their own choices and their own feelings. **They** are responsible, not you. You are **not** responsible for what someone else thinks, chooses or feels. Stop thinking you are, for that is just absolutely **not** in the realm in which it should be! No, that is **not** what you should be thinking! Take what you find beautiful, as you have, Charlie, in creating your pictures. Do what is beautiful to **you** and do not care or think what another thinks. Right now, Charlie, it is your creation artistically that is the concentration you **should** have in your life.

Sue, you are not quite there. You need to finish the task at hand. Finish the task. Work on your writing in your **spare** time. Your photographs, as you take them, even if you can't follow through right now, you **will** have time at a later date. You need to finish up your task at hand. It is nearly complete, but it is **important** that you put your energy there for a short while. It is almost over. For when you leave, you will be leaving with doors wide open. You will be leaving with people wanting you to stay. It is no different than when you left your past Love and **you knew** it was time. It will be the same way in business. You will **know** when it is time. It will be very, very, very clear. You are feeling the urgency, and you **know** it is coming. Yes, Darling, it is. You **will** know. Be patient. By being patient you will have a greater reward, so **hang in** there right now. All that you do with your creative side is not done in vain, you just do not, at **this** time, have the time to put your concentration there. It will come. You see you are using **your** creativity in a different manner. Where Charlie will use her creativity in an artistic manner, you will use **your** creativity in a business manner. That is okay. You see **both** are artistic and **both** are business. There is simply more emphasis on the artistic side of Charlie, and more emphasis on the **business** side of you. Not to worry. And of course you realize you have your separate paths and you have your separate accomplishments to meet. They do not intertwine. They are separate. Complete your tasks at hand.

Now, if you have questions I am happy to help you with any questions you may have. Do you have questions?

Charlie: Yes. I am wondering when I call Denis, am I enabling and interfering in his growing, or is it okay for me to contact him?

Would you call a good friend if a good friend needed to hear from you?

Charlie: Certainly.

Then you should call Denis. You see Denis is on his **own** path and he is learning his **own** lessons. It is not a matter of you staying away; it is a matter of enabling. You see...

Charlie, It is I, Michael. You really, really **need to understand** that Love is Love. Love will **be** forever! Loving someone and **enabling** someone are two different things. For you see Love is totally unconditional. Right now, Denis has his lessons to learn, and **through** those lessons he will learn **so** much! But you don't **want** to see him learn his lessons because it is **unpleasant** for you to watch him struggle. It is about **him**; it is not about you. Stop **trying** to pull something in that does **not** belong to you. Right now, what Denis **needs** to do is go to his Creator. Instead he **wants** to go to you to let you handle it. **Let** Denis find another way. The other and **right** way is for him to go to his Creator; go to the Angels. You see, he is not **liking** what he is hearing from us right now, and so he is choosing **not** to listen. And, Charlie, sometimes **you** do that, too. Please, it is **not about you**, Dear. It is just that he needs to learn **his** lessons. Should you **call** him? Certainly, if you **choose** to... life is about choice. Do you think he might **benefit** by hearing your voice? If you think so, then please **call** him. Do you know it's **okay** to have fun when he isn't? Do you know it's **okay** for you to enjoy the company of friends? Do you know it's **okay** for you to have a Loving, laughing, fun day, whether **he** is or not? He has **his** choices to make and you have yours. Stop trying to get into **his** center, and stay in your **own**, Dear. It is **difficult**; it is a lesson. Lessons are **difficult**, and that is why it is called a **lesson** instead of a **recess**!

We Love you. We Love Denis. Denis has a path, you have a path; **everyone** has a path. On that path there are lessons...lessons that you have **chosen** to learn, and **you** have asked us for help. We have **always** been here to help you, and we remain. Your Heavenly Creator is **here** for you, always. But sometimes, and Sue, you can relate to this...sometimes we have to knock you on the forehead and **push** you backwards... or you have to be **slapped** on the head and **thrown** on your back to **make** you look **up** and remember your Source! Sometimes, when you forget to look **up**, we have to **push you down**. Not that we **really** push you, you see, it is all a metaphor, you understand that, don't you? There really **is** no physical hurting. It is a matter of your continuously choosing **not** to see, **not** to hear, and **not** to learn. And by doing so, instead of walking **up** the stairs, you walk **down** the stairs. You walk down the stairs into the **hole**. And it is in that dark hole that the only Light you see is by looking **up**! So sometimes you **need** to dig yourselves into a hole to look up for the Light! You see? Let Denis find the Light on his **own**, for even by your trying to help him, **he** may not, at this time, be **capable** of learning from you. You see, **he** cannot have you save him. **He**, that is **his** choice, **he** cannot have **you** save him.

And it is now time for you to **internalize**; you must internalize to save yourself. Keep **yourself** in the Light. You have the capability. You have everything that you need to succeed if you **allow** it to be. But you keep getting in your way, and you keep **sabotaging yourself** and you keep thinking that Denis is **your** personal problem to handle. If you would let it **go** and let him **be** and let him solve his **own** problems, you will find

177

that life is easier for both of you. Do you remember, it was told to you in the past; you each have your **own** road to walk. **Walk them! Separately** at this time. Stop worrying about tomorrow and live for the today! And, please, laugh! Have joy! Have fun! You worry about **him** to a point that it is affecting **your** life.

Let Denis worry about Denis, and you worry about **you**. It is time. He has his lessons and he **will** learn them. He has his path and he **will** walk it. He has choices to make, and if he doesn't get **himself** out of that box that he has already dropped the walls on but he hasn't crossed the threshold, he will take an even **more** difficult road than he is on. He must learn to make new **choices**, and **that** is where he is having his problem. He will not step **outside** of his realm of reality. That is not **your** problem. If he **asks** for help, give an answer as you would to **any** friend, but **stop interfering**! He has to learn his **own** lessons; they are not **your** lessons. You have different lessons. You are learning your lessons, except **this** one. You are having **trouble** with this one. Here is an idea. Talk to him as you would talk to **any** friend. Love him as you would Love **any** friend.

Do **not** offer advice **not asked for**. Silence is golden, My Dear. If he **asks** for your advice give it honestly and openly. Stop worrying about the repercussions of your opinion, but you may not **offer** an opinion unless it is asked! You have no **obligation** to anyone but yourself, and right now, Denis is in your path to **teach** you that! You see you are **both** teaching **each other** and helping each other with lessons and you are **both** having a difficult time learning those lessons. Keep **yourself** centered, and treat Denis lovingly as a friend, and remember **his** lessons are **not** yours, and **yours** are **not** his. Your lessons right **now** involve, well... I **do** think **interference** is a little harsh and I don't mean for it to be, but...picture yourself in your **own** bubble. Picture Denis in **his** own bubble. You are in a bubble of Love and protection and so is he. You keep bursting your **own** bubble because you want to get into his. **That** is what is happening, and by doing so you are bursting **both** bubbles. You do this to each other; you are bursting your own and each other's bubbles. Does that make sense?

It is time now that I say good-bye. I will let the two of you have quiet discussion. I will let the two of you discuss what has gone on in this particular channeling. Tomorrow when you channel, we will have **additional** information for you.

Never have fear about calling a friend. Never have fear about **Loving** too much. The fear is **not** about Loving too much, it is about enabling and distracting another from learning a lesson that is in front of him on his own path or her own path. That's all. Just be careful, be wise, and use discernment. Discernment is a **lovely** gift to have and you **all** have it. Ask us, ask The Creator, simply say, "What would Love do?" It will come to you! We will help you. And as always you have our protection, our Love and our guidance.

And now I say good-bye to you with much Love, and much happiness. I want you to laugh and have joy for **that** is just the Song of the Soul! I Love you very much and have a lovely rest of the day!

Thank you. Thank you.

February 4, 2001 at Sue's Cabin at 4:45 P.M....
CONTINUATION...
Prayer and The Language of Light...

Well, good **afternoon**, ladies, and a fine afternoon it is! Hasn't it been joyous? Hasn't it been glorious? Hasn't it been wonderful? It is **fun** to see your joy, even when you are not feeling your best, Sue. And yet, you still have the joyous heart and the eyes of a child as you look, and are so grateful, and look in wonderment at the beauty around you. Ah, **yes**! There was a purpose there, you think? Several things I have to share with you, and actually, Charlie, you were right on. This is, actually, an **additional** message; a **continuation**, for Sue was worn out yesterday. **Both** of you need to be cautious of the energy levels that you have, and **know** how much energy it takes to channel when you choose to do so. Please be prepared for that and **do** so accordingly.

Now yesterday, in continuation, we were talking about your **creativity** with things around you in nature. Creativity with the things that you are currently doing with photography, with your artwork, with your paintings and your poetry... today is a continuation of that. You do know, you will have **everything** you need, My Dears. You are **so** wrapped in fear at times! Let **go** of the fear! Do **not allow** yourselves to be wrapped in fear of any kind. Fear is **not** a part of you! Let it **go**, please! It is very, very **good** of you and it is very wise of the two of you to listen to tapes together and discuss them. Turn your recorder off and discuss things and bring current events into the tapes. For if you have noticed, things **have** come along your path just as you have channeled and asked for information, and information was given to you regarding certain **situations** that were coming up.

Yes, Sue, you **will** have some situations come up in the near future. I will not necessarily say day, time and month. You will **know** and you will **feel** when it is right. You will not really be forced out. It will be **your** choice. You will **not** be fired; it will be **your** choice. Everything that will happen to you is about **choice**. You have **requested** there be **no** choice. That is not optional. A chain of events will happen making it **unbearable**, because it's **against** what you believe. It is **against** who you are, and that is why you will know it is **time** to go. And you **will** know. Do not have a fear of that, you are **far** too in-tuned. We would have to take your brain out for you **not** to know. That we don't **plan** on doing! It will be **staying** quite in tact! And have **no** fear. Actually, Sue, be prepared for your spouse... even though **you** have no fear, fear will come to him. Assure him of **his** options. Look at **your** options, yourself, for you see the door will **never** shut behind you and it will remain open.

There will be **additional** options for you to take a look at. Look at them closely, for what will happen is they will offer you options on a **temporary** basis that could work ideally for you. For it will give you time to **use** your creative talents and it will give you time to earn some money from them, too. And because you work on an hourly basis, you can claim prime dollar amount per hour. Just **let** things work through as they should and as they do. Do not **force** a hand for it will happen as it should. As you spoke of patience, Charlie, please remind your friend to be patient. For **she** has a little problem with patience, as do **you**! All will be fine, My Dears. There is nothing to worry and nothing to fear.

Stop worrying about what someone else can or cannot do for him or her self. Stop worrying about someone else's **choices** they can or cannot make for his or her self. You **all** have the freedom of choice and you all have **everything** you need to be what you are to be. Will you please stop **taking over** someone else's job? You keep trying to take **my** job and it is not for you to have. Take care of you! We will take care of all who **ask** us.

Now I say have a lovely, lovely evening. I will have special Angels sent to you as you work on your Joy Poetry, on your Joy Writing. For I really **believe** that you need more joy in your life, so **ask** for it! Bring it into your life yourself, for you **can**. Bring joy back to you! Think about the lovely day you have had. Think about the lovely, beautiful snow falling. Think about the beautiful snow on the trees. Think about the joy that **should be** in your heart every day. Think about the joy in nature. Think about the joy that The Heavenly Creator brings to you daily in different ways; through sunshine and moonlight and starlight, through flowers blooming and through leaves growing on the trees; in many, many ways. Even today as you were noticing, the sky is blue and the clouds were beautiful with the snow-capped mountains. There is much **joy** in nature. Nature shares. If you have **trouble** finding joy, I will help you. I say good-bye to you now, and I send you with Love and Light. And I **keep** protection upon you always. And Love be with you.

Thank you. Thank you.

-26-
Denis' Automatic Writing @ Why?

2/12/2001
Automatic Writing from Denis:

Dear God, The Creator,

Why did my marriage to Charlene end? I love her now, and then and for a very long time. Why did I treat her so badly? Why did I abuse her? Why did I act the way I did? Will I ever be able to re-connect with her in marriage? Will she ever be able to trust me again?
Thank you.

Love,
Denis

2/12/2001
Dearest Denis,

I know that you are confused about what happened between you and Charlene. Let Me explain:
Your ego is very strong. It controls your thinking. It is a combination of pride and ego. Your inner voices tell you that you must always be in control. When you are feeling "out of control? you "fight" to regain control again. This "fight" has taken the posture of anger, aggression and nastiness.

You don't mean to do this, especially to Charlene, but your ego has been stronger than your heart. Your ego wants to fight. Your heart wants to forgive and forget. Your ego wants to win at all costs. Your heart doesn't care who wins; winning is not even considered. Your ego thinks it must stand up for your dignity. Your heart is not at all worried about your dignity. Your ego wants to preserve your "manliness". Your heart does not differentiate between manly and feminine.

Remember your world is polar. In order for you to understand your heart, you have to understand your ego. Please don't confuse ego with self-esteem. They are not the same. Self-esteem is "Love of yourself, appreciation of yourself and your abilities". Ego is selfishness and carelessness; caring only for yourself. It is preservation at any cost and at the expense of others. When you care about and only for yourself, you are NOT showing Love and concern for everyone else whom you are a part of. You are ALL part of Me. Denis, you came here to learn about ego. This is not easy, as you now know, but you are doing such a good job!

You are separated now from Charlene because you both have many very important things that you are remembering. This can be done best in solitude without distraction. You both are doing such a good job! Please don't think that your Love will ever stop. It won't. When you are ready you will find it very comfortable to be together again. The trust will return. Your work is not done. You still have "ego" issues. I am giving you much help.

Charlene has her own issues that she is working on as well. She is doing a wonderful job! You are both very special. Charlene's learning (remembering) is different from yours. That is why your paths are now separate. You may still see each other if you choose. Your Love is still there. But please don't prevent each other from doing what you came here to do. Your Love for each other will always be there. It has been there for many lifetimes.

Denis, let your ego go! You do not need it to protect you. Allow your heart to govern. It is never wrong. It is never hurtful. It is always going to tell you what is best for you AND for others. Your heart is your Soul. Your heart is "God"...the God within you. Trust it. Love it. Love yourself. Love others. Love is ALL there is!

Love,
 God

27

Helping Others Remember & Spread The Love

February 13, 2001 at 11:50 A.M. Charlie and Sue
Prayer and The Language of Light...

Ah, good **morning** the two of you! How **good** to see you together! How good to see you and talk to you! It feels as though it has been so long, and the reason it feels as such is that **you** have such urgency. You have **such** urgency to move along your path. Steady yourselves. Slow yourselves. For at times, you **get ahead** of yourselves. Try to slow yourselves down and remember to **enjoy the moment**. Enjoy the reason you're here; for you are here for the **experience**. For it is the experience that you will look back on and treasure. There is so much happening in your lifetime right now! Slow down so you miss **nothing**!

We have been constantly with you, Loving you, guiding you and protecting you. I am **always** your Protector, The Creator is **always** your Protector, as well as the many, many Angels that are with you at all times. When you **ask** for armies I send you armies. When you have doubt, I send you **more**. When you have fear, I send you **more**! Remember fear is **not** a part of you. Remember, do **not** doubt yourselves. You listen beautifully. We are so happy and proud of you! You **are** listening well. You **are** learning well. You **are** paying attention. Do you see the joy you get when you take the time to see the beauty around you? Ah! It is a gift, My Dears. It is a **gift** to recognize the beauty that is given to you.

You see The Creator so **Loves** you all, He supplies you with **much** beauty and joy and Love! It is **surrounding** you! Some choose to **recognize** it and some don't. You are recognizing it and it is so lovely to **see** that in you for **you** are growing and your **Spirits** are glowing! They are **glowing** and growing for they are recognizing more and more with each moment. The time is coming now, where you will become more and more verbal... **outspoken**…we might say outspoken. For you will be put in positions, separately on your own paths, where you will be interchanging with people who **do ask** you the right questions. And you are then to provide them the correct answers, for **you** know the answers.

You are **remembering** well. You **do** realize this is all a remembering. It is **not** a teaching; it is a **remembering**. We are helping you, we are teaching you in a sense, showing you **how** to remember. And oh what a pleasure you are... for **you** listen! And you **apply** that which we teach you! And so it is such a pleasure to show you! You are **such** a pleasure to us! You give us much joy! We hope that we give **you** the same joy back to you. You see that is part of the circle of Life! For you give us joy, we give it back and it just goes on and on! For we share **each other's** joy and happiness and Love.

It is that way on Earth, My Dears. As you share your joy and your happiness and your Love, your "**sparkle**", it ignites the **hearts** of those around you. Which is why it is so important for you to be out of your **house** and in the heart of Earth itself; **amongst** those people who need your Light. You see there is nothing for you to **do**, My Dears, except **be**. You just need to be. There is nothing to **do**, for you are not human doings, you are human **beings**! So **be**! Not in your house shut up in your room by **yourself**, for then you just glow for us! And we see that lovely Light, but that Light needs to be **shared** and shined among those that need it.

And you, My Darlings, My Seedlings, have turned into beautiful plants; you are beginning to **flower** and your colors are lovely! You are the flowers needed on **this** Earth. You are the flowers that shed the **Light that sparkles**! You sparkle like **diamonds** and **starlight** in the night! And **you** are the glowing color! The Sunlight basks you and you **share** the lovely, beautiful, sparkling color of your Light and the beautiful fragrance of your Love! You must be **out** amongst the people now, so that **is** where you shall be. That **is** where your path will lead. Your paths will now go separately, but never separate, for your **hearts** are together. But you will be in **different** groups for you will be teaching different people in different ways. And you will be showing a Light in a **different** sparkle and that is good. And you will come **back** together and help each other learn and teach. You will come **back** to help each other, teaching each other, learning from each other's experiences. For you now need to go **out** and it will happen.

Do not worry about **doing**, just **be**. For as you are on your path, your path will **lead** you to where you should go. And you totally are perfectly **on** your paths! You are creating by being who you are. Do not **mistake** creativity and imagination. For you see, by using your **imagination**...that helps you **step out** of the box you put yourselves in sometimes. You need to **use** that imagination. Remember... anything you can **think**, can happen. Anything you can **believe** can be. Anything you **want,** you can have. Be creative. I have an assignment for you both. Go back into your wish boxes, and look at all of the items that you wrote down. And you will now write about each one, coming up with ideas on **how** to have those things **be**. That is your assignment, My Dears. Put it into **motion** now. You put it into the Universe. Continue. It is **not** quite finished.

You are **so** beautiful, as my little flowers are blossoming so! It is almost **time** for you to be out amongst those who need you. You have listened. You have learned. You have applied. You will continue to listen. You will continue to learn. You will continue to apply. For there is **much** that needs to be accomplished, and you are working well. You have this urgency to run. Please don't. If you run, you will **miss** things along your path. Slow yourself down! Listen to your mind by stepping out of it. Step out of your mind to hear your inner self, for it is now the **heart** that speaks. The heart will speak through your eyes, through your ears, through your

188

senses. Your **heart** is what needs to be **listened to** now. You step out of your mind to properly **hear** your heart. And just as you have done in the past, listen carefully, write it down, share with each other, believe what you hear and follow what your heart says. It is the heart's turn now, and here we are...a day from Valentine's Day. Let your heart be your **leader**, and let it begin today!

The Archangels are **all** here amongst you now. They **surround** you. They are around you; they are above you. They are giving you bushels of flowers...fragrant, beautiful flowers, in **gratitude** for all the **work** you are doing; for all the **joy** you are bringing, for all the **Love** you are sharing, for the **smiles** that you give to strangers, for the help that you give one another and to all. For the lessons that you teach, they are **so** lovely and grateful for you! We **all** are grateful to you! And we are **all** here constantly Loving you and helping you. **Know** you are never alone. And know...as joy fills your heart, as your gratitude touches all, as you give to all around you, it is given back to **you** a thousand times again! And Your Heavenly Creator would like to speak...

Ah, My Darling Children! How I Love you! My hand is upon you at all times and I give you Everlasting Light! The Light and Love is with you always! It is as promised, My Dears. And I tell you again how proud I am of you, and I thank you My Dears, for giving Me the Love back as I Love you so! For as you know, there is nothing you can do that can make that Love stop ever, but how lovely, you give it back to Me! And so it is to you a thousand times again! Spread the Love you have in your hearts! Spread it to ALL! For it is Love that will cure all that needs to be cured on this Earth. For it is through the Love you have and the Love you share, the True Light will shine forever on this planet, as it needs to. It is through the Love that is spread to ALL that the fog is then removed, and Everlasting Light is here forever!

Ah, My Darlings, there is still much to learn and there is still much to see and there is still much enlightenment to have, and you shall have it. Please, My Dears, again, do not rush yourselves, and as you go, enjoy! Enjoy with the joy in your heart that I have given you! Enjoy with the Love that I give you! Enjoy with the happiness that is to be yours! Enjoy with the enlightenment that increases daily! Enjoy with the knowledge that you have, the knowingness that you have; the gifts that I have given you! Know I Love you so! All you want will be! All you ask shall be! Please remember along the way there will be lessons, but lessons are fun and lessons can be good! Remember you are not of fear, you are of Love! Remember I am here for you at all times. Remember I NEVER leave you!

Now, as different people are put in your paths, Love them, for many will be put in your path that simply need Love. Show them how to Love for you know! For your hearts are pure and good! For your Love shows all about you! For your auras are bright, bright Light! And there are many that will know of you. You may not know their name but as we know, names are not important. For you will recognize their lovely glow and Spirits! And you will recognize those that need enlightenment, and with that, My Dears, I give you much help! For you are My beautiful little Lightening Bolts! Yes, occasionally, you even have too much charge! But it is okay, for there is nothing you can say or do that will be wrong. All that is going to happen will be perfect. And it will happen in the perfect timing and

190

*it will happen in the perfect way and it is... and will be
perfect! It IS perfect as you are perfect!*

*And now, My Darlings, ah! The Angels are a-
fluttering! There are many Archangels with you today.
There have been more and more. They whisper to you
daily. They whisper to you constantly. Know and Love
them for they are My Gift to you and they Love you as I
do! They protect you. They Love you. They guide you,
and it will be constant. Know them. Love them. Be
grateful. Thank them. Thank them for being with you.
They so Love you and they so Love the attention you
give them! As you are a gift, they are a gift. As you are
Love, they are Love. For you are a part of Me, and I,
you. They are a part of Me, and I am a part of them.
We are all a part of each other. Once the Universe
recognizes that we are truly all one, it will be the way it
will be again. It will be... just as you remembered it... it
will be again.*

*Enjoy your experience, for I want you to! And I give
you much Joy! And I give you many Angels! Enjoy
every moment of every day, every day of every week,
every week of every month and every month of every
year. Enjoy every moment! Let not a moment waste! I
Love you very much! Always know that! Always know
I am with you. Always know you can talk to Me as you
talk to each other. Always know I hear you. Always
know I give you answers. Please remember to listen.
You do quite well, but sometimes what you do is... you
have a preconceived answer for yourself, so you listen to
your answer instead of Mine. For you have already
established an answer to a question you ask Me, and
then you forget to hear Me. Not to worry...I will
NEVER let go of you! Not to worry...I know you Love*

Me. Not to worry…I remember you are human. This is your human experience, and it is a learning, Loving one, so truly, do enjoy it! It, too, is a gift. It is what you wanted and so I gave it to you. Remember this was your request and I will give you what you want and I Love you. I Love you no matter what choices you make. You can do no wrong to Me! You can do no wrong in My eyes, ever! Because, My Darlings, I Love you so completely! And one day you will remember how to Love as completely. You will remember, too! Love is with you, My Dears! Love is with you!

Well, My Darlings, you have done **well**. You are listening well. Continue to write. Continue to share. There will be more **people** in your paths, now. Open up your heart. Open your heart up to **all**! Remember don't pass judgment. See in another the good that he, himself, **cannot** see; see that good in another. You **cannot** say or do **anything** that will be wrong. Nothing can be misunderstood, now. If it is too much it will go over the heads of others. If it is not enough, questions will continue. Answer them with Love in your heart. Answer them **with** your heart! See with Love in your eyes. See **through** your heart! Listen with Love in your ears. Listen **through** your heart! Let the **heart** be the center now, for it is. Always **has** it been, but now learn how to **live through** your heart chakra.

Remember **all** that you have learned. Remember how to **center** yourselves. Remember to **Love yourselves**. For the more you Love **yourselves**, the more Love spills out to **all**! You cannot **Love** too much! You cannot Love **yourself** too much, or another…not as long as you keep **yourself centered** and Love **yourself**. Remember to stay on **your** own path and let all stay on **their** own path. Remember that your teaching paths may now fork in the road, as you teach different people in a different way. Open your hearts! And **that** is all you really need to think about, for there is **nothing** for you to do but **be you**! We Love you! We are all here helping, Loving, guiding, protecting. We are here to answer your questions and Love you through your life. Do you have a question today?

Charlie: Yes, I have one. Is it possible for me to know the meaning of the experience I had, with the car wreck I had on May 22, 1998? Is it possible for me to understand?

It **is** possible for you to understand...but it is **not** something we are verbally going to tell you now. Here is what I **am** going to tell you. We want you to go into a deep meditation, alone, quietly, with no phones on, no TV on, with no music on. We want you to sit very quietly. Say a prayer. Light three candles; a purple candle and two white candles. **Ask for clarification**. Go **directly** to Your Creator. If it is **time** for you to understand, it will be revealed. If you are **not** ready, you will get clarity on **why**. Meditate deeply. Go into your heart. Go into the center of your Soul and search. Do you have another question?

Charlene: I don't. Thank you very much.

Love be with you both. Much protection is **surrounding** you. Sue, you will have changes in your life. They will be coming up quickly. Follow your instinct. Follow your **heart**. You are getting very **good** at listening. When a door shuts, **let** it. Force nothing! **Let** things happen as they **should** and it will be right. Things happen as they should, truly. It is when you force, when you force an issue, when you force a point of view, it is when you **force**... that things are **not** smooth. So no **forcing**; gentle, gentle Love, gentle, gentle behavior. You will travel **miles** by being gentle! You will travel **nowhere** by being forceful. It is no different than when you are teaching about the Love of God. No forcing, no forcing, no judgment; just simply, truly Love! And you will **help** people grow miles! You will **help** them grow into giants! You will help that spark **ignite**! When you are forceful in **anything** in life, it will **not** go smooth. Be gentle and let things happen.

193

It is time for you to **break out** of the cocoons you have been in. It is **time** for the butterfly to fly! It is **time** for the butterfly to have her freedom! So, My Beautiful Butterflies, you have lovely smooth roads ahead and many flowers to land upon. And with that, I say good-bye to you. Know that I am **here** protecting you as I always am, as is The Creator and the other Archangels, your personal Angels, your personal Guides. You have more protection than you realize. So have no fear because you can do **nothing** wrong! Your cocoons are broken open. It is **okay** to fly now because you are two butterflies that have a **Bubble of Light** around you. You will not be caught in a butterfly net! You have wide-open space. You have much to do and much to see and much to explore in your new life! We Love you and we will talk soon.

Know you can talk to **us** anytime! Write down any answers to the questions you ask us. Some you will need to **share** with each other and some are simple insight for yourselves. You can share all that you **want** for that is good. As you listen and re-listen to your tapes you hear **new** things each time. You get new enlightenment and new information and **that** is good. We will say good-bye now as we send you off in Love and Light. And may you have the most **glorious** day! With Love we say good-bye.

Thank you. Thank you.

28

Charlene's Channeling About Her Wreck

February 15, 2001

Charlene is channeling and asking for help in understanding what happened and why, in my car wreck on May 22, 1998.
Private prayer...The Language of Light was spoken...

Ah, My Dear Child, it is I, The Creator. I am always with you. Do not question what you hear. Believe in yourself, believe in Me. Go deep within yourself at this time. Oh My Darling, many are here with you this day. You are surrounded by Angels who Love you so! The answer to the question you are asking is very difficult to put into words that you can understand. It's quite complex, My Dear, but I am aware of your true need to know these things.

As you remember, at the time of this occurrence, you were in a difficult situation. You were in a difficult state. You were in an unhappy state of mind. You truly wanted to leave this planet. You truly wanted to come home, but you are not finished. You are not finished. You have not completed what you came here to do. However, I truly Love you and I truly will not force you to stay, or force you to do what you do not want to do.

This was a day of decision, Dear; this was a day of decision. You could have left upon any of the impacts that you experienced. Each time you chose to stay. Many times you chose to stay. You were certain. It was your choice. You chose to stay and complete what you came here to do. However, as you know, you could not do that in the marriage that you were in, because you were not allowed to BE. You felt that you were not allowed to exist. You felt that you were not accepted.

This experience demonstrated to you that I am in control, that I Love you and that I am taking care of you. You were not hurt. Your passenger was not hurt. None of the people were hurt. No one was injured. It was all under control, as you know. And, yet, this experience was a wake up call to you. It was a wake up call to you to make some changes in your life. You had to get to a situation where you could BE who you are, that you could discover who you are, that you could know who you are; that the world could know who you are, that they might know Me through your work. Through the events that took place at this time, you were shown the importance of remembering who you are, and the importance of trusting yourself and trusting Me. I am always with you. I Love you so. I want you to be happy! I want you to have great joy! I want you to BE. I want you to be who you ARE. I want the world to know who you are. I want the world to know Me through you. I want the world to know Me through your work. You have asked to be an instrument. You are ALL an instrument. You are ALL an instrument of My Work. You are ALL an instrument of My Love. You are ALL part of Me, and I am part of you. I am not separate from you. I am not away from you. I am with you always.

I am aware of how difficult this has been for you. You have learned SO much! You have grown SO much! You have learned, and are learning to trust yourself. You are learning to listen to your heart. You are learning to listen to what YOU want. You are learning to hear Me through what YOU want and what YOU know. Thank you for being you. Thank you for BEING. Thank you for being willing to be you in the world at this time. I Love you very much. I appreciate your effort very much. I appreciate your willingness to stay and complete your purpose. Thank you.

Do not doubt what you hear, My Dear. You have very, very clear reception. It feels like your imagination because your channel to Me is so clear. It feels like it's coming from your mind, and yet, it is coming from the mind of God in you. Let it come. Share. Know Me. Love Me. Trust Me. Trust yourself, and you will be trusting Me as you trust yourself. It has been difficult for you to learn to trust yourself because you put all of your trust and power in another. You have taken it back, and I am so proud of you! Trust yourself. Go into your heart. Ask yourself. Ask Me. Ask your Angels and Guides. You are on your path. You are perfectly where you are to be. Even the accident that you had was not fearful to you. It was not meant to be, My Dear, it was only a wake up call. It was a reminder. It was a reminder that your life is sacred. Your life is sacred to Me! Your life is sacred to you! Live it! Love it! Be! Simply be you!

I hope this answered your question, My Darling. I am always here for you. You don't need to try so hard to hear Me. Relax. Let it come. Let it come. Let it be. Let it flow. Hear Me. I Love you. I am with you always. You are very well protected. You always are, you always have been, you always will be. BE! I Love you!

Thank you! Thank you!

No More
By Charlene Hill

The Gentle,
Trusting,
Innocent girl you married...
The one who worshiped you,
The one who adored you,
The one who gave her life to you
So your life was more comfortable...
Is
No more.

You killed her.
With your jagged shards of
Criticism, Disrespect,
Judgment, Ridicule,
Disgust, Contempt and Anger,
You cut into
The very core of her Soul,
Again...and
Again...and
Again...and
Again...until the
Life-blood of
Her Essence
Poured from her wounds;
Until she lived and loved
No more.

For years I have mourned her,
Yearning desperately for her
Return.
Wrapped in the mourning
Shrouds of
Depression,
What I showed the world
Depended on the day.

Sometimes...
Only sadness existed,
Or anger over her
Cruel demise.
On other days
Love
Would squeeze through
And soak my mummy
Bandages...but
Never could I bring her back!
She is
No more.

Now, my Chrysalis of Despair
Has cracked open.
I stand before you
Naked,
Strong,
Beautiful and
Brave.
I offer you Love again...
But understand:

Never will I be the same.
I am healed now!
I give you
MY POWER
NO MORE!!

29

The Highest and Best Good of All,
Life is About Choice &Life Lessons

February 24, 2001 at 1:00 PM. Denis, Sue and Charlie

Charlie, Sue and Denis are here together to ask The Heavenly Creator, The Archangels, our personal Guides and Angels to join us. In our growth process, we have questions that we would like answered, and we ask with Joy in our hearts. We come before you with Love and ask for the **highest and best good of all**, that our questions are answered and that we are given information to grow, as that is our purpose. We want to get any information we can, pursuing our purpose in the best way we can, **for our highest and best good**. We come with gratitude in our hearts and Love in our hearts. We are very, very thankful for all and thankful that you are here with us to help us and we thank you and we Love you.
The Language of Light was spoken...

Hello! What a lovely happy **day** it is today! How wonderful to see you! How wonderful to see you together! Ah, yes, you have questions. Before you begin with your questions, I would like to share some things with you. I will call it "Review Day". Let's have a review. For often you get sidetracked. Often you have something on your mind and you **forget** the lessons you have learned, the teachings that have been before you, and the many things that have crossed your path to help guide and teach. Let us review a few things.

Each time you come before us, you ask that all is given **for the highest and best good of all**. Sometimes you say, "for OUR highest and best good", meaning **yours**. Let us explain to you what "**the highest and best good of all**" truly means. I will use examples that you can identify with. You go to a friend's house and your friend says, " Oh how lovely to see you! I have baked you a lemon meringue pie." And you say," Oh that's my favorite! I **love** lemon meringue pie!" And in your mind you say, "I will eat half of that pie because it is my favorite". And then when the pie is served you get a very small piece of pie. You get an eighth of the pie **instead** of half, and you are disappointed. Now, let's talk about what happened. The meringue pie was made and it was made because it was your favorite, and you were visiting a friend but all you **see** is your friend and yourself and so you assume that it is just for the two of you, but in another room there are six more people. You don't see them because they are not there visiting with **you**, but they are there. So when the pie is sliced it is sliced evenly, and there are eight people and it is divided into eighths. Had you **known** there were eight people, you would say, "Of course, why of course, that makes **total** sense and is the right thing to do." But you don't know there are eight people because **you** see only two. And so you think your friend is being selfish. You will **not** see what is behind all walls. You will **not** see what is for the highest and best good of **all**. You will **not** have all the information in front of you. This is called "**Faith and Trust**". Faith in God, and trust that all that is happening is **for the highest and best good of all**. Do you understand the lesson? Much that happens in your lives, truly, happens for the highest and best good of all. It is **why** you are **where** you are. It is not just for the purpose of **your** learning, but it is also for the purpose of **other's** learning. Know this, understand this, have faith in this, and believe this.

Now, I have **more** to share with you. It is about **lessons**. It is about lessons that are put in front of you, lessons in your path that **you** have actually **asked** be put there so that you can learn. If we **tell** you certain things you will not learn the lesson. You have to **experience** it. To get answers to all the questions in the Universe, will **not** help you learn. So this I tell you: Your child comes to you and he says to you, "I want to have candy for dinner tonight, and that is all. I want a plate of candy." And you say, "Oh, Darling, no! That is not **good** for you." And the child thinks, "What do **they** know? They don't really know." And how **can** that child know unless he experiences it? And so, the next night you are out and the child fills his plate with candy. He eats jellybeans and he eats chocolate and he eats candy canes and he eats licorice and he eats everything that is his heart's desire...and then he promptly throws up. Now, he says, "I **understand** why my mother and father would not give me candy for dinner, for it will make me sick if I have it as a meal. If I have a little bit at a time it is wonderful! But if I have a plate of it as a meal, for total nourishment, it will make me sick. It does not have the same effect. More is not better." So you see, you could not **tell** that child, he had to experience. Do you understand the lesson?

Yes. Thank you.

Now, as we have **told** you, your paths are in front of you. You each have your **own** path. You all, My Children, learn differently. The Heavenly Creator is here with me, and He is saying," *Michael, tell them that the learning never stops*." And so, I did! And He says, "*Michael, you will answer their questions today because you know the answers...as they also know the answers, but for you, Michael, it is a test of patience*." You see, we **never stop** learning and we **never stop** teaching. And just as patience is **my** lesson, it is **your** lesson. For you three seem to have very **difficult** time with patience, and sometimes it is so you can help **me** with patience! And The Creator smiles upon you, for He Loves you so! He **smiles** at your impatience. He Loves you so deeply! And He smiles at **my** impatience for He Loves me so deeply! As He is here with us, He is allowing me to help teach and to help learn. And now, I say to you, you each have questions…you may begin!

Charlene: Sue's question is how can she overcome the enormous stress that she feels at work?

All you go through… is choice. You put as much stress on yourself as you choose. In actuality, she is learning **much** about stress. She has relieved much of the stress by not **allowing** it to enter. She thinks she had a stressful day yesterday. She did not. What she had was an **exhausting** day, and that is different. She thinks that she was actually doing

202

Title work. What she did was Spiritual work. If she would take the time to meditate on the day itself, she would see how many people she impacted that day. You see, Spiritual work **is** exhausting. It takes **much** energy. It is a **different** energy than physical work. There were many people that were in her path...she does not even realize. She impacted **them** with her Loving Spirit, her smiling face and her ability to let people in front of her know they are important. What **they** needed was important, what **they** wanted was important, and **they** were important. She did not have a stressful day; she had an **exhausting** day! And you may share with her that Spiritual work is **exhausting**, sometimes, but it is **ever** so wonderful! And there are many, many gifts that are shared with the Spiritual work. Did I answer the question?

Charlie: I think so. She was, also wondering how to incorporate more Spiritual work into her everyday work at the title company. She feels like she needs more time to do Spiritual work.

She is **so** funny! You see, she **is doing** just that! Because she **is** being who she is, and by **doing** so, she has incorporated her Spiritual work. You see, she **knows** how to share a Spiritual aura without verbalization, while working. One reason, please tell her this, she is **where** she is, is because she is not **only** in the public eye, she is doing amazing **growth** within a corporation. You see, she is **noticed**. What she does is noticed. They do not understand how she can keep the employees she keeps, accomplish the work that is accomplished, and she smiles and she laughs and she is happy. No one can understand how this is all accomplished. It will reach a point where questions will be asked from **inside**, meaning inside the corporation. It has begun, actually. She has shared a poem; she has shared a book, a **journal** with someone she is not close to and yet has impacted this woman's life tremendously. This woman is sharing information and it will spread. Sue just simply does not **realize** what she is doing because she is simply being who she **is** and by **being** who she is, she automatically does the right things. Does that make sense?

Charlie: Yes, thank you. Sue has one more question and that is she wanted to know if there is anything more she could or should be doing to assist her spouse in his Spiritual growth.

Here again, we have discussed this before. You each have your **own** path. On that path are lessons. Each is responsible for his **own** path and his **own** lessons. She **cannot** take responsibility for someone else's growth. None of you can take responsibility for another's growth. You see, it is from **within**! It is on the **inside**, not the outside! And so the growth has to occur from the **inside-out**, not the outside-in! The outside is the **influence**, but the inside is the **growth**. The only position that **can** be taken in this manner is influence, but the growth comes from within. That is something for **all** of you to remember. You can only be responsible for your individual selves, your **own** person, your **own** growth. No one else is responsible. Do you have another question?

Charlie: Yes. Could I take that a step further? It is very difficult to allow another to learn their lessons when we see them in pain.

Do you think people do not **learn** through pain?

Charlie: Yes, but we feel a responsibility to help them alleviate their pain...

Send them Light and Love! Light and Love; do you know Love is the answer to **all**? Light and Love, My Dear...you see, by **Loving**...Loving is the key to almost everything that you ask! It is **all Love**! That is **who** you are, that is **what** you are, and that is what you exude... **Love**! So you see, you send Light and Love to all in pain. You cannot learn their **lessons**, but you **can** say, "I am so sorry for your pain! I am sorry for your grief. I Love you, and I send you Light and Love and I will pray for you." You see, **that** is the greatest gift of all! It is Light. It is Love. It is prayer.

Do remember please, all of you, concentrate on your meditations for all of the answers **are within** you. You see, we are not teaching you; we are helping you remember! For you **know** it all. It is a matter of **memory**. It is a matter that we help you **remember**. And so you shall! You shall remember **all** that you choose and more! For you see, it is about **awareness**. You are becoming aware, and you are **aware** that you are aware! For now you see much **more**, and you see **understanding**, and you see the benefit and the lesson and the purpose. That is awareness. Awareness has many, many levels. And as you become aware that you **are** aware, you will be aware of many levels of awareness. Awareness feeds off **itself**! The more aware you become, the more aware you become, the more aware you become! Are there more questions?

Denis: I want to continue the process of remembering who I am. I have done a great deal to tear down the walls that I had to protect myself. Is there something more I should be doing?

You **know** you do this through meditation and by **centering yourself**. That is something **complete**, it is **not** a thing you stop doing, you see, you don't just stop. It is like saying, "I have learned all I **want** to learn." There **is** no stopping. You will **never** stop learning. You will **never** know it **all**, and you will continue to yearn for more. And you will **learn** more as you are ready. As you are ready, more will be revealed. What we would like to emphasize at this moment, please, is to **concentrate** on the lessons that have been put before you. Do you think you have truly accomplished **all** that there is to accomplish with the lessons that have been put before you? Before you want to run, would you please continue to crawl? And once the crawling is through, you will stand and you will walk. And once the **walking** is complete, you will hasten your step. **All** of you choose to crawl and **run**! Please! You are just completing the crawl! And you are **not** that good at it! Please, get into a **good** crawl and then we will talk about walking. And we will talk **later** about running, and **then** we will talk about **flying**! Right now, we are **concentrating** on the crawl. You have done a **wonderful** job of tearing the roof off of the box that you had put yourself in. You have knocked some of the **walls** down. The cement is crumbling, but you are not **finished**. There are **lessons** here for you to address. There are lessons here that are not **complete**. You have **more** that needs to be learned. As we have said to you, your crawl is **not** yet perfected.

We come to you with **Love**, we come to you with **support** and we come to you with **armies** of protection. And I can assure you; you have **extra help** to learn the lessons that are not complete. Do not be **impatient** with yourself, My Dear. It is not complete, though. You are **so** impatient! Again, patience is, also, a lesson that **is** needed by all...including **myself**! It is **never** complete, as learning is **never** finished! But you have lessons that are directly in **front** of you. There is a **wall** directly in **front** of you. It is crumbling, but it is not **down**. You have **more** lessons, and they **must** be learned. I must tell you, do not eat a plate of candy...and yet, the lesson must be learned, for you will not gain **anything** if I tell you. It will not, then, be learned. Do you understand?

Denis: Yes, thank you. How can I best prevent my ego from interfering in my life?

Again, **that** is through prayer. **Ask** for help. Ego is a serious **problem** with the entire human race. Do not feel that you are the **only** one overcoming this. Ask Your Heavenly Creator for additional help. Ah! The Creator is telling me right now, that He is sending you **extra** help. And He is also saying to concentrate on this being one of your **heart's desires**. Put it on your heart's desire list, and **state** it in the I AM..."**I am not going to allow my ego to interfere with who I am**!" Meditate on this. Also, be very **conscious** of this. This is one of the things that you can make a conscious **choice** with. Now I tell you this, when you feel, as you can... you can **feel** when the ego starts to take over... **ask for help**. Ask The Creator for **additional** help and guidance and Light. Keep in mind; this is **also** a learning experience. You have **lessons** you are learning through the disintegration of the ego; which is in relationship to the disintegration of the wall that is left, and it **is** in the **process** of disintegrating. They are **hand in hand**; they are related to one another.

Denis: Thank you. May I go on? I have felt that in many ways my life is stuck. How can I become unstuck?

Denis, in actuality, your life has **not** been stuck. Little by little, because of **choices**, remember life is about **choice**...because of choices that have been made, things have been taken away from you. Not because we want to see you in **pain**, but because of the lessons necessary for you to **learn to be who you are**. You feel you are stuck? You are **not** stuck; you have had **amazing** growth in the last year! Think of what you have **gone** through in the last five years! Think about what has taken place in the last five years, and let me tell you...you have grown **emotionally**, what it **would** have taken you, in another lifetime, **three lifetimes**! You have done that in **two** years! You could **not** have done that had circumstances not **changed** in your life. You see, for **you** to see what was in front of you, we had to **take away** the things that were **in your way** for you to see. Do you understand what is being said?

Denis: Not exactly, no.

Okay. Let us use the analogy of...no, let us tell you the **truth**. Your **home** was taken from you, your **wife** was taken from you, your **job** was taken from you, and your **health** was taken from you. Those things were **taken** from you because you did not **see** the **important** things that were in your life. And so **all** was stripped from you so that you **could see** the purity of what is good. Let me tell you that money is **not** the **ultimate source** of happiness. The ultimate source of happiness comes from **within**...not outside you; **in** you, not outside you. The ultimate source of happiness is YOU, your Spirit, your **goal** to be happy. It is not what you **have**; it is **who you are**! So you see, you will be stripped of all physical things until you see that your **happiness** comes from **within**. It is not what you **have**; it is WHO you are! Now, recognize **who you are**!

Let me give you an example. Five years ago you were happy in a lovely home, with a lovely wife, with a lovely family. You **thought** you were happy in a lovely home, with a lovely wife, with a lovely family. Now let's look at that specific picture. Did you have a lovely home? Yes, you did. Did you have a lovely wife? Yes you did. Was **she** happy? No she was not. Were your **children** happy? No they were not. Were **you** happy? No you were not.

How can you find happiness? You were stripped from those **things** so that you can take a look **inside** of you to say, "Ah! I **see** now what makes me happy! The joy of my life is that **I Love who I am**! The joy of my life is that I **know I am Loved by God** above all! The joy of my life is that I know, no matter where I live, or who I am with, or where I am at, or what job I have, **I am Loved above all by God Almighty**! And it does not **matter** if I am rich or poor! I am happy because I am a happy person with a happy, Loving Spirit. I might not have **much**, but I have a sandwich, and I will give you half." You had always **believed** that happiness was on the outside, not the inside. We are trying to teach you that **happiness is within**, not outside of you, but **IN** you. Did that help you?

Denis: Yes, and I am grateful for the information. Thank you. I have a question about my Mother. She is having age and health issues, and seems to be preparing to transition to the other side. What can I do to help her and help my brother and sisters? What is my role in this?

To **be who you are**; to **share your Love**, to **share your Light**. Your Mother **is** having trouble. You will be very instrumental in helping her in her transition. It would be very wise for you to physically see her soon. In that visit you will be very instrumental in helping your Mother by settling her Spirit. Your Mother is, also, having difficulty learning **her** lessons. Your presence will be a great asset. You will be very instrumental in helping your **siblings** as well as your Mother. She **needs to know** that she is Loved. She needs to know **The Creator Loves** her. You need to put aside any and all **past**, and look at your Mother with the **eyes** of God. And look at your Mother with the Love you have. If you have trouble, **ask** God to allow you to look at your Mother **through God's eyes** so that you can feel the intense Love.

Again, not all is revealed to you about **another's** lessons. Just know she has had **her** lessons, and they have been difficult. You will be instrumental. You need to physically go soon to visit, and it will be in that visit. It is not about **doing**, it is about **being**. By **being who you** are in their presence, you will be doing automatically, it is not a concentration it is an automatic thing, you will automatically do the right thing. By being **who you are** you will say the right things. Did I help you with that?

Denis: Yes, thank you.

Are there more questions?
If not, I **do** have a bit more to say to you. You **all** have lessons that are in front of you. Some are more easily learned. Remember, life is about **choice**! Now take a look at the choices you **have** made, take a look at the choices that **could be** made, take a look at your **options**. You have more **help** than you realize. Now, let me share with you. There have been many Masters on this Earth. There are Masters now on this Earth that are teaching and guiding. You, My Dears, **all** of you are Masters in the learning stages, you are not **finished** but you are Masters. You are Masters that are remembering **how** to be a Master.

Now, let's go back to the **crawl**.... a Master of Art, Van Gogh. Do you think he ever **stopped** trying to improve?

Never! Do you think he ever **stopped** learning? Never! He chose to incarnate with a very, very, very difficult lifestyle, to learn his lessons along the way, in a **very hard** way. Did he ever **stop** practicing? Did he ever **stop** teaching? Did he ever **stop** learning? Never! Did he ever feel he knew it **all**? Never. He **chose** very **heavy obstacles** to help him learn.... and it was accomplished. It **all** begins with the crawl, not the run. You, all **three** of you, are **impatient** and so you want to run.

Let me give you an example of what you do sometimes. You are walking down a street and you see a beautiful garden. It is glorious, it is huge, and it is colorful. It is full of red and purple and yellow and white and it is beautiful! Instead of seeing this beautiful garden that is in **front** of you, you are looking at a **rock** that is under the second leaf of the first flower that is red, and **that** is where your concentration is. You are concentrating on a **particle**, or a part of a picture that is the **least** important part of the overall picture. You, sometimes, have your **focus** on the wrong thing. If you want to **change** this, simply **ask**.

Ask for guidance, ask for help, and meditate. Please look at the **overall** picture that is before you. Please take a look at the **entire** thing. Please take a look at **all** that is before you and stop concentrating on that which is **not** important. This is a learning situation that you need to figure out; it cannot be **told** to you, you must **experience** the learning. Concentrate on the **positive** and not the negative. The glass is not half empty; it is half **full**. See the **beauty** before you, instead of the darkness. So, find the happiness and the Joy that is you.

How do you find more Joy in your life? Go back and revisit your Wish List. Meditate on the **options** that you have on each item on the list. **Open** your mind and broaden the perspective. Sometimes you get so **paralyzed with fear** that you cannot **even see** the options in front of you. It is wise to **recognize** it. **Ask for help** to remove the fear. Fear is **not** a part of you! Fear is absolutely **not** a part of **any essence** of a human being! Fear is **not** a part of you! Fear is **tied together** with ego. **Ask for help**, and then please try to **recognize** the help that is given to you.

It is **no** different than the man who asks God to help him and God sends a person to his door, and since that was **not** what the man was **expecting**, he sends the visitor away. He **wanted** God to show Himself. He **wanted** to see the beautiful, bright Angels in his living room. God sends help in **many** ways; so do **not** have a **preconceived notion** of what that might be. It is not to say that Angels **aren't** in your living room, as they **are** there all the time, but my **point** is that they may not be there **physically** for you to see, and you **want** physical seeing. I say to you to **remember your faith**.

Remember your **creativity**. Remember your **knowledge**. You have many, many **options**! Take a **look** at the options that you have on your wish list, and **how** to accomplish them. You have so **many**! If you are in a fearful state, do something that makes you **happy**, by yourself or with others. If it makes you happy to take a bubble bath with a glass of wine, **do it**! Make a list of **what** makes you happy. Make a list of **what can help** you get out of a fearful state. You, also, have many books that **you purchased** for a purpose, or that were **given to you** for a purpose. **They** are there to guide and help. God is sending **constant** help and will continue to do so. Please remember to **ask**. If you have trouble **seeing** your options, remember to meditate. Fill your life with Joy! You are **meant** to have Joy! The Creator wants me to add. "*It is done*!"

You see, you **all** have all the answers. They have all been **given** to you over and over. It is not **new**. You **knew** it all along. I am just helping you remember. Nothing has **ever** been said to you, by me or another, that shook you to the bone; shook your Soul. It can't happen, because you **already know** this information. I am **helping** you remember, and we **all** are learning. It is only recently that I have been communicating as openly, because I had a little **trouble** with patience. So you see, it is **never** over; the learning is **never** finished. We **all** continuously learn. It is **never** finished. It is **no different** than eternity.

If you have no more questions I say to you that you are well Loved, protected, guided and taken care of. You have many **lessons** in front of you and it will continue. So you see, you may overcome **one** obstacle but there will be another; it is not an **obstacle**, it is a **lesson**! There is an **easy** road to learn it; there is a **harder** road to learn it. If you are struggling, then make a shift. **Ask** in your mediations. I promise you it is **all** in front of you. I **promise** you the answers **are** there! I **promise** you are **never** left alone! Do you think we don't **watch** you as you throw your tantrums? Do you think it is **wrong**? It's not. Throw your tantrums if it makes you feel better! Know you are Loved. Know you are taken care of. Truly **know** it, in your heart, for **that** is why you are given the friendships that you have. **That** is why you are given the guidance you are given. It is all about learning. It is all about Loving. It is all about guiding. Thank you for giving **me** the opportunity to learn. I hope that I, too, have helped you. The Creator is smiling…

Ah, My Children! You are lovely and I Love you so! I was smiling and I have such happiness! I Love you with all there is to Love! You are so unconditionally Loved and taken care of, even when you throw a temper tantrum! For you see, you are so beautiful to Me and I Love watching you all learn and teach and help one another. And so soon you will expand.

I Love you, and it is I that am grateful for YOU! For you are learning and teaching so well! Please, please, as all of you are learning the patience that is needed to properly learn and teach, I thank you for helping one another. I bid you a wonderful day and know I am with you all! Have a lovely, lovely day! I Love you.

Thank you. Thank you.

There and Back
By Denis Hill

He traveled his road, as winding it went
Over hilltops, through valleys...much effort was spent.
Occasionally smoothing...but never soothing,
That road seemed nothing but tangled and bent.

Along that old road was a beautiful canyon.
There, something was added; a traveling companion.
The trip now to share, for we were a pair,
Holding onto each other with such sweet abandon!

The road seemed much easier, so we added more:
Some additional travelers, a house with a door,
Sports cars and fur coats, jewelry and cruise boats.
We filled our whole lives with the "stuff" we adore.

Somewhere along this roadway called "Life",
I made a wrong turn...thus causing my strife.
I lost all that mattered and was feeling quite tattered,
For gone were my things... my money... my wife.

I reached deep inside in search of some meaning.
I remembered the Love and the Light that was gleaming.
The Essence of ME...It was awesome to see!
Now exuberance and happiness were what I was feeling!

Through processing all I had learned through my plight,
I discovered that, while I had lost things, alright...
(I had lost all, you see, that had meant much to me),
But you can't lose your Essence; you can't lose your Light.

Your Light is what generated the Love that you are.
It's within you always...as bright as a star!
It never goes out, so please have no doubt,
It is God's greatest gift to you...by far!!

Happiness comes from your Light deep inside you.
It isn't created by "stuff" you subscribe to.
It's not from your money, or from your honey!
It comes from your Essence, your Spirit within you.

It took my losing everything in my sack
To realize this and to get back on track.
I used to look outward, but now I look in...
For you see, I know...I've been there and back.

-30-
Growing Pains

March 20, 2001 at 5:05 PM Charlie and Sue
Prayer and The Language of Light...

Well good afternoon! It is so nice to **see** you two. You talk to me all day, but you two are not as good at **writing** as you used to be. It is I, Michael, and it is nice to see you, although I see you with **heavy hearts**. Have not a heavy heart! Put **Joy** back into your life. It belongs there at **all** times, for you are Light and Love and Joy! You are children of Light. What you are doing now is experiencing the **growing pains** of learning.

Approach **each** day with happiness and Joy and Light. Approach each obstacle as a **learning lesson** and give it thanks and give it Joy and give it Love. **Thank** those that are giving you the opportunity to learn, even when the learning **hurts**. For you are Love and you are Light and you will always be. Let fear be released totally. Approach each **day** with Joy. Approach each **experience** with Joy. Bring Joy back into your hearts. Let that Joy replace that fear! For you have **nothing** to fear. You will **always** be well taken care of as you know, for you are protected in every way! And you **are** being given the Light of God daily as He looks down upon you, as He is **with** you in your heart, as He **surrounds** your very being, as He **encompasses** you in His hands and Loves you! You are **surrounded** by His Love and His Light, and you are given **help** in every way. **Remember** the help that you have and **ask** for that guidance. Sometimes you **forget to ask**. Sometimes you choose, instead, to **fret**. Let that go and feel the **warmth** of the Love! Yes, there are **many** lessons in front of you right now, but they are not just **your** lessons. As has been said to you before, do no eat a plate of candy for dinner. You are **not always** going to understand the lesson if it is **told** to you and not **experienced** by you. Therefore, the

experience is what you are actually, not just **needing**, but **asking** for, so give thanks to that.

Now, you are feeling much **pain** and you are feeling much **turmoil** and you are feeling some **abandonment**. You are NEVER alone! You have been given extra help from The Creator. Charlie, it is **you** that has been given **extra help** to help you overcome the grief and the pain and the fear that presently is residing within you. You have additional Angels sent to you to comfort and Love and protect you. You **always** have it, but you have **additional** help right now. Enjoy that which brings you joy. Enjoy your art. Enjoy those that you want to be with. Make the choice to **only** be with those that bring you **comfort** and **Love** and **Joy**. If certain people bring you turmoil or anxiety, make the choice **not** to be in their presence.

It is a time for **reflection** and it is time for both of you, at all times, to go back **into** and **center** yourselves. Keep yourselves **balanced**, and remember to continuously concentrate on what **you** want and what **you** Love and where **you** want to be in your lives. It is a part of your Wish List, which **neither one** of you have completed going through. You are a little **behind** on your assignments, actually, but we Love you all the same and there is **no criticism** here, just a simple statement. You will **finish** it when you are ready. But reflect back and **do** your meditation and **do** your centering, and **Love** yourself more than you are. For you are thoroughly Loved, completely and totally and unconditionally, and yet, you are not Loving **yourself** as completely as you know how. You are being **critical** of you...Love you! Stop with the **criticism**! You are **not** a critical person. You **think** you are Loving you...you are not. You **think** you are not passing judgment, but at times you are. Look at that and **release** it. You **think** you are looking at a larger picture, but you are not. You **think** that you are looking outside the box, but you are not. You **can** have what you want. Pay attention. Write more, meditate more, pay attention, and look at what you **truly** want for you can **have** it, but you do **contradict** yourself at times.

And this I say to you…it is time to **go back** and pay attention to the lessons that have been given you. And **pay attention** to those lessons and see where they need to be in your **life** at this time. And see what is **appropriate** for you to concentrate on in the lessons that have been given to you. For **some** are very necessary at this very time and place. They are very necessary for you to get all the information that you need to be **who** you are and **what** you are to be. For you are on a **growth** path, and you can move forward **quickly** if you choose, or you can move **backward** if you choose, or you can sit very still and move **not at all**. The **choices** are yours. Life is **choice** and **you** will be the one making the choices.

All will be changing **quickly** in this year. This is a year of many changes for you both. You will be moving. You will both be moving, but in different **ways** and in different **places**, involving both home moves and business moves. It is important that you take a look at your path, Charlie, and **see** it with just **you** and stop worrying about Denis' path. It is time to move forward **by yourself**. You have many choices to make. The road splits and you will make a choice to go to the right or go to the left. Remember **you can always change your mind**! Remember **everything** you do is perfect and there **is** a purpose in all. Now, if you have questions, I will help you with them.

Charlene: Yes, I have a question about my health. Is this pain that I have indigestion, or is it my heart?

You are having **real heart pain**. Much of the emotion will bring on the physical, as you know so you need to make **choices** on your emotional, which will make **changes** in your physical. Do you have any other questions?

Charlene: I am concerned about Sue's health.

Sue is digging herself **into a hole** because she is running ragged from morning to night. She needs to get herself into a better **time-management** program. She is **learning** to treat herself better and we are thankful; we have ridden her **hard** on that, but she is **finally** learning to take care of herself. She **does** Love herself, but she does **need** to have better time-management. She takes **too much** on. She is a goer and a doer, but her energy level is **not** up to par for what she **thinks** she can **do**. So what happens to her is, she takes **all** of her energy and **exudes** it all day. She blesses many but she **forgets** to rebuild her energy by taking quiet time out. She is in **desperate need** of quiet time out. She will have it in two weekends. She has **already** committed herself to too many things. So **that** is her lesson. It is fine to **try** and do too much, you see, she has a Spirit that seems to not **want** to stop. So what happens is she digs herself **into the hole** and wears herself out until she **gets herself sick**. And then when she **starts** to feel better she thinks she is **all** better but she is not, and she **wears** herself out again. It is a **vicious circle** and it is a learning **lesson** for her. So the advice you give her, and let her **listen** to this tape, is that she **needs** to take **more** time out. She needs **more** sleep than most people. She needs to take care of herself in **that** way, additionally, to what she is currently doing. And yes, she will **argue** with you. She will say that she doesn't **need** to, but yes, she **does** need more sleep than most, as she has a very **high** energy level. Her health overall is very good, she just needs to stop **wearing** herself thin.

Charlene: Thank you. Do you have more instruction for us at this time?

Just **Love** yourself. You are **not** doing a good job with **Loving** you. Love yourself more **completely**. Treat yourself in a Loving, good way. Keep yourselves balanced. So give yourselves equal amounts of **feminine** and **energy**, which you are depleting yourselves of. You, Charlie, are **not feeling** very good about yourself as a woman. You are allowing Denis to **deplete** you of who you are, in the lovely feminine that you are. Don't **let** that happen. Don't **allow** that. No one can **take** your energy from you, and no one can take who you are **away** from you. Believe in yourself and **Love** you! Sue, believe in yourself and **Love** you! You don't seem to have as **much** a problem with this. You are becoming better balanced. You recognize that you need to be balanced, and you have done a fair job with getting there and staying there. Charlie, you are **fairly** well balanced but you are, right now, **allowing** someone to zap you of the beauty that you are and the feminine entity that you are. Do not **allow** that. You are a lovely, lovely, wonderful, beautiful, Loving Spirit, Light and Love. Do not let **anyone** let you believe you are **less** than you are! Charlie, do you have another question?

Charlene: I am just wondering how to stop allowing my essence to be zapped.

It is hard because you have **unconsciously allowed** it your whole life. You have **unconsciously allowed** someone else to take your power. You are a very **powerful** being in your own right. You both are very **powerful** beings. Denis is also a very **powerful** being in **his** own right. It might be time… and life is about **choice**, and you and Denis need to sit down and make choices, but Love each other. You can **do** so with a very Loving Spirit, for you **both** are very Loving, you **both** have very Loving Spirits. You **both** Love each other.

Sometimes growth **needs** to happen **alone**. So you need to make the **choice** whether it is best for you both, to be **alone** or to be **togethe**r. What is for the highest and best good for the **two** of you? I suggest you both **do** that through a meditation. **Do** so in a meditation. You could do it **together** if you choose, but it might be best to do so **individually**, alone, not together. As in doing so **alone**, not together…**you** seem to worry too much about **him** when he is with you instead of worrying about **yourself**. And he spends **his** time worrying about himself. He is working **very hard** on his growth. You need to concentrate on **you** and not him. When you are with him you don't concentrate on **your** personal growth; you are too busy concentrating on **his** growth. So you need to **do** so... probably **separately** would be the best, most gainfully done meditation.

Charlene: Thank you. I am concerned about my daughter's health...

Your daughter is on her **own** path and she has **not given any** permission, so I can answer and help you with **you**, and I can tell you to send Light and Love to her.

Charlene: I **do** find myself concentrating on other people, don't I?

Yes you **do**! And you do it **way** too much...for you need to concentrate on yourself. Each have their **own** path and you may **not** influence anyone else's path. It is not to **be**, for life is about choice. So **you** may make choices only for **you**, and **that** is where your concentration needs to be centered. You need to center **yourself,** no one else. Let everyone make their **own** choices and learn when to be quiet and learn when **not** to speak and learn when **not** to tell other people how to handle their business. **This** is very important. It **is** something you do, truly, need to learn. Do **not** offer any opinions unless asked. Do **not** offer any advice unless asked. Do **not** give answers to questions that have **not** been asked of you.

And when they **are** asked of you, let the person know that they may not **like** your answer, and do they still **want** you to answer the question.? That way you have given them fair, fair advanced notice, and **then** you are free to say what you choose. Actually, you **are** free to say what you choose whenever you choose, but sometimes the **wisest** words are the ones unsaid. It is the **unspoken** word, sometimes, that is the loudest. Send her Light and Love. Send Denis Light and Love. Send your children Light and Love. Love your grandchildren. Your grandchildren are **blessings** to you, and you to them.

Are there any more questions for me?

Charlene: I don't think so. Thank you.

Then I will say have a lovely evening. Enjoy your life! Enjoy your movie. Enjoy the people there and if you find it difficult to enjoy **everyone** there, send all Light and Love. And ask yourself, "What is **my** lesson? Am I to teach something here?" And then pay **attention** to what is said to you. For remember, you are the student and you are the teacher, and sometimes it is **through** the teacher that the student learns. I am saying that sometimes, it is through you the teacher, that sometimes **you** the student, learn. And now I wish you **both** the best, the most Love, Light, happiness and Joy! Bring more Joy into your lives for you are Joy! Know you are loved by all. **Know** you are protected and **know** that we Love you so and we are **with** you always. And with this I say good-bye to you! Have a lovely evening. I Love you! Good-bye.

Thank you. Thank you.

What Now?

By Charlene Hill

Only through taking God
My Broken Heart to mend,
Can I go forth and do His Will.
But tell me, will it end?

Or am I meant to feel the pain
Of emptiness inside
For the remainder of the time
That I, on Earth reside?

I'm willing, God to see it through,
Whatever You decree.
I feel so blessed and thankful, God,
That You have chosen me!!

But sometimes in the dark of night
I feel so all alone.
I cannot wait until the day
You come and take me home!

-31-
Jim's Transition...There Is NO Death

April 30, 2001 at 9:15 P.M. Denis, Sue and Charlie
Denis, Charlie and Sue are here asking our Heavenly Creator to join us, asking our Angels and Guides to join us, asking the entire Angelic Realm to join us and help us. We ask for help and understanding as to what is happening in our lives at this very moment. Denis has **specific** questions and would love to have some specific answers and understanding in what is happening with and the purpose of his friend, Jim, leaving this Earth as quickly as he did. We appreciate and are thankful for all the help and understanding we are given. We are very grateful and thankful. We are here in Love and joyfulness and thankfulness as we ask for answers, as we ask our questions, and as we are together. We are here in a body of Love and Joy and thankfulness.
The Language of Light was spoken...

Ah My Sweets, how **wonderful** to see you! I see that you are together with joy and Love and pain. There is **pain** in your life, for there are things happening in your lives that you lack **understanding** in. When you **thought** you knew the answers, when you **thought** you knew the questions; therefore you **thought** you knew the outcome. I say this to you, life is about **learning** and when the learning is complete, it is **over**. When it is over be **thankful**, for the lessons have been learned. When the lessons are learned **here**, there are **new** lessons to be learned on the other side, in a different dimension than you are in now, currently at this moment. You see the learning **never** stops, not for you, not for me, not for **anyone**. You are continuously on a learning streak. You are continuously on a learning curve. You will **continuously** learn. And those in your circle, in your family circle, in your Soul Circle of friends, do **not** think that you will not see them again, for you **will**! And even though they have **left** this dimension that you are currently in, you **will** see them again. And **they** are thankful for that, as are you.

Jim Loved you and **does** Love you today and now and forever, for he is **in** your circle. He is **in** your Soul Circle. Jim is **not** through learning, nor are you, and so you **will** be learning together as one. You see, your **time** element is different, so do not **compare** the two; it is not a comparable thing. Be **happy** for him. Be **joyful** for him. **He** is out of pain. **He** is out of misery. **He** is out of fear. **He** is out of **all** the Earthly feelings that you have. There is **no** regret, there is **no** pain, there is **nothing** that is not Love. That is what he **is** now; he is Love and Light. He is in his **true** essence. Be happy for **him**. Do **not** feel bad. He left your Earth in a very, very **special** place. He was **without pain** and **he was with God**. And he is in the **perfect** place where he is happy. He is without the Earthly things that have been known by **all** of you, and **he is with God** now. He is in a **perfect** place.

And **you** are in a perfect place. You are in a perfect place to continue what **you** are doing, which is **learning** and **growing** and **being**. You are still a human being and **you** are being what **you are** to be! And **you** are doing what **you are** to do. And **you** are learning what **you are** to learn. And in doing **all** those things you are growing. Continue. Do what **you** must do and be what **you** must be, and continue.

Things will fall **into** your path. They will, literally, **fall** into your path. And as they do, you will know they are **gifts** from God, and they **are**. You are **not** forgotten, My Dears, not at all. Do not think so… do not think so. You are **continuously** Loved, taken care of, and your very feelings are **felt** and your very tears, the wetness of your **tears** is felt. The **pain** in your heart is **felt**. The **Love** in your being is **felt**. The **Light** in your very Soul and heart **is seen**. Continue to be **who you are**. Do not get wrapped up in this world and the things that happen **around** you, for that is **not about** you. Have **no fear** of what tomorrow brings! For tomorrow is not important. It is the **now** that is important. And it is the **now** that you must concentrate on, learn from, be in, be a part of; it is the **now**.

Your pain is **felt**, your pain is **seen**, and we send you many, many Angels to **help** you with your grieving. You have much help. But know that your friend, Jim, **is** in a Loving, wonderful place! And he is in another **growing** place. You see, he is just **transitioning** from one world into another. For him it has been days, for you it has been hours; but he is transitioning **well** and he is on a **learning** curve as you are. You can **talk** to him and he **can** hear you and he **can** know what you are saying. He **knows** you so well, for he **Loves** you deeply. You can **talk** to him, he will **hear** you, he will **respond**. Give him a little time to transition. He is **learning** that The Creator Loves him and has **always** Loved him unconditionally. This is a **new concept** for him. Let him **continue** to learn in his quiet place. You **can** talk to him, though, for he hears you and he Loves you. He does not want **you** to suffer in any way for he has **nothing** but Love and joy for you. And he wants you to know that he is **happier** than he has ever, ever been and he can't **wait** to share with you, the Joy!

Now, My Dears, you have questions and you may ask them.

Denis: I have a question. Does Jim feel that he was finished with the work that he was trying to do, with regards to his sibling, or is there something he wants me to do?

Now, you may not **like** the answer to this, but I must share with you, he does **not care**. It is **not** a relevant part of his Eternal Soul and so it was left behind. It is **not relevant**. You see, the **relevance** of life is not about how hard you work, it is about the **accomplishments** in your Soul. It is about the things you **learn** in your very life about compassion and **Love**. It is about things **other** than business. It is **not** about how fast you can input information into a computer. You see, **that** is not the **important** part of living. The important parts of learning are the very **virtues**. And so when he **left** his body, he left **that** behind. For you see, he knew **that** was not an **important part** of his very Soul.

He had **no** regrets, for you see, when you **leave** your very body, you have **no regrets** because you are **not** going to a worse place; you are going to a **better** place. And as **soon** as your Soul leaves your very physical body, your Soul **knows** and **remembers** what you really **are**, who you really **are**, and where you are really **going**, and so they are **very** joyful! And it is **not** about looking back, it is about looking forward! And so I must say to you, Jim did **not** look back. And, therefore, there are **no** regrets and there is **nothing** he felt he left undone. It is always **forward**, My Dear, it is always forward. Whether it is on **this** plane or another, it is **always** forward not backward. One only goes backward to remember a lesson but one does **not** learn by going backward. And if you can remember that, **you** will continue to go forward. Do you have another question for me?

Denis; No, thank you.

Know that you can **always** ask questions. Know that you can **always** have answers. Know that **you** are eternally Loved forever and ever. And know that your answers are always in **front** of you. Know that your answers, My Dears, are **within** you. You can **always** find the answers to your questions.

All is well in **your** world. All is well in **Jim's** world. There are complications that are **not** about you, that are about Jim; about the life Jim lived, the life Jim led. But they do **not** involve you. Not to be misunderstood, but there are complications but **nothing** that is about you. His very Soul, his very essence…happy, happy, happy! Be **happy** for him for **you** do not **know** the pain he suffered! Be **happy** for him for he is in a **joyous** place now! He is **full** of Joy and happiness. **Know** that he is complete! He is **learning**, as are you, but he is in a **complete** place and he is **happy**! I know that is **important** to you and I want **you** to be sure to understand it. He was a **good** man on Earth and he is a **good** man where he is now. He is a **good** Soul. He is a **good** Spirit. He is bright, he is Light and he is happy!

I will share with you, as you begin to lose your Life-essence on this planet your Light dims, for your Soul is **ready** to make a transition. His Soul was dim. He **needed** the Light. He could only **find** the Light he needed on the other side. Be happy and joyful for him for he is **now** complete. He could **not** be complete here. Understand that he did not leave **you**; he only **completed** himself. His Love for you did not **change** and you will **see** him again. You will **see** his Spirit Essence and you will **know** him and he will you. Not to worry and not to fear. Have **joy** in your heart for it **is** a joyful time! You see, Jim went nowhere that **you** will not go.

There **is** not a Soul on this Earth that will **not** be joining Jim. So he is not special and nor are you. You will **all be transitioning** into the next element and it will be a **joyful** time and it will be a **glorious** time! Do **not** look at death as sad! It is **joyful** and **wonderful**! You must **know** it is the completion of one era and into another. And it is the **end** of the human-being physical **trauma** you put upon yourselves! It is the **end** of pain. It is the **end** of the trauma...you are **so** into **trauma**! **All** of you!

My point being, **all** of you will transition into a better place. Your Souls will be happier and **you** will be happier! **Know** that! So it is **not** a time of pain and fear. It **is** a time of joy and Love! Yes, the **pain** you feel, the **grief** you feel **is** a loss, but take a joyful, knowledgeable **jump** in knowing that **Jim** is in a better place. He is happy! He is joyful! He is with The Creator. He is learning on a different plane. He is fully Light and Love in a **group** of Light and Love. He is in a different Soul family... that **you**, too, are a **part** of and will join in **your** time; you are not ready. But I say **this** to you so that you fill your heart with joy and you can overcome your grief with that knowledge. The knowledge that **he** is so happy, so joyful, so full of bliss and wonder and Love and Light! **Know** this!

Now, My Dears, I could give you all a little bit of a speech on the fact that meditation and writing are very **wonderful** for the Soul, and **good** for your very being...if you choose to expand yourself. For you used to do it **far more** than you do it presently. I **understand** your busy schedules. I **understand** your need to do other things, but know that meditation and journaling are the two things that will expand your growth **quicker**. You can **get** your information and the answers to your questions in a fine, **quick** manner if you choose. But it is your **choice**, and life is about choice and you have many choices to make.

Are there any questions?

No, thank you.

And now I say good-bye to you. I tell you to have a lovely week. I tell you to have a lovely evening. I tell you to have a lovely day. I tell you that Love is the **greatest** gift. **Pass** your Love to all. **Pass** your Love to strangers. Now I don't mean physically...I mean with your smiles and with your essence and with your Light and with your Love and with your eyes. Be gentle and Loving and good to those who you don't know for **that** is how we truly, truly **pass** the gift of Love.

And I say now, we send you away with Light and Love, and I tell you good night. Be happy and joyful and **know** you are Loved above all. Good night.

Thank you. Thank you.

Protection, Discernment of Feelings,
Mother Mary, Cloning & Review

May 21, 2001 at 1:10 P.M. Sue and Charlie
Prayer and speaking of The Language of Light...

Ah, good afternoon, My Dears. How **are** you? It feels **forever** since we have last spoken together! You **look** good. You look like you **feel** good. It is a lovely, sunny day. It is I, Michael. I come to you with Love, and I come to you with information, and I come to **you** with gratification. For you see, you think **you** are the only ones learning. You are not. I, too, am learning. I am learning **much** about the human species. I am learning **much** about patience. I am learning much about **understanding** and I thank you for that. For you have been **so** gracious in letting **me** learn through **you** and I hope you are learning through me. For you see, that is the complete circle, the learning and the teaching that we do with each other. And that is the message you have been given many times. You are the teacher. You are the student. You are teaching **me** and I you. And I am the teacher and I am the student. You see how it works? It is a lovely way; it is a lovely circle of life.

Now, let us sit together. I am **here** with you. I am in the middle with you and I share with you things you have already learned, but we will review. For sometimes you take a step backward to go forward. Sometimes you need to **review** to see the big picture and to understand fully, and so we shall. You have grown **immensely** and you don't realize it. Both of you have. You are understanding and learning what discernment means. For when you listen and you hear and you feel with your **heart**, you know that this is **not** about you. You are there to listen and sometimes give advice and sometimes, you are learning, the **best** advice you can give is silence for it does not pertain to you. Very often someone is **looking** for an answer because **they** do not want to be responsible for **their** decisions. They choose to let **you** make the decision so that **you**, then, are the responsible party. Your silence does not **allow** that to happen. You see, you still are listening and you are nodding and you are hearing, but since no one has **asked** anything of you, you remain silent. And **that** is wise. You see how you've grown? You see... in the past you would have jumped right in the **center** of the chaos and you would have **told** everyone what to do. You would have been directing traffic, but not now. **Now** you realize that, "This is not about me and I will keep my peace and I will let someone **else** solve their problems." You are recognizing you have your **own** problems to meditate on, your **own** problems to solve, your **own** problems to think through, and that you are responsible for your decisions. And so it is, and so **let it be**.

Do **not** make another accountable, including **me**. I am **not** accountable. I am trying to **teach** you. I am trying to help **you** learn. I am trying to help you **see** who you are. For you see, the best advice I can give you is for you to **be who you are**. For it is in **being** the complete human being you are, you are total and complete and **that** is what I need to say to you. All you need to do is **be**. And in your **total** being, you can **hear** what is being said to you to help advise you in the direction to take; the right or the left...veer to the right...veer to the left...go straight ahead. You can hear far more **easily** when you are in your **complete** state of being. Therefore, you keep everyone **else's** chaos at bay. They are **away** from you. They are an arm's length from you. They are not in **your** center. They are **outside** of your Bubble of Light. They are **outside** of your aura. For you see, by **protecting** your aura and yourself, **you** cannot be caught up in another's chaos. Now I say this to you...those that have the **most** chaos will do their **hardest** to bring you into it. By bringing **you** into their chaos, you are then the responsible party for **solving** the problems, when the problems do not **belong** to you. Do you understand what is being said to you? For listen to your own **selves** and listen to me and listen to your Creator and listen to your Spirit Guides and listen to your individual guiding Angels. They are **all** there to serve you.

There are others, outside of your Bubble of Light, outside of your aura, outside of you, that are **not** there to serve you. Keep yourselves **enlightened**. Keep yourselves **protected**. Keep yourselves in your Bubble of Light. In doing so you can **never**, **ever** be harmed or stray. I say **this** to you…your Creator will not **let** you stray. You see, He knows where **everyone** is, He knows what path they are on, and He knows what lessons they have chosen for themselves. Therefore, **all** are in the perfect place at the perfect time, learning the prefect things that will contribute to **their** overall growth. All are given the information needed to follow the path before them. It is not **your** path, therefore, these are **not** your lessons, therefore, they do not have an understanding for you. The less understanding you have, means the lessons are the **least** needed to be learned by you. The **greater** understanding it has for you, the more that lesson is going to contribute to **your** learning process. The less the understanding means it is **not** going to contribute toward **your** learning process. It is not **your** lesson.

It is I. It is I, The Mother. It is I, The Mother Maria.
I am here to share with you something. It is <u>most</u> important at this time. The Earth is needing the feminine energy and you are here to contribute toward that. <u>Know</u> that. Abide by that. Help Mother Earth, as it is very important at this time. Feminine energy will overpower the male energy at this time because that is what is needed to heal the Earth. All balances out in the end, but, now, the feminine energy is needed greatly. You are here to contribute. It is your greatest contribution. Know that. Abide by that. I am here helping you. I am here guiding you. I am here protecting you with all. Now, call on me if you need me. I am always here for you.
I Love you.

Ah My Children, it is I. It is your Creator. I am here to share with you, I am here to tell you, I am here to engulf you, to encompass you, to make known to you...you are so protected! You are so Loved! Unconditionally! My Dears, I want you to pay attention to <u>unconditional</u>!

You see, sometimes I have watched you both have grief. You have grief and you are learning. You have grief if you think that you have made a mistake. I tell you this...there are no mistakes. For you see with each turn you make, with each step you take, it is all a learning process and it is growth. There are no mistakes in growth, My Dears. There are <u>no</u> mistakes to be had by you. Each step you take, each breath you have, I Love you more and more each day, each moment, each second. You both are learning a great deal right now. You don't give yourselves the credit you deserve. Discernment is a very, very gracious, gratifying and loving gift I have given to you. And you are utilizing it and learning how to. Thank you. I am grateful for that. You see, gifts are given to many and many gifts are not utilized, but you are learning. And you are learning very well. Thank you, My Darlings!

Now, I bring you much Love and I bring you much help. You are totally surrounded at this time and always. You are surrounded by many, many Angels that will protect you from harm. Nothing can break through. You have your own armies, you have all you need, want, or could ask for. Know all is happening in the exact way that it should, in the exact time element that it is to happen. Know that there are <u>no</u> mistakes, there are <u>no</u> errors and it is as it should be. You are *learning how to have faith. You are learning what faith means. You are doing well!*

I look down upon you and I send you Light and Love and I send you more Angels than I can count. You have more help than you know what to do with, but you don't realize you have the help there for you. Listen to yourself! That is all you need to do, for they are whispering in your ears and they are telling you the right things and you are so very protected. No negative energy can enter your aura! I tell you this, as it is very important right now. It is not that for all, but it is for you, right now. You see, when you ask it is given. Be careful what you ask for, My Darlings, be careful. Judge properly. Don't judge at all. That is how you judge properly.

Now, Michael would like to share some more information with you, but I want you to know you are deeply, deeply Loved, protected and taken care of. You will be given some more gifts, as it is needed. Utilize what you have and know that I Love you and thank you. Thank you for your friendship. It is so wonderful to know that you are My Friend! It is so wonderful to know that you are My Loving Children! It is so wonderful to see your Light glow! And the greater your Light glows, the more Light I give you. I Love you, My Dears. I am with you always. May you have a lovely day!

So, let's continue. We were talking about **previous** lessons. Let us chat about one that we have had before, and that is about **names** and the very **unimportance** of names. You may call **me** whatever you choose. I will **always** know who you are. It is not your sex, it is not your hair color, it is not your

234

height, it is not your weight (you guys really are hung up on your weight), but let's look at your Light. **That** is how I know you. I **know** you by your glow! I **know** you by your Spirit. I know you by your Loving, Loving, glorious Spirit...not your name! Now let us look at the Light that is yours and the Light that is mine and the Light that is Our Creator's and the Light that is of each. **That** is how we know each other, you know. So, if I came to you as I am right now and I said, "Good morning! Good afternoon, good evening, happy Monday! It is I. It is I, Arizona", you would **know** it was me, for you **know** me. You know me well. I could call myself **anything**, but you would know me. You would **know** me by my attitude, you would **know** me by my lack of patience, you would **know** me! All we would have to do is talk a moment. All you would have to do is **feel** my Spirit. All you would have to do is **feel** my Light and you would know me.

Now, you have had talk of cloning, and you have some knowledge on this. Yes, there **is** cloning going on in the Universe. There **is** cloning going on upon your own Earth. There is cloning going on in the Universe, which you are familiar with and aware of. But one **cannot** clone Spirit. One **cannot** clone Light. So in cloning a physical body, you have a **cold** physical body. You have **no Light**. You have no **energy**. You can take a picture and you can copy it; you know that, you are artists. You can take a negative and you can copy a negative and copy it many times and have many photographs of the same picture, and they look exactly the same. You **cannot** take a Spirit. You **cannot** take the Light energy. You can **never** clone an Angel. You can **never** clone a Light. You can **never** clone a Spirit. You can **never** clone The Creator. We are all, you, me... all of us... are a part of The Creator. We are **all** a part of the Light of The Creator. We, therefore, are all **God-like**. Those that are **not** of that Light energy, **want** that Light energy. Those that are in the darkness, if they were to come in your path, they will **never** be able to enter your aura. You are well protected, but they can **cross** your path. You can be **influenced** by others if you choose, that is why we say do not **get caught up** in another's chaos. Each, in the midst of their own chaos, have lessons to learn. You each have your **own** chaos to deal with and it is enough. You don't have the chaos, maybe, that others have, as you are now in the Teaching and Learning Program. You are teachers, and therefore, **that** is your main lesson. Recognize **who** you are to teach and recognize very **often** the lesson you are to teach is silence. Recognize what the lesson is you are to teach, for very often it does **not** mean wrapped up in **words**. Words sometimes get you in trouble, in fact. **Feel**. **Feel** the energy around you. Do this with the **gift of discernment** that you currently have. Utilize it. Perfect it. Know it. You are **learning** discernment through words. Now begin to learn it through **energies**. You actually have both been in tuned with this, probably **longer** than you have words. You are both quite in tune to the physical **feel** of different energies. You will be **perfecting** that feel. You will do **more** with fewer words. You will be listening and praying more. **Utilize** the gift of prayer. It will be instrumental, using your gift of discernment. As you feel things that are **not as holy** as you Love, or **not as Light** as you Love, send the energy that is **lacking** the Light you are familiar with... **send** it Light and Love. **All** can be cured; **all** can heal with Light and Love. Now **do** this with your feminine energy. Be the **nurturer**, the Loving, Loving nurturer. I am not talking the **physical** lover, I am talking the Spiritual **healer**; doing so with the **nurturing Love** that is you.

Time is of the **essence**. You need to get together again soon. Sue needs to go to work now. Soon this will not be an issue, but today it is. Soon you will be getting together more **frequently** to share with each other, things that you will take care of individually. For you **each** have your issues and you **each** have your lessons and they are given to you differently. And you are learning them very consciously, sharing with each other and growing from each other. You will learn and teach one another and learn together. Then you will go about life on your **own** paths, on your **own** road in front of you, teaching those that pass and cross your path. And then you will get together to share, and that is good! Know that **everything** that is in front of you, as you know, is a teacher or a student, and so approach each with **dignity**. Approach each knowing there **is** something to share between you. Even if you don't recognize that which is in front of you, even when it does not **feel** as Light and Loving as you are familiar with, **know** there is a lesson or a teacher there. Then learn the lesson. If you have questions, please **ask**. If you are unsure, **ask**. All will be given to you in a Loving manner.

Now I must say good-bye. Before I leave, do you have any questions?

Charlie: I am a bit concerned about whether I am to say or do anything in regard to my friend, or do I just simply send Love and Light to her?

Oh, Love and Light! Send Love and Light! Both of you **have** been sending Love and Light to her and continue. She is on her **own** path but she is also feeding you some information that is **helpful** to you. You see she is helping **you** learn discernment. So recognize what she is **doing** is a gift to you, too. You see, gifts are wrapped up in different packages. Please don't worry about her; she is Loved and well taken care of. She is helping **you** learn. Bless her for that and **thank** her. She has her own lessons that are **not** about you, and she will learn them. Remember what we talked about just today, earlier. Know when to be silent and when to listen. Take all the information that is **given** to you and process it. **Ask** what it is you are to learn and **ask** what it is you are to teach. Be thankful for that which is given to you. But, **bless** her. Bless her for what she has given you.

And now My Darlings, I say good-bye, but I am here with you. I say good-bye, but I know we will speak again soon. I say good-bye, but I am **not** leaving. I Love you. Have a marvelous day!

Thank you. Thank you.

-33-
Allow Spirit to Lead & Unraveling Pain

May 29, 2001 at 4:45 P.M. Sue and Charlie
Prayer and speaking of The Language of Light...

Ah, My Dears, how **are** you today? So lovely to **see** you! I know it has been a struggle for you to get together; your lives are so busy. I need you to know we will be reviewing again.

Much is **happening** right now all over the Universe. Much is **happening** on your world right now; much is **happening** on your Earth right now. There is much chaos and time is flying. You will feel it, you will know it, and you will turn around and you will say, "Where did the time go?" Things are happening very, very fast! **Protect** yourself, **guard** yourself, **Love** yourself. Protect yourself with a Bubble of Light as I have taught you. For there is **much** chaos and many will try to bring **you** into their chaos. Remember to stay centered. Remember you are an **observer**. Remember you do **not** want to get caught up in something that does **not** belong to you. Remember this, as it happens **so** quickly, and soon you say, "How **did** I get in the center of this?" And it is because you were **not** paying attention, but it was not **yours** to have. It is a chaos that belongs to others. They will come to you for advice. Remember that the **best** advice is silence sometimes. Remember it is not, sometimes, for you to **give** the answers, but for you to help direct others to **their** answers. And **that** is how you become the Master you are. You will recognize **how** to show another to come to their own answers. You will **guide** them but you will not be the one directing.

Now, we have **talked** about this before and we will again. I have talked to you about **who** you are, about the **human beings** that you are. Yes, you are Light and Love, but at **this** moment, in **this** time, in **this** dimension, you are fulfilling the body and the need to be a human being. This does **not** change your Spirit. You are simply **embodied** in a different way.

Now, the **easiest** way to be who you are is simply to **be** and that is all. Just **be**. Do not force the lead! For Spirit will guide you and with Spirit's guidance, there **is** no struggle. It is an easy, simple path, which has been broken by Spirit, and so it is simple and easy and gliding through. It **is** no effort. Both of you at times, **struggle** with that, for you feel that **you** must take the lead. You will pick the direction and ask Spirit to join you as opposed to letting Spirit **lead** you. Do you see the difference here? There is a **great** difference here!

So by simply **being** that Loving being, Light and Love that you are, and allowing **Spirit** to guide, everything happens in a gentle, Loving, easy way. You will have no rocks in your path. Sometimes you jump ahead of Spirit. For very often you are so **impatient** and you know where you are being lead and you want to go **faster** than you are supposed to. I have discussed this; the crawl, the walk, the run. So I implore you again, **allow** Spirit to guide you in everything!

Now I have some further things to discuss with you. As I discussed before about the chaos, things **are** going to happen and they **are** going to happen quickly and they **are** going to happen in a **way** you will not understand. Have faith, have faith, have faith. **Know** that you are Loved, protected and guided in **all** you do. There are those that are going to be around you… things will **change** in their lives, in your lives, and they will be **outside** of what you think you have planned. Know that **all that happens** is for the highest and best good of all. **Know** that. And if you cry, you will be comforted, and if you have fear, you will be comforted and you will be shown that there is no fear to be had. And if you panic, we will remind you to **center yourself** and **Love yourself** as we Love you.

Always remember that what happens **is** for the highest and best good of **all**, and **you** do not know what is behind those walls. For **all** that happens, happens in the perfect time in the perfect place to the perfect ones. **Know** this. Know that **all** that happens has God's Blessing upon it. Know that **all that happens** has been **agreed to**, prior to incarnation. I share this with you so that **you** can see things with the Love in your eyes and the Love in your hearts. Help each other. Help each other for yes, there are shadows and they will be coming forth. But **you** have **nothing** to fear. For you **know** about Love and you **know** about prayer and you know **how** to get what you want when you want it and when you need it.

I do ask of you... it is time to **write more** than you are writing. You have been lax on your writing. It is **time** to journal more. It is **time** to write down your questions. It is **time** to go into yourself, into your hearts and **feel** and **see** things wholly, with your eyes of Love and your heart of Love. **Meditate** more and remember that you have the Light of God...and remember the meditation. Fill yourself with such Light, especially when you feel dark. For when darkness tries to invade you, just **fill yourself** with Light. Send the darkness away! For it is your Light alone that will Lighten any shades of the dark.

You have much Light that is falling from Heaven to you. You have a **rainbow** of Light around you. You have a **tunnel** of Light coming from Heaven to you. It is non-stop! It is an **unending road** of Light! It is an **unending path** of Light and Love! You will never, ever be without! And you will never, ever have too much! And you will never, ever feel you have enough! And that is good, for it is an unending flow and it continuously flows **to** you and it continuously flows **from** you! And that is good!

And so the lesson today is **be who you are**. Be happy. Be joyful! Be Loving. Be who you are and **allow** Spirit to guide you to **where** you are to be, to **who** you are to become, to your **end** result. Learn the lessons you are to learn, for it is by **not** learning those lessons that you become stalled; you become not moving at the pace you choose to move at. If you become stuck...you **are** never stuck... but if you **feel** you are stuck in a rut, it is because you need to **learn** the lesson that is in front of you that you are having difficulty learning. **Ask** Spirit to guide and help and then it will be.

What questions do you have today?

Charlene; A while back you told me that you could not unravel something that I had in my life and I would like some clarity on this. I don't know what it is you are speaking about.

Let us go back...to the age of two, and **that** is where the unraveling begins. At childhood...you were a baby...you were a toddler when it began. You need to go back through the shadows and **re-teach** yourself. And **reclaim** who you are, and **reclaim** your Light and your Love, and **reclaim** that you **deserve everything** you want. Go back. Love your parents, for they did what they believed was right. Forgive them, send them Light and Love and know that they did not, **intentionally**, hurt you. But **claim** the hurt; **claim** the pain, **release** it and claim your Love again. **That** is where you begin to unravel.

You see, only **you** can do that. Only **you** can go back through and **recognize** where those hurts took place. **Recognize** how they snarled up and tied knots around your heart. **Recognize** the fact that you are Light and Love and **deserve** the best in everything. Please, it is **no wonder** you do not have an **easy** time centering yourself...you never allowed **yourself** to be in the center! Give yourself that gift, please. **You** center **you**. Love you. Put your Light and Love and **yourself** in the center and **allow** that Light and Love to radiate through you. **Untie** the knots that are around your heart from childhood and from your teenage years and from your twenties and your thirties and your forties. Begin anew. Learn to **Love yourself completely** and allow yourself to Love completely. Begin with **you**, My Dear.

Release the tapes that you play over and over without meaning to. **Release** the things that you were taught as a child and **re-teach yourself**. Tell yourself, " I **deserve** the Love

241

and Light My Creator fills me with daily. I **deserve** it! I deserve **everything**! I **deserve** to be Loved completely and totally! And I **deserve** to have the physical wants that I need and want. I **deserve** to be spoiled. I **deserve** to be the queen that I am. I **deserve** to have the wealth and the riches. I **deserve all**, because if I have **all**, it will not **change** who I am. I will still **be** Loving, and giving and I will still **be** who I am. I will **be** my Light and my Love; I will **be** that. I will be **all** The Creator has asked for... for He has asked **nothing**. He has asked me simply to be who I am, and so I shall!"

And **that** is why I say to you, please **be who you are**. Be your Light and Love. **Release** the binds; release the ties that have bound you. Release that which **was not** perfect. Release it **all** with Light and Love. I tell you this, don't expect **another** to be perfect. Love **each** for who they are, for you are all different, as you have different Spirits. Let us **all** grow in our own way, for **I** am still growing, too. And so from **you** I learn patience. And so from **you** I hope I am **learning** to teach properly. And so from **you** I gather **so** much and I thank you.

All must learn in his or her own way. Allow it. Do not expect another to **be** exactly like you; to **feel** exactly like you, to **look** exactly like you. The flowers in the garden are all different colors and different shapes with a different number of petals. And **all** are very beautiful, and **all** are created by Our Creator and Loved as such. And **all** is perfect. And **all** is in its perfect perfection! And petals from the flower drop off and change, and the leaves on the trees change color and the tree itself grows dormant and new blossoms arise, and the tree itself grows taller and the roots go deeper. And so it **is**, and **allow** it to be. Growth looks **different** on each person. **Allow** it to be.

Be **thankful** for all that is put in front of you. Be **thankful** for that which you do **not** understand, and **ask** for guidance so that you may learn and grow. Be **thankful** for all that is brought in front of you and has given you the **opportunity** to learn and grow. Be **thankful** for the questions that you ask. Be **thankful** for those that come in front of you and just need to **learn** from you. Fill your hearts with **joy,** for **that** is who you are to be. Be joyful and Loving and happy for **that** is who you are! Questions may be asked... but don't take them **so** into your heart so that it **breaks** your heart! **Be** who you are, you are Light and Love!

Lighten up! Just Lighten up! Do so by **asking** for more Light and you will be given it. Fill your hearts with joy and Love and Lighten up and be who you are! Do you know, if you **can** Lighten up and be who you are, you will **feel** like you are perfect; you will be in the perfect place. You allow the minute to drag you down. Don't **allow** it any longer! Now I tell you this, center yourself by allowing **yourself to be the center** of your Love. **Center** yourself. **Love** yourself. Be who you **are**...all else will fall into place. There is not one person, human being, on this Earth or **anyone** on this Earth that can help you be **more** perfect than you are. It is your road to walk. There is not one person in this world that can **make** you be a happier person. You **each** are responsible for your happiness.

I am going to help you grow, but to **grow** you have to be allowed to make mistakes! Otherwise, how can you **know** what is Light if you don't know what is dark? How can you turn right if you have never turned left? How can you know up from down if you have never experienced it? So **know** that. In the experiences that are coming in the near future, know that you are only here for the **experience**. Help each other remember that, for you **do** help each other grow. Thank each other for that.

Do you have any other questions? Remember that you can ask questions any time! The Light is there to fill your heart and your Soul, and your glow is **overflowing**! Sit and bask in the Light and enjoy! And know The Creator Loves you so! And I Love you so! And we **all** Love you so! You have **more Love** than you realize; **more help** than you realize. And so now I say good-bye. And I say have a lovely afternoon, and have a lovely evening, and have a lovely night and have a lovely day, and a lovely every **moment**! And I say good-bye with Love and joy as I hand you both a bouquet of beautiful flowers! Smell the fragrance...remember to smell the fragrance...don't pass the flowers up without **noticing** their beauty. I Love you both! Have a lovely day and I say good-bye to you.

Thank you. Thank you.

-34-
Time, Dreams & Taking Care of Health

June 3, 2001 at 6:20 P.M. Sue and Charlie
Prayer for protection and of thanksgiving...and speaking The Language of Light...

Well good evening, My Dears! It is I, Arizona...ha, ha, ha, ha! It is a **joke**! It is I, Michael, and how lovely to **see** you for we have some things to **share** today. I urgently tell you, the essence of **time** is important right now. I need to share with you, certain information regarding the **time** element. You feel very rushed. You feel very **urgent** to keep moving, moving, moving at a fast, fast pace. But beware, My Dears, things must happen in the time element that is allowed. For you see, the seedling does **not** grow to a mature, twenty year old tree overnight. Nor can you. So just as we have urged you to allow Spirit to be the leader, and you be the follower, we tell you this again. For you feel an **urgency** to push ahead and push forward, for yes, time is of the essence and things are happening oh so quickly and it shall continue. But try very carefully **not** to move ahead of yourselves. For things **must** happen in the time allotted for such.

And now I tell you this; there is much that will be happening in the near future. You, yourself, have said, " Time is flying by so fast! I cannot believe that 2001 is half over! It is June already! And yet yesterday, I was worried about complying with Y2K 2000!" Yes, it is happening quickly and it shall continue. And many people and many situations will be put in your path, for **each** thing that is put in your path is an **instrument** to help you grow. It adds growth to your totem pole. You see, **all** helps you grow. You only remain stunted if you choose **not** to learn the lessons. So I urge you to **look at everything** that is put in your path and look at it as **clearly** as you can and **ask** if you need further understanding. Write about everything you have questions on, for there is learning in **all**.

Pay close **attention** to your dreams because you will be getting much information now in your dreams. Write them down; ask about them, as you did. Ask about them and we will give you answers. There will be **much** significance in the things you are shown. Pay attention; **everything** has meaning now. If you have an urgency to see someone or call someone, **follow** the urging. They need to hear from you. If you have an urgency **not** to be around someone, **follow** your instincts; **follow** your discernment. Continue to ask for guidance and help and protection. You **have** it, but by **asking** for it, we know you are **aware** of the need. By being **aware**, you protect yourself even more. By being **aware**, it will be easier for you to see, understand and learn. Look at each person in your path as a teacher or a student. Love them, or send them Love and send them away. You will know.

Through it all remember your smile! And **through** it all, remember joy! And **through** it all, remember the Light that is you! And **through** it all, you shed your Light through your eyes and your smile and your glow! And **through** it all, you will **attract** many. You will meet new friends and you will meet new neighbors and you will meet new people in your path to help establish who you are and help **teach** you what you are wanting, yet, to learn. For you are not **finished**…and just for the record, neither am I! For **together** we will reach **greater** heights and **greater** depths and we will find new plateaus and climb new mountains. For **together** we will learn and teach one another! For **together** we will have such **fun** doing so! For it is the joy that we have for each other, in our learning and our teaching, that makes it such fun! And **through** it all we will help each other and we will help many more, all of us **together**, for we will grow and grow!

Take the time to **take care** of yourself. Please **do** that. Remind each other to get the rest you need and take proper care. Take **care** of yourself to get enough sleep so that you have enough energy to **carry** the energy that you need to carry; to **transmute** the energy you need to transmute, and to

continue channeling and sharing the messages that are given. Take **care** of you! And **give** yourselves the pleasures that you want and need! You see you **can** have the pleasures of many things **without** overdoing it. You can have the pleasures of not just friendship and lovers, but the pleasures of wine and the pleasures of entertaining and the pleasures of the friendships **without** over indulging. You see the **key** is moderation. You need to practice **moderation** for it will give you better health. It will help you remain in a healthier state, both mentally and physically.

You can put certain people **on** your path if needed. If they are in your mind or heart, they may have **information** that will be helpful to you in your learning process. Those that come to tell you things, for you are such a good listener, remember that is what you **are**... a **listener**, not a problem solver, but a **listener**. For by listening and asking certain questions, **that** is how you can help put them on the road **they** need to be on. And **that** is how you can **help** them determine the answers they need to determine. You will do just fine, but stay **out** of another's chaos. You do **not** need it at this time. You **never** need it, in fact, and what it is, is called an "energy burnout" when you get involved in another's chaos. **Save** your energy; **save** it! **Save** it to use it **properly** and to use it correctly and that way **all** is better served by doing so; the teacher, the student and of course, the Spirit.

At this time, The Creator is **helping** you and **clearing** the fog from your mind and you will have more insights. And you will have much greater **understanding** of things as they take place. **Document**. You have not been **good** about documenting. Document your dreams. Begin today. Write down everything you can remember. **Through** it you will have greater **understanding**. You will recognize things and you will say, "Oh yes, I am quite **aware** of what is going on and I am **not fearful** for it is all taken **care** of...and all will happen for the highest and best good of all." **Know** that **all** will happen in the time that it must, so do **not** have worry and

247

do **not** have fear. There are people that have **lessons** to learn in the timing that takes place. It is not **about** you, and you have no need of further understanding of this. It is simply for you to know that all is **perfect** so do not worry.

Now, My Dears, I want you to have a restful, peaceful, joyful, wonderful evening. I want you to write. I want you to go to bed early. I want you to sleep in a lovely, very soft, dreamy, peaceful, Loving evening. You will sleep well but you will sleep so that you **do** wake up remembering your dreams. Please **write them down** upon awakening. You can share them and discuss them together. My Dears, do you have any questions before I tell you good night? I am **always** here to answer your questions, and I say to you, enjoy your lovely evening. I will **be** here. Your Creator, of course, is **always** here. Spirit **never** leaves you. You have many, many Angels that enjoy your company; more than you really realize, for you attract the Light of **all** and it is good. For their Light shines upon you and increases your own. And so, My Dears, **continue** to Lighten up! And have a lovely evening and we will talk soon. My Love is with you. Good night now.

Thank you. Thank you.

-35-
Changes and Transformation

June 7, 2001 at 5:25 P.M. Charlie and Sue
Prayer and speaking of The Language of Light...

Well, good afternoon! I see you are **loaded** with questions. Well, let's **talk** awhile. Let's see what we can **help** you with today. First I must share with you that everything you are asking, you **already** have the answers to. They have **been** given to you over and over and over, but let us review.

Love is **not** something you learn; Love is **who you are**. You are Light and you are Love. It is not a learned trait; it is **your very essence**. You cannot Love too much, nor can you be Loved too much. Your Creator Loves you intensely! There are no **words** in your language to share with you, to explain His Love; to give you the complete, entire picture.

All that happens is by **choice**. As we have discussed, you have made many choices **before** you even incarnated, and now your choices are coming forth. And yet you don't **remember** the choices you made and the lessons you chose to learn. So here is where **faith** comes in. And by letting Spirit **guide** you and having **faith**, you understand that **all** that happens **is** for the highest and best good of all, so that the lessons you chose to **learn** can be accomplished; accomplished by **all**. Follow your **own** path. Walk your **own** path and do **not** ask another to walk it with you, for each have their **own**. We have discussed this. Sometimes those paths are side by side, sometimes they are crossed, and sometimes they are far apart.

Enjoy **all** that is in front of you and learn **all** that can be learned by each experience. **Enjoy** the lessons; don't make them so hard. You see, very often you are making things **far harder** than they **ever** need to be. You **do** this to yourself! It is not meant to be so hard, but you toil and toil instead of just simply Lightening up and following the Spirit's lead. Do **not** pass judgment on **another's** lessons; **how** he chooses to learn or **what** he chooses to learn at this time. It is not for **you** to decide.

Your bodies are **changing** and you are having different **reactions** to different things. You can take as much medication as you want; it will change **nothing**. Because you see, you are **transforming** now. And you will **see** subtle changes in yourself. People will **see** subtle changes in you; nothing they can identify...is your hair color different? Are you wearing glasses? Did you used to wear glasses? Are you taller? Are you shorter? They cannot identify the changes in you. This will happen more and more frequently as you are changing.

Sue is going through a **metamorphosis** at this very time. She is not understanding what is happening to her very body, but her **body** knows. She **is** doing the right thing by being calm, by Loving herself, and being **good** to herself. She is understanding **part** of it is balance. She is understanding that her work in the work force is nearly over. It will happen in a fine, fine way, not to worry, not to fear. Roll with the flow as you are being changed; as you are metamorphosing into who you are to be.

Just as you two were so silly...muscle-testing teas, you can do so with decisions... for your **heart** knows the answer. It is your **mind** that is confusing you. If you have confusion as to your choices, you need to meditate on them. Very gently and quietly **ask** for guidance. Write more, for your hand and your body, very often, know how to **write** things down that you are **afraid** to think in your own mind. Have faith. Have trust. **All** that is happening **is** for the best and highest good of all. And it **is** the highest and best good because you are either learning or teaching.

I tell you to have a lovely evening. And I tell you to **stop** your fretting and stop your worrying. I tell you that **no matter** what you do, you are perfect. And I tell you that **no matter** what you do, the lessons that need to be learned **will** be learned. And I tell you that whatever happens, there is a shorter road and there is a longer road; and it makes no difference, for the lessons will be learned regardless. So have **no** fear. Have **no** fear. You make the choices that you think are **best** and you meditate and you ask. You have **been** given all the answers needed to make proper choices. I tell you that you have; you must simply concentrate and instead of worrying so about whether to turn right or left, why don't you simply **follow** the Leader? Let your **heart** lead with Spirit, instead of your mind. Have **faith** that all **is** happening for the best and highest good of all. **Believe** it!

Are there any more questions?

Now, My Darlings, I say you will have a lovely evening. Lessons will come to you in your dreams. Are you writing them down? Please **write** them down and **share** them with each other. Write them down as you remember them. Those lessons, that are coming to you in dreams, will be repeated. They will be repeated in different ways. All is well and all is good. Have faith. Clarity will come. Clarity will come, but you must **listen** for clarity. Remember packages are wrapped up differently and they come in different sizes and they come in different shapes. They come in different colors and they come in different ways.

And now, My Dears, I will say good-bye to you. I will say have a lovely, wonderful glorious evening! As I, Arizona, say good night and I Love you. And I know you will have a lovely evening! My Love to you! Good night!

Thank you. Thank you.

36

Time and Timing, Mother Mary, Setting Goals & Age

July 2, 2001 at 1:05 P.M Charlie and Sue
Prayer and speaking The language of Light...

Well good afternoon, My Very Wonderful, Impatient Ladies! How wonderful to **see** you! How wonderful to talk to you! You gave me a grand opening, I must say, because what I want to speak with you about is **time** and **timing** and how timing is all so relevant. As you just said, there are **no accidents**; there are **no coincidences**. Everything happens in the **time and manner** that it should. For, events **line up** so that they fall into place; so that the people are in place, so that the events are in place.

The reason that I am discussing this with you, Sue, is that you **say** you want things to happen for the best and highest good of **all**, and then you say, "But **I** want it **today**!" So you see it would **not** be for the highest and best good if we listened to **your** timetable. So what we ask, My Dear, is that you patiently **know** that your Creator has the best timetable of all! Remember, one of **your** lessons is patience. And remember your Creator **knows** what is best for **all** and the highest and best good of all will take place in **God's** time. **Know** that, **believe** that, **remember** that, **have faith** in that. All will happen as it **should** and as it does, you will **know** and you will **see** and you will **understand**. Okay, My Dear?

Timing is **most relevant** in everything that takes place in your life. And I'm sharing with you now that things are going to fall into place for you both. As we have discussed before, you are not on the **same** paths. Different people will be put in both of your paths. They are instrumental in your learning, your teaching, your growing, and you are **being initiated** into new and more knowledge and gifts and revelations. Those that cross your path are there for a reason. All learn in their **own** time frame, not in yours. All teach in their **own** time frame and not in yours. Each person, each Light entity, each Soul, has **its own timetable** for learning, has **its own way** of learning has **its own way of listening and hearing**. And that is why **no** judgment should **ever** be passed on how another learns differently from you. For **you** are growing rapidly. You are learning much. You are **ingesting** as much as you can as you continue to grow and learn and teach. If you pay attention, some of the very words out of your mouths to **others** are the things that you, yourself are needing to remember and learn; for I had told you that before. You will be teaching that which **you** need to learn, and so it is, and so it will be.

Now, Charlie, I tell you once again, the most **important** lesson for you right now, in this moment, in this space, is **silence**. You have many that are going to come to you; many in your own family will come to you. And you listen cautiously, and you listen with your heart full of Love, and you listen with your heart and not your mind. And as you hear, you say, "Let me, Dear Creator, let me hear with the ears of Love and the heart of Love. And Please remind me, what would Love do?" And it will be.

Silence is your **most important gift** to others at this time. Smile and Love. It is through your **silence** that your essence truly comes through. You see, you can Love with your heart and you can Love with your eyes and you can Love totally and completely **without** telling someone what to do. When you **are** asked, when you **are** asked a question, when you **are** asked advice, before you answer anything remember... the Master is one who **teaches**. He teaches the younger Master **how** to find **his** options. And **that** is what you will do. Share. Share what options you see and help **them** discover more. And that will be your greatest gift to your children; allowing them to learn **through** you.

It is I. It is Mother Maria. I come to you with Love and gratefulness. For you see, the feminine energy is so needed on this Earth at this time. Which is why the two of you have become relatively nurturing for you are listening to your Soul and you are listening to your Angels. Nurturing is needed. It is through your Love. It is through the Love you share and the Love you give. That is what people see. That is what they are attracted to. All you do, you do with Love. You see, Love is the greatest gift to share. It is the greatest, most healing, most wonderful. And with all you do, you do with Love. It is seen, it is recognized, it is felt. And by doing so, you raise the vibration of the very Earth. So you see your Loving nurturing natures continue to be what you are. As you have been told before, just be. For through your very being you are doing so much. And that is why people are drawn to you. For your essence is Love. And those that have built the brick walls around their hearts still recognize it and they miss it and they are attracted to it. And so you will help those break down the brick walls once again. And that is done by Love; simply Love.

Do you have questions for me today?

Charlie: Yes I do. I have been having difficulty dreaming and planning goals and hoping. Part of it, again it is interesting that you are speaking on time. Part of it is that I don't know if I have enough time. I feel that I am starting over and, yet, I am middle aged.

Do you think **age** is **relevant**?

Charlie: That's what I'm concerned about…that I don't have enough time.

Age is **not** relevant. All will happen in the time that it is supposed to. Age is **totally** not relevant! You forget…you are here for a sort, short, short, menial time when you think of the overall essence of your entire Soul Life, which is **eternity**! What you are **doing** and what you are **being** is what is important. For you see your very **being** is what is sharing with other people the lovely Love and the **beauty** that you have within you. Now you talk of hope. What **is** it you are hoping for? Are you hoping for more Love? You see there is an unlimited supply. Are you hoping for more…what? For more what? Be descriptive. I tell you, you have an unending supply of unconditional Love! Are you unhappy? Are you unhappy on this Earth? Are you unhappy for the decisions that you had made prior to incarnating? I tell you this, you have done a **fine** job, and your **purpose** is in the process of being met. For you **have** met many of the goals that you set out to meet and you **have** helped many, many people grow and learn and that **was** your goal! So I tell you this, you **have** accomplished more than you give yourself credit for. So what is it that you further want that you have not received?

Charlene: I feel like the goals and the dreams and the plans that I had for my life... I feel that I have totally failed.

Ah! I tell you this, not only have you **not** failed, you **have** **accomplished** much! And you have **allowed** yourself to be in **pain** to accomplish it, and all are grateful! Now, because you are a High Soul, you are a high level being, your **Soul** knows this, even though your **mind** doesn't. And so you **have** accomplished all that you **asked** to accomplish, and you are in the **process** of completing that. You are not finished, yet, My Dear, and therefore, you are going nowhere! And when your time is through you will **know** it and it is not through yet. And your Soul **knows** this and so you see... can you **feel** the laughter within you?

Charlene: Oh yes! I just feel like, on the Earthly plane, I have worked hard and have nothing to show for it.

And so, when you leave this Earth, what **is** it you care to take with you? This is not your **true** place of **being**. This is **not** your **essence** for life. This is very momentary. So what **is** it that you choose to have that you think will last you through eternity?

Charlie: I feel that I would be able to accomplish more good if I had more abundance to share.

Then **let it be**! Stop getting in your own way! You see you get in your way so much for you are **afraid** to succeed for if you do someone will **pass judgment** on you...and who would that be? You **allow** others to manipulate you, even unconsciously. Don't **allow** it anymore, Dear, and you will be fine. For you were meant to live in abundance and, yet, it is **you** who have sabotaged yourself for you are **afraid** to have abundance. Now, you **get rid of the fear**, and it is there. Do you understand?

Charlene: I understand what you are saying, I don't know how to do it.

Hum...and how often are you **meditating**? Hum...now I share this with you, you have come a **long** way in your learning. You have come a **long** way in your releasing and you are **not** finished. When you **have** let this out of your system, this **fear** of accomplishment, this **fear** of abundance; for you say you want it but I tell you this... it is only **you** who are denying it. When you **release** that and **allow** yourself the abundance you deserve, it is there! You have **no** other lessons to learn in that respect.

There are **others** that do. When you just simply allow and you say, "Thank you", it will happen. However, let me say this to you...you build yourself a very magnificent highway...it is magnificent! You can go anywhere and everywhere and you can go there quickly. And then you build all these brick walls in the center of the highway so that you cannot go through. First you build a magnificent highway...then you build yourself **blockages**. And you do that for you are **afraid** someone will say, "That's not fair. She has a better highway and a better car than I have and that's not fair. I want what **she** has and I want her to give it to me now." And so you find it easier **not to have** than to have **more** than another. But you see, you have **learned** your lessons and so you **shall** have what you want.

Others have **not** learned their lessons, and it would **not** benefit their very well being to be given abundance. For abundance would **misguide** others and some would not be able to see that these are gifts from God. And without seeing where it **comes** from, it is useless. Instead, for those that forget The Creator, those that forget their Spiritual Being, those abundances must be taken away so that they can be pushed down to **look up** to say, "Thank you", to say, "I Love you", to say, "Help me", to say, "I believe in You". You see there are **many** lessons that must be learned and with each individual, they learn differently. Do you understand?

Charlie: Yes, I do, thank you.

I share one more thing with you. Your Creator and the Heavenly Essence, not only encourages you **not** to be negative, it **warns** you about negativity. **And in no way, shape or form, would a Heavenly Being <u>ever</u> share a negative thought or attitude with you**. **Know** this! When you receive information, before you listen with your mind and ears, **feel** it with your **heart** and you will know. For **you** have the gift of discernment. For you see, I am not saying to you that there are not **tricksters**, but they are **not** in the Angelic Realm, and it is **not** Your Heavenly Creator. It is **not** your Spirit Guides, for there are many who look after you, guide you, Love you, protect you. There are others who **want** to confuse you, trick you, and mislead you. With the gift of discernment, **you** have the ability to know the difference.

Charlene: I find that I have been writing a lot of the negative feelings down. Is it helping to get it out of me, or is it making it stronger?

Actually, it depends on what your **motive** is. If you are writing to release, and you are writing for guidance, you should be getting answers that you should also be writing down. Your answers should **never** be negative. If they are negative, clear. Clear the house, clear the air and start again. No one should answer you in a negative way or in a negative form. You have a **clear passageway** to The Creator. Along that passageway are many Angels. **None would answer in a negative way**. So, are you journaling away negativity or are you writing and asking for answers? Either you can do. I suggest if you are writing away negativity, and I assume, asking for help... write down the answers. If you think it **serves** you better, you may write it down and then **burn** it. Send the negativity **away** into the night with Love.

Charlene: Sometimes when I feel negativity and I write it down, I feel unworthy of the answer.

That is an **old tape** you are playing in your head from many, many, many years ago and even lifetimes ago. You **are** worthy of all and you are **unconditionally Loved** and you **can** have anything you want. **Never say you are unworthy.** Your Creator Loves you unconditionally. How **can** you be unworthy? As we have said before, all happens in the **perfect** time and place. Don't **ever again** feel you are unworthy! **Release** those tapes and **do not allow** any person to make you feel unworthy. And **do not allow** any person to make you feel guilty. Don't **allow** guilt. Don't **allow** fear. Release those things into the Light and let your abundant Love take over for you.

Charlene: Thank you.

Do you have more questions?

Charlene: I have been listening to tapes from Tony Robbins and I have been feeling that some of the messages are divine guidance.

Know this...you are **all** Masters. **All** have something to offer. Now what we just said to you was that people will be put in your path. Sometimes they will come by tapes, some by telephone, some by book. All have something to teach. And recognize that there are lessons to be learned always. We have said before that learning is **never** complete for there is always **more** to learn and there is always further to go and grow. Can you Love too much? It cannot **happen** for Love is eternal and it multiplies over and over and over again. So can you be Loved **too much** and can you Love **too much**? Never! And the **more** you Love, the more Love you are given over and over. And the more you Love others, the more you Love yourself over and over. So **allow** the Circle of Love to continue.

Your paths will soon start in **different** directions for different reasons. You two will **always** have a heart connection and if you doubt yourself, call each other, for you have **such** a heart connection you can almost read each other's minds and soon, you will. If you have a fear, **share** with each other. For not only does your gift of discernment accomplish what **you** need it to accomplish, but when the two of you share **together** you are always right on...in case you have not noticed. If you discuss something, you **both** know when it is right or wrong. If you are afraid you are not **hearing** something properly, or feeling it properly, share it with the other and you will **know** you were right.

Now, is there more that we should discuss? Is there more that I can help you with?

Many things will come into your path and many things are going to **change** for you soon. Your families are going to grow. They are going to move on. They are going to rely on you for your Love, for it is your Love that helps them grow. Words don't need to be said, for they **feel** your Love. Do not have fear. Do not have worries. Know that **all** that happens, happens for the highest and best good of all.

As we have said before, there are many that will be **leaving** this Earth plane. It is **nothing** to be frightful of, for life is eternal and your Soul will live forever. You will help with several transitions of other people as they transcend into the next plane. One of the **hardest** things for humans is the loss. It is **so** hard even when you **know** eternal life is there. Loss is a **human** feeling. It is not going to be easy for **one** person on this Earth. Do you think it was **easy** for Mother Mary when her Jesus died? No. Did **she** know what eternal life was? Yes. Was it **easy** for Mary Magdalene? No, it was not. Was it **easy** for anyone? No, it is not. You, too, will feel a sense of loss when it is **your** turn. That is **not** something we can take away, but we will be here **always** to comfort.

If there are no more questions, I will say good day, I will say good morning, I will say good afternoon, I will say good night, I will say happy Monday, I will say happy day, happy sun and happy moon. I say I Love you and I am with you always and we will talk again soon.

Charlie, it is **time** for **you to channel more**. You **know how**, you are hearing correctly, you have been **shown**, you have been **taught**, and the time is **now**. Both of you will have your **third eye** opening. It will get wider and wider and wider and you will be able to see more **clearly** and you will be able to see **more**. Continue to tape all of the sessions and when it is time we will help you edit…but not yet.

Now, My Dears, I say good-bye and I say I Love you. I say good-bye but I am not **leaving**. I say good-bye and we will talk soon; as soon as **you** choose. When you have questions, just ask. The Creator has given me permission to help **you** grow and in doing so, the Creator has allowed **me** to grow through you. You see the circle continues. The Creator **never** leaves us. He is smiling on us now as we share and learn together. We will continue to do so. Good-bye, My Dears. Continue to **be**! Be your happy, joyous selves, and know I Love you! Good-bye now.

Thank you. Thank you.

37

Know All Happens Perfectly in God's Time
& Our Connection to Nature

July 10, 2001 at 1:50 P.M. Denis, Sue and Charlie
Charlie, Sue and Denis are together. We ask the Heavenly Creator to join us. We ask The Archangels, we ask our Spirit Guides, and we ask our personal Angels to all be with us. We are here in gratitude and Love. We ask for any information you can give us that will help us grow and help us learn. We thank you. We come with thankfulness in our hearts and we thank you for helping us. We thank you for joining us. We thank you for guiding us through our life-lessons as you have done. Thank you.
The Language of Light was spoken...

Hello My Dears. How are you this morning...or is it afternoon...on this day in your life? You **do** get quite hung up on time. Realize...realize now and realize always...time is **not** of the essence, My Dears. You have eternity. Eternity is ahead of you. Sometimes the stress you feel and the stress level that you put yourself through is because you **allow** yourself to go through a "time crunch". Know this, it is **not important**. Stop putting those **binds** upon yourself and around yourself. Stop with building the fences that fence you in...that put **boundaries** around what you can **do** and what you can accomplish. You see you sometimes allow yourself to **sabotage** your own good doing. Let time go. Try **not** to let **time** interfere with what you want to accomplish.

By **putting** the time limits on things, you sometimes **hurt** yourselves. Realize that all that will happen, happens in **God's** time, not in yours. And with **that** belief and understanding you can **relieve** yourself of all of that stress. For regardless of what time element **you** want, you must **realize** that when you ask for things to happen for the highest and best good of all, that **that** means **God's** time. Remember that...allow that to **be** for it is. And you can **relieve** yourselves of all the **stress** regarding time when you realize that it is **God** leading, not you. It has been said before and it will be said as many times as you **need** me to say it, for we are not working on **your** time frame, My Darlings.

As much as we Love you and we want all that is **best** for you, **we** can see ahead. We can **see** things that **you** cannot and so we **truly** know what **is** best for you. Know this, understand this, remember this when your schedule, as **you** have determined it, is not met. This has to do with job changes and different changes in your lives, which **you** think should take place this moment. Know that things happen at the **perfect** time, the perfect place, on the perfect day and the perfect hour at the perfect minute. Know it **all** falls into place for the **best** and **highest** good of all. For if one job is **not** available to you, **know** that is because there is a **better** one around the corner. What does that mean, around the corner? Does it mean in one day, in one hour, in one week? Well, I tell you this. It means at the **perfect** time and the **perfect** place. Know this, believe this, understand this and be thankful for this; for we want what is **right** for you.

When we say we want what is **right** for you, we say we want what is best for you to **learn** what you must learn and to grow into who you are and to believe in yourself and in others and in God and in me and in all that you know **exists**... even though you cannot touch it. And so I say to you, have faith and maybe **that** is the purpose...faith. For you see, faith can **heal** many wounds, as does Love. Love is the **greatest** healer of all. Love is the greatest **conqueror** of all. And therefore I tell you...I say to you...**Love** with all your hearts. Love **all**. Love **all** that come into your path. Be good to **you**. Be **kind** to you. Love **you** as I ask you to Love others. For Love really conquers **all**; for it is the **greatest** gift The Creator has given you...has given us all.

And now, what are your questions?

Charlie: We are all three concerned about all of our children, and I want to thank you for helping my daughter to heal.

Prayers work! Yes, she **was** healed over and over, but you **knew** that she would be, and she will be healthy once again. And then **she** will **choose** whether or not she will **stay** healthy. And it is not about **you** for silence is golden. Do remember the Golden Rule. Love, Love, Love for you **cannot** Love too much! And sometimes the very **best** advice is silence. All of your children have lessons, and they will learn them. They are actually **all** very High Spirits. And they have **chosen** to take a lot on this lifetime. Love them **through** their learning and Love them **through** what they must go through. They all must learn in **their own** way, as do you. You all have a **different** Spirit, and you all learn in **different** ways. You are **all** different. You **hear** things differently, you **respond** to things differently and you **react** to things differently. Therefore, all of you **learn** in a different way.

And the way that your children learn has **nothing** to do with **you** and you must stop internalizing everything. For what you at times do is if anything goes wrong... or in **your** opinion goes wrong... anything that is objectionable to you... you take on **responsibility** and feel it is **about** you. I tell you, it is **not**! You must stop doing that, for in **doing** so you take on more grief than is yours. In **doing** so you hurt for other people when their heart hurts. And I say again, everyone must learn in different ways. It is **not** about you. You **hurt** for your children...part of this is mothering, part of this is **wrong**... for they must learn their own lessons. And that is why I say Love them. For you can **never ever** Love too much. Even without words, allow them to **feel your Love** for that is **comforting**. They can learn their lessons with the comfort of your Love. **Do not tell them what to do**, for you learn differently than they. **Do not give advice not asked for**!

And when they **ask** for advice, tell them the truth. First say, "If you are asking what **I** think, I will tell you but you might not **like** it." And give them the option of hearing it. If they still want to know, say, "I don't want to hurt your feelings. I will tell you the truth if, truly, you **want** it but I am afraid it will hurt your feelings." even if it does not. (What you are saying is that you Love them so much you don't want to tell them something that might hurt them.) And if it is right, and you know it **will** hurt them too deeply, say the truth again, "This is not about **me**, this is about you. I can **help** you see your options and your **choices**, but I cannot **tell** you what to do." Use your discernment to decide if the truth is beneficial or harmful but still be honest.

All of your children are old enough to be responsible. It is **wrong** to take on **responsibility** for another. You have been told to center **yourself**. You are responsible for you! It is not **about** you! They have the choice to learn their own lessons. But do not **abandon**. Give them Love. Send them happy notes. Give them happy phone calls. Let them know that they are, simply, Loved. As Our Dear Creator Loves us unconditionally, Love your **own** children unconditionally. Unconditional Love is the highest and best good of **all**. Stop worrying and centering yourself around another. Keep your center around **you**. If they have to learn lessons in a certain way, then it will be. You must realize that The Creator sees **all** of your children and Loves them. **None** of them are forgotten. They have many Angels surrounding them. All your children learn lessons differently. Center yourself around what **you** need to do, not what **your children** need to do, not what your **friends** need to do, not what **spouses** need to do. You all need to center yourselves around **yourselves** and figure out your **own** lessons, not another's.

Now, as you all know, **changes** have been many, as we told you there would be. And they are **not** done and they are **not** complete. You have changes in **every way** in your environment right now...for you don't have enough water...for you have too much rain...for the topsoil gets washed away...for the flowers bloom in their beauty...for the trees are dying from different insects. I tell you, Mother Earth needs your Love, too. Denis, do you have a question?

Denis: I am curious what my connection is to my little groundhog friend.

Actually, you are **all** very connected to nature. And you are **very** connected, not just to your little groundhog friend...you are connected to many. You are connected to the birds. You are connected to the flowers. You are connected to the trees. You are connected to the wind, the air, the clouds, the Sun, the moon. You are **very** connected to nature. And just as you can talk to your little groundhog friend, you can talk to a dog on the street. You can smile at a baby in a stroller. You can just **be**. You can always just **be** and you will fit into nature beautifully. Sometimes you look at his little face and you read different things, so **listen**...just sit and listen. For **everything** has a message to you all...everything. Look at the stream, look at the water, watch the brook, look at the rocks in the stream, look at the leaves as they flow in the wind and they almost talk to you. Listen! For they **do** talk to you.

Enjoy outside. Spend **more** time with nature. Spend **more** time in your favorite, quiet place. Be alive! Touch the trees, smell the flowers, smell the grass, smell the pine and **enjoy** the beauty of it all for it truly is most beautiful! And **that** is what you really Love about this Earth. And so by Loving everything you are sending Love deep down into it's core and **that** is what is needed now. **Recognize** the beauty and the Love and **spread** it and **enjoy** it and **share** it. Write about it and very **special** writings will come through; special poetry, special stories. Enjoy! For, you see, that **is** what life is. Life is growing and growth and **living**!

You see, sometimes you forget to **live** your life. Instead, you just sit and you are stagnant in your life. **Live** it!! **Be** who you are! You are a human **being** living a **glorious** life! For there are many things you can **do** to improve your life that are not monetary. Meditate on that and you will find some **amazing** answers.

And now, if there are no more questions, I say to you be **happy** with what you do and who you are. I want you to be happy! I want you to have **joy** in your hearts! I want you to have unending, overflowing Love! I want you to fill your **hearts** with joy! I want you to have a happy, happy, Loving day! I want you to grow and prosper and be happy! Your Creator is with you **always**. He is proud of **all** that you do. He is proud of all the **growth** you have made. He is proud of your Love. He is proud of your friendship. He is proud of **you**, as is the entire Angelic Realm, as are your Spirit Guides, as are your personal Angels. Yes, we are **all** here. We are clapping our hands for you! We are sending our Light and Love to you! And we want the **best** for you as you grow in the Light of God!

And now I say good-bye, and I **want** you to enjoy, enjoy, enjoy! We shall all talk again soon. We can talk in the privacies of your own homes, or we can talk together, or we can talk with more friends around us. It is **your** choice now. Different gates will open up on behalf of you all. I Love you and I say good-bye, but I am not leaving. I will **so** look forward to our next conversation.

Thank you. Thank you.

-38-
Denis' Automatic Writing

7/11/2001
Automatic Writing from Denis:

Dear God, The Creator, Michael, Metatron and all other Angels watching over me,

It has been awhile since I wrote to you. I am sorry for the delay. I write with an open heart and I ask for guidance. I ask that you tell me where I went wrong and how I can get back on track. I ask to know who I am and I ask to know my purpose.
I am grateful for Your Love and for Your Guidance.
Thank you.

Love,
Denis

7/11/2001
Dear Denis,

It is so nice that you are writing once again! We have much to tell you. You are a very special Spirit. You have a clear connection to us and we will help you and guide you whenever you ask.

Before you came to Earth, you chose to learn about Love and Compassion during this lifetime. You are a leader and a Master. You will help many, many people to see Love and to choose Love. You will be a teacher, but first you must be a student, for there are some very important aspects of Love that you must remember. Once you remember them for yourself, you will help others remember them, too.

1- Make a list of all the things that stand in the way, block or prevent Love.
2- List why they prevent or block Love.
3- Then write how to avoid these things.
This exercise will help you to see where the work needs to begin.

Remember that NOTHING negative will ever come from any Angel or Divine Being.
This should be your model. This will help you to see where you went wrong and, also, how you can correct your direction.

Your purpose is to Love. Love everything and everyone. Love every situation and circumstance; realize that God has made them all perfect. You can learn something from each one. Your purpose is to Love every moment of your life. When you do this, JOY is present in your life.

The example you set for others to see is to teach them. You will notice others watching you as you go about your life from now on. They will be inspired by you. They will be touched by your Angelic presence. You are a performer, performing Love for all to see. Just be YOU! You are awesome! You are everything. You are Love. You are irresistible. You are contagious. Others want to be just like you. You are magnetic because of your Love and Light. Don't cover it up; don't hide it. Allow it to shine bright. Smile. Laugh. Praise. Share. Hug. Kiss. Touch. LOVE!

Filter everything through Love. Interpret everything through Love. Reply to everything with Love. Be a beacon of God's Light. Allow others to find you. Allow others to see your Love. You will never run out of Love, no matter how much you give away.

Remember the vision we showed you of who you are? You felt the power and the energy of you. You felt the Love and exuberance of you. And you felt the creativity of you. Don't forget this vision; we will show it to you often. For this is Who You Are!!

Denis' exercise :

Things That Block Love & Why:

1- **Criticism**   Makes you feel "less than"; inferior

2- **Judgement**   Creates a "power-over" situation.

3- **Indifference** Creates a feeling of being "invisible".

4- **Abuse**   Creates a "power-over" situation.

5- **Distrust**   Love cannot exist without trust.

6- **Disrespect**   Creates a very one-sided situation.

7- **Discouragement**   Sucks the life out of any relationship

8- **Anger**   Prevents intimacy.

9- **Abandonment** Shows a desire for no connection.

10- **Inconsiderate Behavior**   Creates a one-sided situation.

11- **Uncaring Behavior**   Shows a desire for no connection.

12- **Un-sharing Behavior**   Shows a desire for no connection.

13- **Devaluing Behavior**   Creates a "power-over" situation.

14- **Negativity**   Destroys hope.

15- **Fear**   Blocks intimacy.

16- **Cruelty**   Creates "power-over" situation.

17- **Blame**   Creates a "power-over" situation.

18-**Accuse**   Creates a "power-over" situation.

19- **Attack**   Creates a "power-over" situation.

20-**Suspicion**   Blocks intimacy.

How To Avoid Things That Block Love:

1- Criticism: Realize that things are not "up to you" to judge. It is not your place to point out the shortcomings of a person or effort. Realize that there is more than one point of view on every subject and that everyone reacts to a situation using their best judgment and ability. Assuming this, don't ever make another feel "less-than" or "inferior". This hurts and prevents Love.

2- Judgement: God does not judge. We should not judge. Everything and everyone is perfect; All is as it should be. None of us is smarter than God. Judging hurts people by creating a "power-over" situation and prevents Love.

3- Indifference: We should never act indifferently toward another person as it makes them feel "invisible" and totally not important. In reality, everyone is equally important and special. Indifference hurts and prevents Love.

4- Abuse: We must never abuse someone, as this is the worst form of injury. It creates a situation of "power-over". It leaves the victim feeling violated, powerless, angry, disrespected, resentful and it destroys trust. This causes great harm and prevents Love.

5- Distrust: When we distrust another we are turning off Love. Love cannot live without trust. Just as we must have faith in God, we must have faith in people. Distrust prevents Love.

6- Disrespect: When we disrespect another person, we are telling and showing them that we think very little of them, their reasoning, their abilities, their knowledge, their morals and their worth as a person. Disrespect hurts and prevents Love. It is a one-sided situation.

7- Discouragement: When we discourage another person we shut down their creativity, their wants, their needs and their desires. This sucks the life out of a person and prevents Love.

8- Anger: When we are angry we build a wall to keep out intimacy and Love.

9- Abandonment: When we abandon something or someone we are stating that we have no more interest for connection. We are shutting down Love.

10- Inconsiderate: When we are inconsiderate we are refusing or failing to honor the needs, feelings or desires of another person. This is very "one-sided" and prevents Love.

11- Uncaring: Uncaring Behavior shows that we have no further desire for connection with that person or situation and blocks Love.

12- Un-sharing: When we are unwilling or unable to share with another we are stating that we do not trust them with our feelings, thoughts, things or ideas. This shows that no further connection is desired and blocks Love.

13- Devaluing: When we devalue or belittle another, we are claiming to have "power-over" them. This hurts and prevents Love.

14- Negativity: This destroys hope and prevents Love.

15- Fear: Fear blocks intimacy and prevents Love.

16- Cruelty: When we are cruel to another we are claiming to have "power- over" them, disrespecting them and intending to purposely cause hurt. This blocks Love.

17-19 Blame/Accuse/Attack: When we do any of these things we are refusing to accept responsibility and choosing to pass it onto another. This creates a "power-over" situation that causes harm and prevents Love.

20- Suspicion: This involves many different things: fear, distrust, anger, judgment, etc. Suspicion blocks Love.

-39-
Love or Fear?
By Charlene Hill

There are just two choices: Love or Fear.

If we Love enough, there is no room for Fear, and if we are full of Fear, there is no room for Love. Anything that makes us feel anything other than Love, is based in Fear. Resentment, indignation, jealousy, envy, judgment, negativity, anger, rage, retaliation, shame, hatred, etc. are all based in Fear.

God is Love and only Love. So is our essence only Love, and that is why anything else doesn't feel good to us.

We need to try to embrace our fellow human brothers and sisters, even if they do or say things that we disagree with. Some of them have lived very difficult lives, full of discrimination, loss, illness, humiliation, poverty and judgment. Some are acting out of true Fear, and haven't learned any other way to be.

When we hear about people doing horrible things, we need to remember that they are acting out of Fear. We need to try to forgive them, not for <u>what</u> they do, but for their not <u>knowing</u> what they are doing. In reality, acting out of Fear is insane. Even as Jesus said while on the cross, "Forgive them for they know not what they do." Some are so full of Fear that they have forgotten the value of human life.

Right now, our world is full of Fear. Anger and Hatred are running rampant, and many innocent people are being killed. Genocide is being done in Darfur and Somalia. Wars are raging all over the planet. We need to pray that all come to their senses and stop the wars. We must remember that we are all the same, that we are all sons and daughters of God, that we all want to live in peace, and that we are all the same race...the HUMAN race. We must remember that every living creature deserves respect.

Especially here, in this blessed land of ours, we must be united. We are all Americans. We all love our country. When our leaders make erroneous decisions that put so many of our young lives in jeopardy and threaten our security throughout the world, we must work together to repair the damage. We can decide to worry and fret that others may take what we have and leave us with none, or we can decide to trust God to provide and learn to share and to Love.

We stand as beacons of God's Light to all of the Earth. Only in America can we have the freedom to follow our dreams and be examples to the world. We have so many huge problems to solve, and we must all work together to solve them.

As for me, I choose Love.

Love and Light to you!

40

Denis' Vision of Himself

7/14/2001
Automatic Writing from Denis:

Dear God, The Creator and Archangels,

I come to you with an open and loving heart. I come to you with gratitude.
I ask that I can see myself as I really am and that I can see where I am and
where I went wrong.

I ask to see my lessons so that I can learn them and understand them; so
that I don't have to continue making errors and so I can get back on my
proper path. I ask that, with Your help, I can remove all barriers and
blockades that I have put up along my path; that have been preventing my
forward motion.

I ask that, with Your help, I can restore my Love for myself and my belief
in myself once again so that I can Love others as I should.
Thank you.

I Love You very much!
Denis

7/14/2001
Dearest Denis,

Hello! It is so nice to hear from you.
You have been noticing all of the beautiful Nature around you.
This is wonderful!

Denis, close your eyes. We will show you...YOU!
Now, close your eyes and picture this:

There is a huge ball of Light the size of the moon. The Light
is shimmering when it is not beaming out. It is almost too
bright to look at, but you want to look anyway.

You sense a vibration coming from within the ball of Light. The vibration is very high and very intense. The vibration is intoxicating and it draws you closer to it.

You have no fear of it because the vibration is communicating Love, Joy, Compassion, Excitement, All Possibilities, Enthusiasm, Understanding, Forgiveness, Creativity and Exuberance.

There is a Kindness and Gentleness so profound that you would gladly hand it your tiniest, newborn baby. Yet, there is such Power and Strength that you know that nothing could defeat it.

You have never felt such Love! It is overwhelming! You cannot breathe...you cannot speak...you cannot laugh...you cannot cry. You are in total awe!

Denis, you have just pictured YOURSELF!

This is Who You ARE!!

Your Loving Angels

41

(Sue's Son, Tim, was badly injured in a car accident)
Chaos, Tradition & Don't be Pushy

August 2, 2001 at 7:55 PM Sue and Charlie
Prayer and speaking of The Language of Light...

Hello, My Darlings! How lovely to see you! I have some information for you.

There is chaos, as we have told you, and it is very, very wise of you to hold the chaos at bay for it is not **your** chaos. It is someone **else's** chaos, and many will try to draw you into it. Sue, I am not at this time referring to Tim's accident. I am referring to things that are coming up in the future for both you and Charlie. There is some **additional** chaos that will come up and affect you both. It will **not** be, necessarily, about you. You will not be in the **center** of it but it will involve you and others will try to **bring** you into it. You may Love, you may guide, you may just **be who you** are which is pure Love and Light; for it is your Love and Light that helps and guides others. It is your very **being** that helps guide and Love and protect. You see people are **comforted** when you are around and it is because of your very **aura**. It is because of the very Light that comes from you. It is because of the Love that shines from you. Remember to **center yourself** around yourself.

As I have said before, the **weather** around you is changing. There are more tornadoes, there are more hurricanes, there are more typhoons, there are more storms...yes there **is** cloudy weather ahead. So this I say to you...if this cloudy weather is crossing your path, these tornadoes are **crossing**... not staying. They will only stay if **you** choose to become the **center** of them. Do not. And therefore I tell you once again to **look** before you cross. **Feel.** Use your discernment and know when to go forward when to go backwards and when to **stay still** and be silent. It is time, truly, to be **using** your full discerning ability. It is time, truly, to step ahead and to go about **doing** what it is you will do. And that is **being** who you are, The Light and Love...who you are. You see **simple** things are what will change. The **simple** things are what will change the people around you and about you. It is the **simplicity**. You see, you make things **far** too difficult. Go back to the simplicity of life and you will see.

And again I see questions all over both of you. I see them all **over** you and yet you say, "Oh, I should **know** the answer to this. Michael will yell at me!" I will **not** yell at you and I **will help you see**. I will help **guide** you. I will help teach you and by **doing** so, you see, you teach others. It is **not** about anger because I never get angry with you! And it is not about **my** thinking you should know something if you don't. You see **my** job now is to help guide and teach. For you have **within** you the Master you are and I am only trying to bring it out in you. I am only trying to **show** you who you are. I am only trying to help you **believe** once again in yourself. I am trying again to show you and to teach you to **be** and that is all...simply to **be**. For when you are being who you are, you are in a state of perfection for **that** is what you are. You are Light and Love and **that** is perfect.

Now, Charlie, I know you have questions about Denis. I am **not** saying cut the heartstrings. It is no different than when I tell you both to cut the **apron** strings from your children and **allow** them to grow and experience and be who they are to be. Now is the time to **cut** the strings and be the fullest of who **you** are. For you cannot be the fullest of who **you** are when you are too **concerned** about another person and **his** very being. Center yourself around **yourself**. Let Denis walk the path he needs to walk and you walk the path **you** need to walk. And I share with you that at **this** moment in time your paths are not together. Do you understand, Charlie?

Charlie: Yes, I understand. Thank you. I do have a question about my daughter. Would it be beneficial or helpful to share with her that she will determine whether she stays healthy?

No. And I tell you why. She **has** that information in front of her. All she has to do is put her hand out and you will hand her the tape. She has not **asked** you for it and you are **not** to give it to her at your insistence. If she **asks** to listen to more tapes you may hand that one to her. But I share again with you, be **careful** of what you say and you be careful of how fast you walk. For that does not mean if she steps in your home that you put the tape on for her listening enjoyment if she does not **ask** for it. You **both** must be very cautious about being pushy. We have shared this with you before.

It was a good question, Charlie. **Never** criticize yourself. You do that frequently and I tell you again...Your Creator Loves you so! And you are **perfect** in His eyes. You were created as such. You listen to **those** tapes, Charlie, **not** the tapes in your head. **You** listen to **those tapes of Love and joy! You** listen to them for **your listening enjoyment** and if another cares to, that is fine. Sue has given away many tapes. She probably does not even **realize** how many she has given. And that is the purpose of the duplicate tapes. She gives them **without** even taking a look or wondering which one she is giving, because it is always perfect. And **that** is what you are to do, too, My Dear. And so, if someone **asks** for a tape, give it. For you will find out that every one of these tapes is in your very **head**. The reason for the tapes is for you and Sue and anyone else to **listen** to. You will be **amazed** at whose hands get on these tapes. That is much of the purpose. You will find that you **will** end up with a full set of tapes between the two of you. And at one time, not yet, you will be **writing a book**, and those tapes that are **not** in your hands...well I guess that they were needed somewhere else. We repeat for a reason, My Dear. And I say "**We**" because The Heavenly Creator is with **me** here always, as He is with **you**. He is guiding every **word** I say to you. And it is very Loving and

278

wonderful! For you see, I learn, you learn, we **all** learn! It is wonderful how the circle of life works and how dimension crosses dimension! It is very glorious!

You have learned, through different experiences, **not** to be pushy. You have **pushed** several, and you have pushed Sue's husband more than you realize. Both of you have, and yet, he Loves you both and he will continue. He knows where to go when he needs to. Be careful of how **far** you push though. For it has been said to you more than once that silence **is** golden. You see, you are now emitting a specific **aura** about you and you have others **curious** for it is not understood.

Sue has everyone at her **work** in total amazement for it is not **understood** how she can be happy, due to her injured son. It is not **understood** how she can still bring joy to another while in her **own** crisis. But she will say it is not **her** crisis. You see that is the difference, for she **knows** this is a learning experience. She **knows** that all is **perfect** in God's world and she is a part of it. You see, when you are a part of God's world, you **know** that all is perfect and as it should be. You **know** that through these experiences you truly **sharpen** your faith and your Love and your trust, and it just becomes bigger and brighter and more glorious. And so it is a **curious** factor **how** that happens so others will be asking, you will see. It is through **many** things that doors will open. Your tapes are one. There are other things coming in the near future that will cross your path and will be quite amazing.

Sue, you are going to the female Doctor for a reason. It is **not** medication. As we have told you before, you can take or not take whatever pills you choose. It does **not** matter. You have special protection as you always have and always will, and medication does **not affect** you. You are changing and you are transforming and it is in the **transformation** that you are feeling that you are not yourself. Well guess **what**, My Dear...**you are not**. You are transforming into your butterfly. And so, let it **be**. If you **think** you feel better if you take a pill,

279

take it, but it will **not affect** who you are and it will **not** affect the changes that are going on about you. For the changes, My Dear, are not **physical** and so there is no **pill** for that.

It **will** come out, Sue…your Spiritualism **will** come out and it **will** be revealed. You will reveal it in what **you** think is a funny way. It will start with a friendship with this woman. She will ask you a specific question and you will look at her and say, "If I answer that question you will have me committed." She will laugh at you and say, "I **doubt** that, highly!" And you will look back at her and say, "Ha-ha! But you are talking in **medical** terms, and I am talking in **Spiritual** terms." And **that** is how it will begin and you will **share** and she will **not** know what to do with you. She will **want** to put you under hypnosis and she will **want** to experiment with your mind. And you may **let** her, for she can be **trusted** and she is a good person and she is bright and she **knows** what she is doing and she is not harmful. **Know** this! She is in your path for a reason.

So, My Little Dears, do you have more questions for me?

Charlie: I was given some sage. What is the proper way to use it?

How do you **want** to use it? You can **cook** with it, you can **burn** it, or you can **eat** it. I must share with you. There are different traditions. In many cultures sage has been used to clear and to cleanse and you can use it that way. It is **you**, yourself, that does it, My Dear. It is **not** the sage. The **sage** does not do it, but it is your **heart** that does it. It is your **Light** that does it. The sage is simply a tradition. It has been a tradition…a Native American tradition. It is not bad, it is not wrong; it is as good as you **want** it to be. Tradition is tradition and if it makes you happy, **do** it. But is that the **only** way to cleanse a house? No! Is that the **only** way to say, "I am not feeling comfortable and I think there might be some dark energy here." All you have to do is say," **Remove yourself…be gone and let Light and Love fill my home.**"

And then take the Light and Love and **protect** it with a Bubble of Light. You see you do not need **anything** but your very **heart** to do **all**. It is your own **heart** and your own **tongue** and your own **intentions.** Do you see?

Charlie: Yes. And that is how I felt with the Reiki and other things we have learned. It is not the exact movements or chants etc but it is the **intention**.

It **is** the **i**ntention. It **is** the **Love**. It **is** the **heart**. It **is** the God within. It **is** the Light and Love. Yes, you can use your hands in a specific motion, and you can say, "se-he-ki," or you can say, "Michael, please help me **find** this!" You see those are the same things! Do you see? You just **ask** for help in **any** way you choose. This is only **tradition** and tradition is fine. There are traditions in many religions and in many cultures. Just because they are different does **not** make one right or wrong.

Charlie: Why do I feel such overwhelming negativity when I am in Utah and there are churches on every corner?

Because **you** have a new **understanding** of Spiritualism versus the structure and the overall being of religion. You have been on the inside. You see your Spirit **knows** Spiritualism. Both of you **know** Spiritualism. You were **born knowing**. You were **born** with Souls that **know**. As human beings you were **taught** that you might **not** have been in the know... as much as you truly **were**. And, therefore, you thought, because you were **taught**...that Spiritualism came from a structure, but it did not. It took you several years to realize it is **not** the structure. It is **not** the name of a religion. It is the Spiritualism **in your heart**, and once you **realized** that you **found** yourself. You could not **find** yourself in a structure because it was not **there**. However, that is not to say there is **no** Spiritualism in religion, for in some religion there **is** Spiritualism. Do you see the difference?

Charlie: Yes, thank you.

Do you have any more questions for me? If you do not have more questions now, you will later. We will talk again soon because it will not be long and you **will** have more questions for more growth. Different things will come along your path and you will have curiosity about where it leads. And so I tell you this now...have **faith**. As things change in your life, as they do because life is **about** change, and as things happen and change, **know** there is a White Light upon you. **Know** that there are Angels surrounding you, **know** that you are protected and Loved above all. And **know** you have much Love shone upon you every second of every day. The Light **shines** upon you now and forever!

And with **this** I will tell you to have a wonderful evening and I will tell you, you are **never** alone. I am **always** with you. You have **many** Loving and comforting you at all times. Both of you have been a bit **short** on the joy in your lives lately. Please **find** that joy again. Hold onto it and Love it. I will say good-bye now, My Dears. I Love you and The Creator is with you always.

Thank you. Thank you.

Denis' Automatic Writing @ The End?

8/4/ 2001
Automatic Writing from Denis

Dear God, The Creator,

Is this the end for Charlene and me? Are we to go our separate ways?
Am I supposed to leave her alone? Is she supposed to leave me alone?
Please tell me where this relationship is at this time. My heart is open and
my mind is open to receive the message that you have for me at this time.
Thank You. I Love you!
Denis

8/4/2001

Dear Denis,
Thank you for bringing your questions to me and I will
try to answer them. Your relationship with Charlene is
now quite different than before. You are now very good
friends with much history behind you but with different
futures ahead of you. You are both, now, on separate
paths. You both have very important things to
accomplish on your path. You have agreed to do these
things, and you must. You cannot do these things while
attached to each other. You must be separate.

You have learned a lot from each other and you have
experienced Love together. You have produced and
raised wonderful children and, now, grandchildren.
You have done your dual duty and now you must do
your own work. Denis, this is the addiction we have
talked about. You are addicted to Charlene. You must
break that habit. You are strong and resourceful and
are now ready to complete your work. You will know
what you must do very soon. Charlene will be okay.
She will be very sad for a while, but she will get over it.

You both have some very good memories to look back on, and a few not so good. That is all a part of learning and living.

You both must realize your freedom. You are both, now, free to create, to grow, to expand, to learn and to think. You, now, both have peace and quiet. Neither of you needs to tolerate being mistreated by the other or disapproved of or criticized. Please morn, cry and feel sadness and loss, then spread your wings and fly! You are free! Free to paint the canvas any color you choose, free to make any music you like and no one to tell you or suggest that you can't. Please don't worry...your Love for each other and your Love for your family will never die. It will always be there but you both must now break the addiction to each other.

I hear every prayer that you say and I feel every pain that you experience. Thank you so much for allowing me to experience human life experiences through you! By the way, I Love your drumming! I Love the way you (I) feel while you are playing the drums. Don't worry about Charlene. I am taking very good care of her. I Love her very much, too. I Love you.

God

-43-
Family Members

August 6, 2001 at 1:55 PM Sue and Charlie
Prayer and speaking of The Language of Light...

Well, good **afternoon** My Dears. How are you today? Busy, busy, busy as always, I see. It is wonderful to **talk** to you once again, and as always, I am here to help you. And, as always, I am here to help widen your path so it may be clear and it may be firm and it may be **easy** for you to walk upon. For my goal is **always** to help you and to help you for the best and highest good of yourself and the best and highest good of **all**. For at times, as we have talked before, **you** do something that might be for the best and highest good of **another** and for that we are grateful. In fact at times you are unable to see clearly that it doesn't necessarily mean that it is for your **own** highest and best good, but for another. And now you come to me, I see you, with questions **everywhere**! I have talked to you both recently, and I told you that you would come with questions again. You will **continuously** be tested with your faith. You will **continuously** be tested with your knowledge and your Love...not by us, but by those you know. And I tell you this... **fear not**, for **fear** is **not** a part of you! We have said it before, we will say it again, and we will say it continuously to you. Yes, you will **continuously** be tested. Put yourself in your bubble of Light, surround yourself with Love and **know** you are Loved above all. So, upon saying that, what can I help you with today?

Sue, do not **worry**. There is **no fear** about Timothy. All has passed and **now** the lessons are **his**. Do be careful not to **take** his lessons away from him. It was fine for you to say that you trust **his** judgment for you put the burden back upon him. Tell him that again and again and then he will be afraid for he knows how **you** feel and he will **not** want to upset you. He will do exactly how **he** feels. Not to worry and not to have fear.

Do not even be upset and do not let your feathers get ruffled by your ex-husband for he is **not** as self-assured as you are. He has less **faith** than you have, and he **thinks** he controls so much when, as you know, he has control of nothing. **Let it go** and smile and **be who you are** for this should **not** affect you. As he once **knew** the buttons to push, he no longer does and it frustrates him. Let it go and **surround** yourself with the Light and Love that you are. Put yourself in the Bubble of Light so **no one** can touch your buttons in any way, shape or form and you will be well **protected** as always.

Charlie, it is time for you to do some reevaluation of what you are hanging onto. You cannot make room for anything **new** if the old is more important so you must get rid of that which is **not** very important or you will have no room for the new and for the growth. It is no different, Spiritually, than it is physically. You must get rid of the old to **make room** for the new. That even includes going through your closet for you see...how can you fit into your brand new clothes of a smaller size if you continue to hang onto the old? It is the same **physically** as it is **emotionally**. Get rid of the **old** and keep the **new**. There will be no **room** for the new if you hang onto the old.

Charlene: I understand.   That goes along with the belief systems and...everything...physical, spiritual, and mental.

Yes. And so, My Dears, what else can I do for you? As your days start out so sunny and lovely and your Sun is shining so brightly and you say, "Oh my goodness! The heat is so **hot** it is almost too much!" and, therefore, we send the rain and you say, "Oh my goodness! The rain is so hard!" You see sometimes you simply will not be happy because you choose to see too **much** Sun or too **much** rain and when you simply have enough you forget to **appreciate**. And so when you have too much sunshine you are unhappy and when you have too much rain you are unhappy. And so I tell you to find the **middle** road of your life so you will **remain** happy and content at all times; or allow too much Sun or too much rain in the middle of your path. Do you see? For if you see the beauty in **all**, you will continuously be happy. Sometimes, instead, you choose to complain and that is your choice. I say **choose** to be happy. It will make your life **so** much easier! I say find the brightness and the joy! I say find the sunshine! I say find the rain and enjoy every aspect of all! For if you can find **every** aspect of all, you will be the true Master you are to be.

And now, Charlene, you say, "How can I be a "friend" when I so **Love** him?" And I say to you to treat him no differently than you would **anyone**, for you Love all. When he is in your path or you are in his path you treat each other with the graciousness and the politeness and the joy that you would **any** member of your family or **any** friend. That is different than crying after every time you talk! For now you must become **friends** to be Lovers for you have **forgotten** friendship. You can be a friend **without** telling another what to do. Remember to keep quiet when quiet is needed. Remember to give no advice unless **asked** and remember to give advice in a proper way. Give it graciously and Lovingly. Be gracious, be joyous, and keep your Spirit **quiet** when it needs to be.

Once you are a parent you remain a parent, but as the parent, you are still the child. And as the child you are still listening and grateful for all that is said to you for you are **always** learning as the child. And even as the child, you are, at times, teaching. And as the parent you are doing **both**. You show respect as respect should be shown. You show Love as Love is to you, for **that** is who you are and what you are and you show it to all. If you are treated disrespectfully, **stick up for yourself** without putting another down. You simply, joyfully say, "**I am so sorry but I do not believe that or I do not** accept that and I respectfully must tell you please, do not treat me that way again", or "Do not talk to me that way again". There is a right way and a wrong way to address it. Practice the right way and it will come easier and easier to you. Learn to Love all, even those that are hard to Love. When you need special help, ask. Ask to see Love through the eyes of The Creator so that you, too, can see Love that is not felt. That, again, is the true mark of the Master.

Now your questions are?

Charlie: I am concerned about my mother's health. She seems very weak. I would like some insight as to how I might help her?

Well, you are right in what you see and what you feel. You have a very wonderful discernment when it comes to the health of others. And that is one gift that you have that you will be practicing more and more...the gift of healing. Your mother doesn't want to be healed... for to be healed she must listen to truth. She cannot hear truth because what is not true is what she is needing to believe, for she has believed it her whole life. She chooses not to change. However, as she asks, you may discuss and you may share that which she asks you. Otherwise remember when to be quiet. How can you help her? By listening, by Loving, You see Love is the best for that is what heals all. Your mother and father are aging and the circle of life will be complete soon, but not yet. There are still more lessons. Your mother is not in as ill health as she would like you to believe right now, but she is very much needing your Love and she is very much needing additional attention. Do you understand? I am not telling you she is in perfect health...

Now My Dears, do you have more questions? You have grandchildren coming up soon for you are both grandparents and much joy will be had here in the near future! Love with all your heart as they wrap themselves around you with the Love they have for you. They so Love you! They so unconditionally Love! Take your lessons from the children.

Is there more that I can help you with today? You will have many questions. They will come up and I am here to help, here to share, here to guide. You see, I want what is best for you. I want you to grow **easily**. I want you to learn your lessons as you can... quickly. I want you to learn them happily. Not **all** lessons are happy lessons but you can learn them with as much joy as you can. See the joy in **all**, Sue, as you did with Tim's accident. You saw the **miracles** that existed through the pain. **You saw miracles**. The miracles are not over, yet.

Is there more that I can help you with, My Dears? As the Sun was shining so brightly, soon the rain will come. See it with **Love** this time. See it with **joy**! See it with fondness. See it as the trees and the grass and the flowers. They have more color and they bloom more beautifully. Sunshine is wonderful for growth and yet too **much** Sun will burn the flowers. And rain is wonderful to help them grow and yet too **much** will drown them. It is no different, My Dears, for **you**. Find the joy in **all**! Find the **middle** of the road and see the beauty that is there for you. Smell the flowers and enjoy. Count your **blessings** not your heartaches. Smile your smiles through your tears. We are **always** here to comfort and Love. We are **always** here to Love. Many Angels are **here** for you. All you have to do is simply **call** and we are there. Protect yourself with the Bubble of Light and you, My Dears, cannot be harmed. Not **ever**!

Now I say to you...I want you to **enjoy** your days. I want you to enjoy **all**! I want you to recognize the teacher that you are and the student that you are. Share, Love, grow, **be**! I am telling you this...all has been given to you for you to look at, for you to analyze and for you to embrace. And now it is your **choice** to learn, to see, to hear, to feel, but it is there. The Love of The Creator is **with** you always. The Angels are **with** you always. I am with you always, too. Any time day or night it does not matter. We are **always** here for you. And so when you **ask** I will tell and when you want to know the secret, **look inside yourself**. There is so much I can **share** and so much you must **learn**. And now, My Darlings, I say good-bye. Have a wonderful day! May Love be **with** you and may Love encompass you. Share your Love. Share your Light. Share your glow. Good-bye, My Dears. I will see you and talk to you very soon. I Love you!

Thank you. Thank you.

Charlene's Channeling...Changes & Choices

August 20, 2001 Charlene Channeling alone...
Prayer and speaking of The Language of Light...

Ah, My Dear! You are **listening** to me. You are **hearing** correctly. Please **don't** question what you hear. I will put into your mind that which you should say and do. It feels like your imagination. **Let** it come. **Let** it be. Don't question. Set aside your mind. As I have told you before, be mindless. All is as it **should** be, as you know.

Many changes are **happening** and will continue to do so. Thank you for listening. Thank you for trying. Thank you for clearing the **clutter** out of your life. You will feel so much **better** when it is gone. You already are feeling Lighter. Can you **feel** it? As I have told you before, soon **you will be channeling for many**. This is **part** of what you are here for. Thank you. You have **asked** to be an instrument. Thank you for agreeing to **be** an instrument for us.

It is I, Michael. I told you I would work with you. Thank you for trusting and believing. Thank you for allowing **me** to learn through you. We all **learn** as we all **teach**, as you know. All is well and good. All is as it **should** be. We so Love you! We are so **grateful** to you for doing this. Hear me. Set aside your mind. Listen to yourself. Feel the Light of God as it **surrounds** you, as it comes into your head and you are **filled** with that Light and it emanates throughout this room, coming from your body and it is coming from God **into** you. Bring it **in**. Feel it. Fill your body with God's Light and Love.

Do you have questions at this time that I can help you with? For as you **know** I am here to help you in **any** way I can. What is it that I can **help** you with this day? I am here to practice with you and I will stay always. I will be here always with you whenever you **want** to practice or channel or simply hear...simply listen. I am **always** with you. God, Your Creator is **always** with you. Your other Angels are **always** with you, too. Your room is fairly brimming **full** of Love and Light and those that are with you. Please don't feel lonely. Please **allow** yourself this time. Learn and grow and **be**. I know you miss the **human** touch and you will have extra help with that until you **allow** it into your life.

Many **changes** are happening.

You have many **choices** to make. We are here. We are always **with** you and we will help you make them. By listening and feeling in your **heart** you will **know** what is the right thing to do. There will be **no** doubt; you will **know** it. If there **is** a cloud of doubt, do nothing. It will be made and manifested to you very **clearly**, what it is you are to do, where you are to go, who it is you are to speak to. We are talking to you always. Thank you for listening. We speak to all of you. Those of you who invite us in and **ask** for our guidance, we are most **grateful** for! Thank you. This is part of the teaching that you are to do...to instruct others to **please ask**. Please **ask** when there is doubt. Please **ask** when there is fear.

You are all so **full** of fear! Let it go. Let it be. There is **nothing** to fear. All **is** happening exactly as it should. There is **no** way that any of you can do it wrong. This world is **so** into right and wrong, up and down! Let it go! It is not true! We Love you. We are **always** with you...you are **never** alone. Never! None of you are **ever** alone! And yet, you feel that you are wondering through this world that you do **not** understand, and you feel that you are wondering through it by **yourself**. Your Creator would **never** do that! Your Creator would **never abandon** you and leave you somewhere you don't understand; somewhere where you **don't understand the rules**! Your Creator would never **do** that! He Loves you so! He has been with you always! He is **part** of you. He is part of me! He is part of **all**! Help others to learn this. Help **others** to know that they are not alone.

As you continue on your day today, Charlie, know that we **are with** you. **Know** that we are helping you, guiding you, Loving you. Thank you for listening. Thank you for getting rid of **some** of the clutter in your life. As you do so, you will **continue** to feel Lighter and easier and brighter and freer and happier. Please continue to **do** so.

I know it all seems overwhelming to you, but as you do a little bit every day, it will become less overwhelming. We are helping you. We are Loving you. **Allow** the new. **Allow** new thoughts. **Allow** new beliefs about who you **are**, what **you** can do, **your** strength, **your** power and **your** Love. Grow and continue to **be who you are**. Oh! You have **such** a future before you! Allow it to **be**! We want it for you **so** much, as does Your Creator, as does your Spirit! **Allow** it, please, My Dear. **Let go of the grief**! Please **let** it go. And we will **help** you fill that space in your heart with Love, with peace, with joy, with happiness, with pure Light and Exaltation of God!

See? Doesn't **that** feel better? It can feel like this **always**, if you **allow** it. Simply **allow** it. Carry this feeling within your heart today as you go about your day. It is a lovely cool day. The Sun is shining...the breeze is blowing. Don't stay in the house all day. Try to get outside a bit and see this beautiful Earth. We Love you. We are **with** you always. Good-bye for now.

Thank you. Thank you.

-45-
Health & Miracles

August 23, 2001 at 4:30 PM.   Sue and Charlie
Prayer for protection and thanksgiving and The Language of Light was spoken.

Well hello, you two. How are **you** today? Just as we have **told** you things are changing fast. They are changing all around you and there is **much** growth and there is **much** learning and there is **much** teaching. You can **see** how you can grow and learn and teach through different things that happen in your life. I share this with you now...I share with you that it is **not over**. I share with you that there is **more** to come. I share with you to **take care** of yourselves physically and mentally. Be as healthy as you can be, for it is in your good **health** that you can learn **through** that which you need to learn through.   And you can teach **through** that which needs to be **taught**. And you can **hear** the things that need to be **listened** to.   And you can pay **attention** to that which **needs** to be paid attention to.   And you can **help** those that need your help, for there will be many and there will be more and you have **much**, yet, in front of you.   But as you are seeing, you can still smile.

You see the **miracles**, you see the **growth** and you see the **greatness** that is a part of your lives. And because **you can see it**, you teach others.   For very often it is through tragedy that **joy** is found and **lessons** are learned and **miracles happen**. As it was said to you today, Sue, "miracles seem to be a part of your life" for you **expect** them and, therefore, they are.   So **expect** what you are wanting and it will be.   Be **realistic** in what you choose to do. Be **realistic** in what you choose to learn, and be **realistic** in what you choose to teach.

Miracles are happening daily.   They are happening and are surrounding you both. Pay attention and dwell on the **positive** and not on the negative.   And believe it or not, you will stay balanced. But you **stay** balanced through your good health by taking **care** of yourselves, eating properly, drinking plenty of water and exercising...oh, was that a bad word? Exercising is **still** a part of your vocabulary...**try** it! It is right up there with **writing down** things that you need to write! It is right there together. Here is an idea...you can actually exercise and meditate at the **same** time! And then you can **write things down**...that which comes into your mind and those things that you want answers to; and the answers will be given. I **tease** you and yet I tell you...you are in good health and will remain so. But you must **do** so by getting the proper amount of sleep and balancing yourselves out. And you are **trying** desperately to do that. Continue. Sleep is very important now...eating properly is, too. Everything will fall **together** for you and your effort has not exactly been your top priority. **Do** make it a priority, now, to **take care** of yourself for you must have good health to balance out that which will be asked of you. It **is** being asked of you now and it will continue to **be** asked of you in the future. Pay attention.

And just as we have told you before, do **not** take on that which does not belong to **you**. Recognize the things that **others** are learning at this time and many of those things are being learned **through** you. You are helping to teach but do not make **yourselves** the center of that teaching for very often it is a reflection **off** of you. Very often, **you are the conduit** that is being **used** to teach and to grow. So you are being **watched** carefully as you endure different things and cope with different problems and heal different wounds. For it is through **your** healing yourself that **others** learn to heal themselves... do you see? You are being watched.

Sue, you are being watched because of your positive attitude, for your smiles and the Love that you still spread in **spite** of the turmoil that you are living through. And again, I tell you, this is not **your** turmoil. Yes you are a mother, and yes you behaved in an appropriate way, and yes you **prioritize** as you should. And now let your **son** learn as **he** needs to learn and let your **other** sons learn from him as **they** need to. And you may guide. And you may be **quiet** when these things are not your lessons to learn. You will simply guide, and as things are **asked**, you are welcome to share but do not involve **yourself** with that that does not belong to **you**. Be good to you! You have been given a **gift** and that is a gift of **time**. Take advantage of that which you can, and you have decided to do so.

Both of you, your children **are** your children and you are a mother and a grandmother always. But remember that which **belongs** to you and that which does not. And remember as a grandmother you may **not** tell the parents what to do, for it is now **their** turn to learn to be a parent as you learned. If your children **ask** you for advice, be cautious in how you give it. And never, ever, ever **belittle** their **parenting**. For if you **do** so it will isolate them **from** you as a parent to a parent. Yes you are **always** going to be a mother. You are **always** going to be a grandmother. Love them, Love them, Love them... for Love conquers **everything** but it does **not** give you the right to tell **them** how to be a parent. Nor do you have a right to **tell** them how to live their lives, as they are all adults.

Remember that you must always learn to Love **yourself** completely before you are **able** to Love another. Do not waste your **energy** at this time, for your energy is quite valuable. It is **important** for you to keep all energy protected. You will be **using** it wisely and you will have things in **front** of you to handle and, therefore, you need to be in your **healthiest** physical/mental state. You **are** in a healthy Spiritual state, and you will **stay** there. Do **stay** there.

When you have doubt or when your faith begins to lapse, remember the White Light. Remember the **meditation** of the Light from Heaven directly from Your Creator into the crown chakra. Let it fill your every **cell** and then protect yourself with a Bubble of Light so that you, yourself, are **overflowing** with the Light from The Creator; the Light of Heaven, the

glow that is Christ-like. The intenseness of your aura will, again, draw **many** to you. **Protect** yourselves with the Bubble of Light. **Accept no negativity**. As you feel it, send it **away** with Light and Love.

Now, do you have a question?

Know you are Loved. **Know** you are protected. **Know** that you are doing God's Work. **Know** that you have much help. **Know** that you are Loved above all. **Know** you are precious. Do not become overwhelmed with **where** you are on this Earth, for **that** is not your Soul-essence. Your Soul is **not** Earth-bound. You are here to do the work you **agreed** to do and you **are doing** it well. You are teaching, you are spreading joy, you are spreading Love and you are helping many. You do not **recognize** or know the amount of people you help through the different things that you both do. Know that you will **never** recognize those you help, just know that you **do** and that must be your purpose, for you do it so well.

If you have no questions for me, I tell you I **Love** you so. I Love you so! Know I am **with** you always to help and guide and Love, just as **you** help and guide and Love others. Know I am with you. Know I am **always** with you. Know The Creator is with you always. Know that He smiles **upon** you as we help each other. Know that He is so **proud** of the work you do. And now, My Dears, Light and Love remain with you always. I will say good-bye and I am not **leaving**, but I say good-bye. We will talk whenever you need it. You are both on a **wide** path in front of you and you are both **doing** all that you have been asked and you are doing it fine! You are doing it **well**! All are **proud** of you and the joys of Heaven will be yours! Just know that you have many **armies** to help and many **armies** that are joyous for **all** you do. Love be with you, and we will talk again soon. Good-bye now, My Darlings.

Thank you. Thank you.

-46-
Allow God To Be The Leader,
There Is NO Death & Be Who You Are

September 10, 2001 at 12:35 P.M. Sue and Charlie
Prayer and speaking The Language of Light...

Good afternoon! It is so good to see you both. How wonderful to get together again! You know, I must **clarify** something for you, first. You both do realize that at **all** times, your questions can and will be answered; that at **all** times we are here to talk to you. There is no special **criteria** for you to get answers to questions you have. You do not **have** to be together, you do not **have** to be in a special room and you do not **have** to say a special prayer. You just have to **ask** and know that the question will be answered. You just have to **ask** and know we are with you. You see, you simply just have to **ask** and know that we will be with you to **guide** you, to **help** you, to **give** you what answers we can give you. Just **know** this.

Now, we understand that when **two** come together it is **greater** energy and the Love flows even **stronger** and the Light is **brighter** and the attraction is **greater**, for all the Angels shuffle to be near you. For when there are **two** or more gathered, the energy is that much **greater** and you draw the energy to you that much **faster**. And we **all** join together in joyous and wondrous Love of one another! But this does not mean that this does **not** happen when you are alone. It can **always** happen and your questions can **always** be answered. But when **two** or more are gathered in His Name, it is that much **grander**!

Now, so **good** to see you! Happy day! The Sun is shining and the sky is blue and it is lovely, and it is always wonderful to share this great time with you! I do see many questions around you but first, let me share this. We have said this before and so we share it again...Stop needing to take the

298

lead. Simply **follow** and all will happen as it should. Not all is **about** you that happens **around** you. You know we have discussed this over and over, and sometimes the more you make it **about** you, it will be more difficult **for** you. Again, we have discussed this. So when things happen that might affect your life, even though it is not about you, **let it be**. And Love all those around you, through it. For it is **you** that are leading others to the path of being the **follower** of God. For you see, when it appears that you are the **leader**, you are the best **follower**. For it is **then** that you are **hearing** the message the best. You are **hearing** with your heart and **others** are lead to follow in the way **you** are leading...when in fact, you are simply the **ultimate follower**. Do you see? It sounds like a trick but, My Darlings, it is not. It is when you are the finest **follower** that you then become the leader.

Now, we have discussed this. The chaos will **not** be ending, My Darlings, so simply be thankful, be Loving, fill your heart with joy and Love and do **not** try to **take over**. If you just simply **let** the Spirit **lead** you, you will get there in the shortest and least painful way. Do you understand what I am saying to you? Simply **allow**. Simply **allow** the Spirit to be your Grand Leader and be thankful and be joyous and be happy! Question, sure. You may **question** all you want and we are here to **answer** your questions. Just remember who the **Leader** is.

And now, things will happen quickly, as I have told you. Here we are already into September and **much** has altered your lives and much will continue. For just as there is birth, just as there is the **beginning** of life, there is the **end** of life and that is the completion of the circle. You will both have a **taste** of this in your life. It is **not** to be fearful! It is **not** to be frightened of. It is simply the way it **is**. It is simply the **truth**. It is simply **life**. Neither one of **you** have a fear of death, in fact I know at times you have both **welcomed** it, but complete your life-stay here. It will be wrong to **alter** it for you still must complete what you have **promised** to do. For it is **you** who have promised and it is **we** who will help you complete it. And we will **help** you and we will **guide** you and we will **Love** you. And all that you think you should have, you will have that and more.

Do not put a **limitation** on what your life **should** be. Do not put a limitation on the joys and the wonders that you think you **should** have, for you will have it all and more! If you let your Creator…give it to **Him** for **He** has a **far grander** picture than you! You are **limited** in **your** imagination and **His** is not. You are **limited** in what **you** think you can do, but **She** is not. You are **limited** in the gifts **you** think you should have, but **The Spirit** is not. So **allow** it to be and know that it **shall** and simply be grateful and be thankful and be Loving.

There is **much** joy and Love around you. Do not **forget** that. Remember what belongs to **you** and what does not. I don't just mean that in a **physical** way, but remember that **anger** is not yours. Remember **envy** is not yours. **Hate** is not yours. Grief…grief **is** a part of life and it is short-lived. **Love** is yours and **it** is **unending** and **it** is the answer to **all**. Some **around** you might be angry, so send them Light and Love to help heal their wounds. Remember **you** are Love, you are **not** anger. You do **not** hold grudges. You are **Love**.

Remember this, both of you. For there are people **around** you…Charlie, there **is envy** around you. You do not hold envy in **you**, but there are others who hold envy **because** of you. You **laugh** at that…it is not funny. There are **some** who see you as a very, very great talent. There are **some** who see you as one who **has it all**… and it is in your **own family**! **Send** them Light and Love. Love them. You do not need to **share** with them anything unless they ask. Love those around you, both of you. For in your own families, there are those who do **not** wish **you** as well as you wish them. Love them through it. Love **everyone** around you. No anger, no envy, no spite, no judgment, no fear…let that all go and **send** it into the Light with Love. As you know, it can attach…**send** it away! Remember your Bubble of Light to **protect** you! Protect **everyone** and send **away** that which does not belong to you and **be who you are**! Remember who **you** are and **be** that! It is **so** important, cspccially as it becomes uncomfortable for you as this year comes to an end. Whether it is family, whether it is business, whether it is play... **protect** yourself and do **not** lower yourself to another's standard.

You **know** who you are... **be** that and **do not let** another drag you down. And if one **tries** to drag you down, make new choices about who you **want** to be around and who you **want** to share your Light with and who you **want** to share your Love with and who you **want** to share your life with. Life is about **choice** so make your choices wisely and never stop **being** the Love you **are**! Do not **allow** another to say you are **less** than that, for you are not. Know it, believe it and **be** it! Be the human **being** that you are today by **being** who you should **be**! Love **yourself** immensely! By Loving yourself, you draw Love **to** you.

And Love those around you and **they** will learn to draw Love to **them**. You see many do not realize that by Loving yourself first, you **emulate** Love. Now, those that are **most difficult**...Love the greatest and Love the most. Send them Light and Love and **do** not pass judgment and **do** not be harsh. It is hard sometimes, when people **don't tell the truth** about you, but **you are better** than that, and **you** can let those things bounce off that Light Bubble that is your protection. It does not hurt you. Words do not hurt **who** you are! You **know** who you are so I say to you...be **it**; the Love.

Now, believe it or not, the **chaos** that is around you both, the **chaos** that will continue on this planet...you have a wide, smooth road ahead of **you**. Your prayers are **heard**. Your Love is **seen**. Your Light **glows**. Your wishes are about to come true. Now, **your** wishes will come true and others will have a **hard** time with the easy road, it appears, **you** have. They do **not** know. They do **not** know your background.

301

They do not know **anything** about you. Do not **worry** about those that pass **judgment** on you. Just remember to **protect** yourself and not let anything that is **not** you, **attach** to you. In many ways your lives will become **easier**. If you do **not** abide by the lessons that have been taught to you, it will be harder....learn the lessons...you **have learned** them well.

Allow God to be the **leader** and it will all be fine. Encourage one another to **stay** on the right path and it will be. For different things will **happen** around both of you and take you in different directions. But you will **never** lose one another and you will **never** lose the encouragement of each other and you will **never** lose me and you will **never** lose The Creator and you will **never** lose the armies of Angels that surround you. You have **always** had and will **continue** to have more help than you realize. The lessons will now change but because of all you have been **taught** and all you have **learned**, it will not be difficult for you. Stay focused. Stay in the Light. Surround yourselves with the Bubble of Light, encompassed in Love, and **know** and **see** in your mind the armies that surround you. You, My Dears, are **untouchable**!

The lessons you will teach will not be as obvious to **you** as they are to others. You are where you **should** be for a reason, so **stay** in that place. Continue to teach. Continue to smile. Continue to teach with your silence, for you teach **many** about silence. And you **will** be asked questions and you answer them in the appropriate way. Listen! Listen carefully. Please start **writing** again...I recognize and I know, as The Creator does, how **busy** your lives are. We recognize and know that you must take careful care of yourselves, carefully. I recognize, as we **all** recognize, that need for you to sleep when tired; rest when needed. Take care of **you**, for you are **important.**

Do not be so **concerned**, Sue, about your job. Let it happen as it will, but keep in a positive way. You are gifted **more** than you are recognizing. Continue **being** gifted. Continue with the **gifts** that are surrounding you. Others would **beg** to have the position **you** have right now. Think carefully about this. You have been released of responsibility and you are being paid...and you are being paid **handsomely**. Continue. When it changes it **will** change abruptly but it will be fine...not to fear...not to worry. Fear and worry are not a **part** of you. It will happen in a very nice way, so let it **go** and just **be who you are**.

Charlie, continue on the road **you** are on. Buyers will come. Sellers will come. People will come to your garage sales. Continue releasing those things that **need** to be released from you. All will happen as it **needs** to. All of the things that you are holding onto...some have negative meaning, some have positive meaning and some have absolutely **no** meaning, so release. Those will come and they will buy, so **let** it happen. Read a book...enjoy yourself...here is an idea, **write** while you have your garage sale. Journal. It will **all** be fine and your phone will ring and your art will begin again and you will see **new** creativity. Remember that many lessons are **learned** from the student. You are in a position as teacher now. Learn from the **students** in front of you and they will learn from you.

Now, what questions do you have for me? What questions can I **help** you with? What questions can I answer before you continue on your lovely day? For it **is** a lovely day! Remember to be grateful and thankful. Remember to look up at the sky and **see** the beauty of the color there. Remember to look at the mountains and **see** the beauty and the strength that is in front of you and let it **be** you. Look at the warmth of the Sun and the chill of the snow on the mountaintops. Love it. Thank it. **Be** it. For you see there is **both** warmth and chill in everything so **notice** the things around you. Identify with it, analyze it and see what it brings you. Above all be **thankful**. Be thankful for **everything** in your path, thankful, thankful, thankful, for you see the **more** thankful you are the **more** gratitude shown, the **more** you are given. Recognize when we say the more you are given, it is not necessarily a concrete **thing** held in your hand but the gifts that are there to be shared. Identify the gifts that you **want** that you don't currently have or know how to use. **Ask** and it will be **given** unto you. **Ask** and it will **be** yours. **Ask** and you will **be** shown. **Ask** and you will **be** taught. **Ask** and it will be **you**!

You always have **such** questions about your children! Do not question. Simply enjoy and Love. Many of the things your children and your grandchildren and your grandchildren to come will go through are **not** lessons to be learned by **you** but lessons **to** be learned by others. Give them the opportunity to teach that which **they** have agreed to teach and do not think that it is **yours** to take over. You must **remember** and use your discernment. It is one thing to help; it is **another** to **enable**.

Know that the children coming onto this Earth now are **great** teachers. **Allow** them to teach. Love them, enjoy them, listen to them and laugh with them. Take your adult mind and put it on the floor **with** them and **be** them and they will Love you. Enjoy the things they Love. Laugh with them. Do **not** be the parent. Do **not** be the adult. Be the **child**. Show them that you **can** be the child. Show them. Do not offer your children information not **asked** for. Love them. If you find the **need** to help them, **ask them** first. Remember they are all adults. They are not children. Allow **them** to make the mistakes that **you** were allowed to make. Allow them to learn the lessons in the way **they** need to. Again, we have discussed this but it **is** important now, please remember it.

All those in your path **are** there for a reason, so smile and be Loving and kind for that is **who** you are. Remember not to pass judgment because someone wears clothes differently than you, wears their hairstyle differently than you, wears make-up differently than you or has a point of **view** that differs from yours. Make no judgment about this.

Now, if I have **missed** something, what can I help you with? I am happy to answer any questions you ask.

Charlie: I would like to ask and request help with my teaching today, that I might touch each one and encourage each one in their creativity.

Ah, your request is not just **heard**, it is **done**! And it shall **be**, which is why we said earlier to pay attention to **each** student and remember to listen carefully, for sometimes it is the student that teaches the teacher. So go with open heart and open Love and listen carefully for you **will** touch each heart and each will learn from you differently, but there **is** something there for **you**, too, to learn. You will have much help, My Dear, for when you walk into the room look around and picture the **army** that is above you and **smile** and **they** will smile back. It will be a successful day and you will **leave** there feeling good.

Now My Dears, it is time for you to get on with your lovely day. So I say to you, **enjoy** your lovely afternoon. Enjoy yourselves. Enjoy those around you. Fill your life with Love. Fill your life with laughter. Remember your laughter, remember your joy and remember we Love you! Now My Darlings, I will say good-bye. And I tell you to have a most **beautiful** day and I am **with** you always, and The Creator is **smiling** upon you and there is much Light and Love **surrounding** you. Hold **that** into your very **aura** and have a marvelous day! Good-bye now.

Thank you. Thank you.

September 11---Nearly 3,000 were killed in the attacks at the World Trade Center in New York City; the Pentagon in Arlington, Virginia; and in rural Pennsylvania.

September 11, 2001
The United States of America Was Attacked
Denis' Automatic Writing About It

9/11/2001

Automatic Writing from Denis:

Dear God The Creator,

I am shocked by the events that happened...the attack on America, but I am not very surprised. Will there be more attacks? More Chaos? How can we turn this very bad event into a very good situation for the Human Race?

I Love the relationship that I have with You and the Angels. I feel like I am learning much and remembering more. I can feel the changes in me. Thank You for Your help!

I am grateful for the opportunity to work on the CD for the Salt Lake City Olympics. Things are really coming together. Will You please tell me if we can expect success from this project? Please guide me to do the right things to ensure success.

What special messages do You have for me? I have seen the eagle.

Thank You so much for Your Love.
Denis

9/11/2001
Dear Denis,

I told you about the chaos ahead several weeks ago. This is only the start. There are people on Earth who enjoy death and destruction. They are happy when others are in pain. Their beliefs are very different than yours and it may be very difficult for you and others to understand them. Send them Love and Light.

Please don't allow yourself to get caught up in this chaos. It is not about you. You are safe. Your family is safe. This is only the beginning. More and more Humans will be leaving as the cleansing takes place. Love will prevail...darkness will not. Your role is to hold the Light. Hold the Love. Amid all of the chaos will be the Light Workers who will be teachers and comforters. That will be you. There will be nothing to fear. This is ALL part of the "Plan". Everyone has already agreed to their role in this plan.

The vibration is raising higher and higher and some cannot handle it. The vibration is Love. The opposite is Hate. When a guitar is in "tune" it is pleasant for all to hear. When it is badly "out-of-tune" it is very difficult to listen to. As the vibration of Love is increased, raised higher, the vibration of Hate is even more noticeably "out-of-tune".

Denis, yes, you are changing. You are listening very well. Your dreams are very active and you are learning day and night. I Love you so much! The world needs your messages...especially right now.

Just ask Me and I will help you write as many songs as you like. Remember...I inspired every hit song there ever was! I LOVE to do this! Just ASK!!

Love,
God

-48-
Be Who You Are and Live In Your Light
Your Country Needs You; The Planet Needs You

October 7, 2001 at Sue's cabin at 9:45 A.M. Sue and Charlie
Prayer and speaking of The Language of Light...

Good morning, My Dears! How lovely to **see** you in a lovely
place. You are **growing** daily, you are **learning** daily, you are
changing daily and it is so **fine** to see the **growth** in you both.
You don't **recognize** it in yourselves or each other. It is fast,
it is furious and it is wonderful! For you are not just growing,
you are listening and wanting to learn.

Pay **attention** to yourselves. Pay **attention** to your bodies,
pay **attention** to what is on your mind and in your heart.
Finally, when you are tired, you are laying down and sleeping.
Finally, when you know you are **not** in the perfect place for
yourselves, you are making **changes**. For you see, you are
listening, finally, to yourselves and to your hearts. You are
listening to what you need to hear. You are **hearing** what
your Soul needs. You are **proceeding** as you should and **all**
are proud of you! You are doing a marvelous, marvelous job.

Please stop being so **hard** on yourselves. Stop wondering if
you are doing things **properly** for you are. I tell you, you are.
Simply, continue **doing** and **being**, for that is all you need to
do. You need to **be who you are**, and simply continue. I
hope that we have always said things in a way that you can
understand. Continue to hear things with your **heart**, not your
mind, for it is your **heart** that knows. And your mind
sometimes **does** have a harder time comprehending, but your
heart and Soul know. As you have been told, **see** with your
heart and **feel** with your heart and **learn** with your heart; for
the heart knows. I know and see **many** questions on you, but
first, let me share some information.

Yes, I have **heard** you say, it has been a tough year. The year is not over. Continue to pray, continue to be who you are, continue to lift up, continue to be above that which is not you. Continue, simply, to **be who you are** and **live in your Light**. Both of you, live in your Light, for your **Light** glows above all. You **both** have had things to face this year, and as I say the year is not over. You have come across and will **continue** to come across, **others** who, also, have had difficulty with challenges that have been put in front of them. It is with **your** guidance and help that **they** will get through it. For it is with your Light and your Love and your **own traumas** that you have gone through, that others look at you with a different Light for they **believe** you. You see, different experiences are put in front of you for different reasons.

Charlie, know that **sometimes** one must be **alone** in order to learn. Listen! For it is with the different traumas that are put in front of you, and by getting **through** them as lovely as you do, with the Light that still glows, with the words that you speak of faith and of Love and of God and of Angels...that **others** can look at you and say, "Wow! She has **not** lost her faith. I can **listen** to her and I will, for if **she** can do it, **I** can do it!"

Sue, you are in a very powerful spot, for you work with so **many** and are very visible. And when others ask you about your son, you say that the **power of prayer** has gotten you **through** it. Do you see the **impact** you have on people? You do not complain. You do not get angry. You give joy and gratitude. And you see, it is **with** that joy and gratitude that others step back and say, "What? How **can** she be grateful? But if **she** can be grateful, **I** can be grateful, too".

Yes, you have **both** had things put on your path that make you **stronger** and make you **grow** and above all, it has **increased** your own faith. And never **once** has it challenged your Love. But I share with you, it is through **lessons** that you **teach**. And so just as you both recognize now, why Sue still has her job, recognize that **all** is done for a purpose. Please **know** it. Simply **know** it. Have the faith and trust that you have and you will look back and you **will** see. You will look back and you will say, "Oh my Heavens, yes! I **see** why things took place the way that they did, now." You see, you are very, very wise, as you have **always** been; wise in the knowledge that comes from the **heart** not the head. Wise in the knowledge that comes from the **third** eye...not the first and second.

And so, yes, I see your struggles. Yes, I see your fear. Please, My Darlings, be not **fearful** for you will be taken care of. Be not fearful! Yes, you must, and you are helping yourselves, but **be** not fearful My Dears. For it is **through** these struggles that **you** will teach and others **see.** And **through** that knowledge that they have of you and what you have gone through, do your words **have** the strength and the ability to be heard...do you see?

Now, let us continue. This year has been a **struggle** for you both and you wisely have tried very hard to concentrate on yourselves; meaning that you have tried to stay **out** of other's chaos. It is not over, My Dears. You both **know** that and you **are** aware of it. Your heart knows it and that heart of yours **tells** you, and you know it. Be cautious. Be careful. Live in your Light. Stay **out** of other's chaos and do **not** be dragged down by another. For it is hard, sometimes, for you are human.

By **protecting** yourselves with a Bubble of Light and **living** in your own Light and **being around** those that are Light-beings, as you both are, you will give each other strength, hope and the grace to get **through** what you need to get through. For it is strength in numbers, My Dears. Stay **away** from the negative and **do dwell** on the positive. Live in **your** Light and the Light of others. Be very, very cautious to **protect** your own Light. Graciously **give** it! Graciously **send** those in the dark your Love and Light, because it will be **given** to you triple and double and multitudes back to you. For God is so

good and you will **continuously** be bathed in His Light! The more you **send** the more you **get**.

Now, you have questions about the world. You have questions about the United States. You have questions about **everything** that is going on; the terrorism, the killings. No, it is **not** over. It is **not** over and will not **be** over for a while. **Why do you think you are here now**? Your Light is **so** needed! Yes many are killing in the name of God. You will be one to teach **who** God **is**. You will be one to **help** those who are so confused.

How **simple** it is! It is simple. Sometimes you **try** to make it far harder than it is, but you know better. It is simply all about **Love**. Those that are coming onto the Earth **now** are true Light-beings, so Love **every** baby you see. You can **see** it in their faces. They are Light-beings...they **all** are. Love your grandchildren to no end! Let them **be who they are** and experience that that **they** want to experience. For you will be great teachers; teaching the children to **stay** the Light and Love that they **are**.

Help your own children **remember** who they are, for guess what? **They** are Light-beings, too, for they are the parents of the Light Children, as **you** are the parents...you are Light-Beings. Not **all** are, but every **baby** now is. Love **every** child that comes in your path, for that child will **recognize** you. They will recognize you and smile and laugh at you. As long as they are **allowed** to be who they are, that is how they will be to you. Some are not **allowed** to be who they are. Many are **taught** right away to cry and to be fearful. So when **you** see children, Love them. Send them Light and Love. The babies that are spread around this planet are **all** Light-beings, and will shine and show.

Just as the United States have **become united**, the nations of the world are uniting, and all have the **same** goal. That goal is **peace**. They do not **want** to fight terror with war; for **war is**

311

terror. But the rulers on your planet are not **women**, they are men. And that is how **men** believe problems are solved. Even in the animal kingdom, as you witnessed yesterday with the elk, the **males** believe that the way to get what they want is with a good **fight**. Humans are no different. The animal kingdom is, to be honest, **more fair** in some ways. Nature does have a reason for **all**... even war.

Light is needed **more now** than ever. The Light **will** overcome the dark. And do you **want** to know why? Because the dark will kill **each other** off. Unfortunately there **will** be casualties along the way but there **is no death**, as you know. What do you think the **pain of a planet** does to the Universe? It is **no** different than you walking into a room with negative people...you **feel** it and it is **hurtful** to you and does **not** feel good. How do you think Earth **feels** among the other planets? You must **overcome** with Light and Love. And you **can** and it **will** happen! **That** is why **you** are here and **that** is your **ultimate** goal. That is your **ultimate** purpose.

It is not about **one** relationship, it is about **many** and you touch many hearts. You don't **even** recognize it as you go, and that is the **beauty** of it. Because if you really recognized it, you would **concentrate** on it and **that** is not what it is about. It is about **being who you are**...just **being**! It is far more **simple** than you are making it. For in your **being** the Light and Love you are, you **spread** Light and Love and joy! Be that! Touch others with that! For we must **heal** this planet. For we must take the negativity and **send** it into the Light and Love. **Send** it into the Light of God. Send **darkness** into the Light...send **Light** into the darkness.

You will feel **much** darkness soon. Please, please, again just as we had **so** challenged you to **protect yourselves** as much as you could with a Bubble of Light and to stay **out** of other's chaos, we implore this of you again. For it is very, very **important** now that you **fill up** your Bubble with the Light and the Love of God and **ask** for help daily, to **do** so. We implore you to **shine** your Light…**show** who you are! And you **do** so even in making another laugh. For **laughter** is contagious and laughter is **joy** and joy is **Love**. You see it **all** comes back to **Love**. The **only** way to **tame** the chaos that is not yours, is with Love and Light. And so, My Dears, **that** is what we share with you today, and **that** is **so** important. And I want you to **picture** Light and Love and I want you to **be** Light and Love as you are. By **being who you are**, you will **glow**! You will glow and you will **shine** above the darkness! And you will **shine** amongst the chaos! And you, alone, **protect** yourself with a Bubble of Light, with the chaos all around you. Have no **fear**…let fear go! **Protect yourself and be who you are**.

Now, what questions do you have that I can answer…if I have not answered them yet?

Charlie: When I channel, it sounds like the still small voice that I have always heard…Am I hearing right?

Yes! You see! Your **hearing** is fine! Listen to that very small voice, but **turn up the volume**! You are keeping it in a small closet…turn the small closet into a very large house! Listen to that small voice…**it is not small at all**!

Charlie: But it feels so easy…

It IS easy!! We have told you and told you and told you and **told** you…you make it so HARD! It is so easy! It is so easy! That little small voice is not at **all** small and it will **nag** you to death until **you let it out**…and I am not kidding! You see, it is so easy, and **that** is the hardest lesson for you. **It is so easy**.

Charlie: It has been with me always…

Yes, that is **exactly** true. And if you choose to hear it just for you…that is ok. Use it for your joy. And if you choose to **share** it…that is better. But have no fear and have no worry

and do **not** believe that anyone in the Angelic Universe is criticizing you My Dear. For we Love you with **everything** there is to Love! When we try to help you, we apologize if you have had **any** negative feelings. **Never in a million years have we come to you with negativity...only with joy and Love.**
Do you have more questions?

Charlie: Could you please tell me the importance of the vision that I had years ago, about the American Flag?

You are here for a purpose! And just as I have told you about that purpose, you are **helping to unite the nation** that you live in. For America truly does **need** you. It is all...it is very simple, My Dear. It is very simple, for you are all touched with **why** you are here. **Do you think you were born in this country by accident**? Never! Do you think there **are** accidents ever? There are not.

Charlie: I just wondered if there were something more I should be doing.

Be who you are. It is **so** simple. **You are here for a reason**. It is **so simple**. You are afraid to believe it **is** this simple, because your life on Earth has **not** been simple. It has **not**. It has been **hard.** And, therefore, it is hard for you to say, "If my life has been **this** hard and **this** complicated, how can you tell me that when I am in the Light of God, it is so simple?" And **that's** why you have trouble, My Dear, because your **life** has **not** been simple. But I am telling you that your **purpose is**, and I want you to **know** it and I want you to **believe** it. I want **you** to believe it, I want **Sue** to believe it and I want **every person** on this planet to believe it.

For you see, you have **made it hard**...not meaning you personally, but **humans** have made their lives **difficult** when it didn't have to be. Now different lessons are learned in different ways and, therefore, situations have been put in front of you to help you learn a lesson and sometimes there is **difficulty** in that lesson...but **being who you are** is very simple. It is **very** simple. And being who God **wants** you to be and living in God's Light is so simple! That is **not** to say and **not** to be misunderstood, with the fact that different lessons that you have **asked** to learn here on this Earth have been difficult...for there is balance. Lessons sometimes are not so simple. The **human** lessons that you have asked to learn, that **help** amplify and understand the Light and Love that is you...sometimes human **lessons** are difficult. Does that make sense? For the **lessons** are **human**, the **being** is not. Do you have other questions, My Dear?

Sue, Sue, Sue, do **not worry** about your husband. He **knows** who you are. He actually is **threatened** by who you are. He will come to you **when he is ready** and do not force **your** opinion on him. Forcing is absolutely **not** going to work and both you and Charlie have learned that. By **forcing**, it at times, has a **negative** effect. By **speaking**, which is different than forcing, and answering questions; **that** is what you need to do. If you say too **much** in answering questions, as we have told you, it will **not** be heard.

You witnessed that, Sue, with your sister. She absolutely, and you saw it...it was almost as though she had a shutdown. Not only did she **not** hear it, she will not repeat it because she cannot **remember** it. However when she is **ready** to hear, her **Soul** will remember **who** to go to. Her **heart** will remember **who** to go to. Her heart **knows**. So all will be done and said in the time that it needs to be done and said. Charlie, you, too, have witnessed this with your own parents. So just be cautious and I specifically say this to you, Sue, for you will so **want** to **share** with him and enlighten him. He will enlighten when **he** is ready. He **knows** where to go. His heart and Soul know you, and **he** even knows you, but he is still in shutdown and he **will** be for a while. He will, also, **feel sorry** for himself for a while. Send him Light and Love.

Is there more that I can help you with, My Dears? I just **so** Love you! The Creator **so** Loves you and He gives you **all**

your needs and **all** you want. He spiritually sees your Light
and He gives you **more** as you want it and need it.

Charlie: It's difficult to keep the joy and knowledge and Love and Grace
and information when you want so to shout it from the hilltops! It's
difficult to just wait until we are approached, especially with those that we
Love. We want to share it and give them this wonderful gift!

Yes, and opportunity **will** arise.   And **as** opportunity
arises…you forget that the Universe is working **with** you, not
against you!   You see, there are two ways of learning and
teaching and one is by running in like a bull and screaming it.
Now, how **many** will listen to you? None. And the other is
by quietly smiling and being who you are and being the
Master that you are and by **knowing** when silence is truly
golden. And you see it is the **Master** in you that knows that.
And yet it is the **child** in you that says, "I want to scream my
joy!" I understand what you are saying, and it is the Master
that, sometimes, must quiet the child **into** the knowing. Now,
just **think** about it.

You can think about this one logically for a moment. Running
into the china shop as a bull…running into the china shop as a
child with hands waving and joy, and you will break all the
crystal…all the delicate crystal. Let the child in you calm and
be the Master in you, and no crystal is broken. And by **being**
the Light that you are, you will bring **more** Light and
brilliance to the crystal around you, therefore attracting **more**!
Do you see the difference?

Therefore, we share with you that you will bring **more**
brilliance to those around you by being the **Master** instead of
the **child**. Both are beautiful in God's eyes, but you will do
more good and spread **more** Light and Love and joy by being
the Master rather than the child. As I say, **both** are glorious in
God's eyes, but you will do **more** by being the Master. Do
you see?

What else can I help you with today? Do you have more questions for me?

Charlie: No, I don't think so. Thank you.

So we will say good-bye now and in doing so...one more thing...remember the Bubble of Light and continuously **add radiance** to it. For your Heavenly Creator will give you **all** you want and need until you are **so** bathed in it you won't want to do **anything** but sit and pray and be thankful and Loving. You **do** have things to do and accomplish and you **will** and you **are**. Remember that **each** person on your path is **there** for a reason. Remember to laugh and remember to keep joy in your life. With that I say good-bye and have a lovely day and you will have a lovely evening. You will laugh, you will have joy and you will have fun! Don't forget to have fun. Fun is **important**, for laughter spreads Love, too. With Love I say to you have a lovely, lovely wonderful day. I Love you and we will talk whenever you choose, for I am **with** you.

Thank you. Thank you.

49

Everything Is Happening As It Should

October 21, 2001 at 5:30 P.M. Charlie and Sue
Prayer and speaking of The Language of Light...

Ah, My Children, how lovely to **see** you! I tell you pay **attention** to that which is around you. For you see as the summer fades into fall and the fall fades into winter, you, too, are changing. For as the seasons change they show you **new** life, **new** growth. For you see change is **good**! Do not **fear** change for nature does not. As summer changes into fall you see the **beauty**. It is a **new** growth, for you see, summer dies out as fall begins. And autumn is **so** lovely and **so** beautiful. There are **new** colors. They have a **different** vibrancy. They are **beautiful** and you acknowledge that. Look at the fall sky, for as you see the sunsets you both have been in **awe** of the beauty you see. You lovingly speak of how the Creator draws a **beautiful** picture on the sky of life, and it is true. Do you think **you**, My Dears, do not imitate nature? You are a **part** of nature. You are a **part** of the overall creation, and yet, My Dears, you **do** imitate nature. And **you**, too, are going through the changes that **you** need to go through.

Both of you have recognized **physical changes** in yourselves. You have recognized the need for sleep. You have recognized the different changes that take place in your own bodies daily, and you find it curious. Ah, it **is** curious, isn't it? For you see...you, too, **are** changing and you are breaking **out** of the cocoon that you have been in. And...My Darling, Beautiful Butterflies, you are **learning** to fly! We have talked to you many times about your crawl and your walk and your run. My Dears how you grow! Your **growth** is immense! I do not know if you **recognize** how fast you are growing...and you wonder why you feel change in your bodies? Oh, My Dears, you have come a very long **way** in a very short **time**! And yes, you **are** changing. You are **recognizing** your own Spiritualism and you are **seeing** and recognizing the need to listen. For in **listening** you learn and grow. And you have done **so** well! And you are now looking back and saying, "Ah! **Now** I **get** it!"

Sue, you have said, "Now I **see** why I must just stay where I'm at...for they seem to know **more** about this than I do." And **that** is why you are still in your job. Charlie, you are where **you** are for a reason. Stop worrying about **why**, and simply **be**. You see...every day is a new delight! See it as such and stop the **worry**. For **all** takes place as it should and it **will**, regardless of your struggling. Instead of struggling...enjoy and **be**! Your job, Dear, is to **be**! **Both** of you...just **be** and Love and enjoy and be happy! Happiness is the **gift** you are given! Take the time to **enjoy** it! Sue, you were talking to your husband just today, worrying about time off. PLEASE stop! Do what **you** need to do. You see...it is **important** that you be happy. It is **important** that you be happy as a couple.

Charlie, listen...if you are **feeling ready** to be a couple again, please **do** so. Listen to your **heart** and **trust yourself**. You have come a **long** way with your trust... now finish it **up** and you will know. Love. Simply **Love** and address everything you do with Love and you **cannot** be wrong ever! You see there **is** no wrong, there is only **growth** and there is **learning** and there is **being**. There **is** no wrong. But when you attempt to do **anything** in your life, and you **do** it with a Loving heart, it can only **be** perfect! Do you see? There **is** no right or wrong. There is **perfection** in all you do. So if you, personally, are **ready** to be a couple again, **do** so. For what you would be **saying** is, " I **trust** my inner voice. I **trust** you, Denis, and I **trust** to go forward." Now you can **still** trust your inner voice if your inner voice says, "I still need some time alone." You see it is all about **trust and you**.

I find it quite **interesting** right at this moment, that **both** of you are worried about where you will **live** tomorrow. And I say, "Who cares? Why do you **worry** so? You are **well** taken care of." Do you **really** think that you will **not** be taken care of? Look outside and look at your birds and look at your fox and look at your bunnies and look at **all** that you see right out your back yard. And through that, you must say," Our Creator takes **care** of all of these and He, too, will take **care** of me." Do not **worry** about where you are tomorrow, for **wherever** you are it is where you **should** be. It **will** be the perfect place...whatever you **choose**. Ah, that **word** again! It is about **choice**. For you see, it **IS** about choice. You are in total control, or you can **allow** the control to be that of your Angels and Guides and let it **go**. Just have trust. But truly, you are **always** in control. You are a **very** free Spirit and no matter **what** choice you make it is right and perfect, do you see?

Both of you are worried about your grandchildren. Please do **not** worry. They are all very special, powerful Spirits; and have **chosen** to come into the families that they are in. They are here to teach the parents that they **chose** to be their parents. Please trust that **we** are taking care of them, as is the Heavenly Creator. And **all** is as it should be. Your job, My Dears, is simply to **Love** them. Love them unconditionally and allow them to **be who they are**. You can **help** by the Bubble of Light and prayer. Send Love and Light to those that you are worried about.

Yes, the year is **not** over. But that does not mean that **you** should not live and Love every day of every week of every month of **every** year! Do not worry...for certain things **need** to happen. They **must** happen. Know and understand there **is** a reason for all and not **always** do you need to be made aware of it. That is where your **trust** and your **faith** come in. For many times it is **not** about you. You are here to spread Light and Love. Many, many things that happen on this Earth are **not** about you.

It is true you are the center of your very **own** little worlds and you **should** be. Keep yourselves in the **center** of your own little worlds and know and believe and understand that what happens **outside** of your little world is **not** about you but

320

needs your Light and Love. Do you see...do you understand? It is important.

Faith and **Trust** and **Love**...those are three **key** elements. Make your life as easy as you can. You see you try to make it **harder** than it should be. Please don't. Make it happy and joyful! Make it Loving and good and wondrous! For **that** is where you belong...in a joyful, wondrous world! And **that** is what **we** want and plan for you. That is what **you** want. You keep allowing your **mind** to rule your heart and your mind **wants** to sort it all out and file it very neatly and then analyze it. Stop. Just say, "Stop, for we **offer** it right up! We offer it right up into the Light for **that** is where it **all** belongs; into the Light." And all will be **perfect** as it should be...and all **will** be just as it should be. And those people that **need** to be on your path, **will** be! You see you cannot **prevent** that from happening and you cannot **analyze** it to death until it does happen...do you see? You simply have to **be**, and that is what I ask of you.

Now, what questions do you have...for I will help any way I can.

Charlie: Is there anything we can say to our children to help them not be frightened and worried?

Let them **come** to you and **ask** the questions that they have. If they do **not** ask, there is very **little** that you can do. For each is on their **own** path and each must learn in their **own** way, do you see? Use your discernment in giving information to those that do **not** ask. As we have told you, if you give too much information, it will **not** be heard or remembered. They will ask questions that will give you reason to answer. You see it is **not** up to you to push them onto the path that **you** think they need to be on. So, simply send them Light and Love. They will get to where **they** need to be. And they will get there on **their** path when **they** need to be there. Let them grow at **their** pace and Love them...just Love them!

Many gifts will be given to both of you. Just continue learning and being and practicing and doing what you know to do... and **all** will happen as it **should**. All will continue to happen as it **must**. And know that **is** what should happen, as it does, do you see? Not to worry about jobs, either of you. Things will **fall** in your lap...you are so funny! Things will **fall** into your lap. They are **there** because you must learn or you must teach. Remember the goal. Instead you are looking for other reasons. If something falls into your lap it is most likely because of the **person**, not the job. Do not think it is to tell you the **job** you should or should not be doing. It is the **person**, the Soul, the very being. It is **that** that you should pay attention to...**not** the job. All will happen as it **should** and words will be spoken and things will be said and you will teach or you will learn. You are the teacher or you are the student...and sometimes you are **both.**

If there are no more questions, I tell you to have a marvelous day! You see, you Light up the day; you Light up the night. You are very Light beings and you are so **very** needed and you are **so** treasured and you are **so** Loved. **Be who you are**. Worry not, for there is **nothing** for you to worry about. You know that whatever happens, happens because it is **supposed** to. Sometimes things happen because you **asked** for them to happen. Many choices were made by you **before** you incarnated and your Soul knows what is best. Your Soul knows what you need to learn and what you need to teach and **you** know it, too.

Now I say good-bye to you and I leave you in the Light of God, and I leave you with Love **surrounding** you. And when I say I leave you, **I never** do. You are very protected but we still ask you to protect **yourselves** continuously. You have armies protecting you from every direction: North, South, East, West, up, down, right, left. I Love you very much. You are Loved by all. Have a wonderful evening. Good-bye.

Thank you. Thank you.

50

Have No Fear but Protect Yourself At All Times

October 26, 2001 at 7:15 P.M. Sue and Charlie
Prayer and speaking of The Language of Light...

Well, good evening, good evening, good evening! It is so **nice** to see you. It has been a lovely, busy day for you both, I see. Well, you know you **can** just call up and chat. You do it with each other and it is **fine** to do it with us. It is good to see you. It is good to talk to you. It is good to be **with** you. Yes your lives have been busy, and everyone around you has been busy. Yes, **everything** is changing. It is changing very quickly. I have told you very frequently that there would be change and chaos. It is here and it is now. You are feeling it and you are doing well with it. You are doing very well keeping yourselves **centered**. You are **hearing** well. You are **listening** well. You are **Loving** well. Your hearts are hearing well and you **are** doing just fine! Stop second-guessing yourselves for you **are** doing just fine.

Charlie, I am especially proud of you, for **you** are moving over the line. You have moved **beyond** the limitations that were holding you back. You are getting rid of that which you no longer need and you can **see** how it helps Lighten your load. You **don't** need to carry that whole load...Lighten it. And the **more** you Lighten it, the better you will **feel** and the better you will **be** and the better you **do**.

There are still **many** things ahead of you. There are still many things and much chaos. It is just the beginning. You have prepared yourselves well, for you **are** emotionally preparing yourselves and **have** prepared yourselves. As shocking as September eleventh was for both of your hearts, it wasn't. It was almost **expected** and it was known. You see, all is happening as it **should** and as it has been discussed and **agreed** upon. **Remember** that in the upcoming days. **Nothing** is happening that should **not** happen. I will give you a hint.

Do not think you are **alone** on this planet. Do not think **you** are the only ones that are shedding the Light and sharing the Love. It is **not** just the two of you and you do **know** that. There are **other** entities that are Light entities. They will be there to help and guide and you will **feel** the shift as it happens. Now, this is only to help prepare you for when the **time** is right, it will be disclosed to you and you will know.

Do not have fear **ever**. There **is** nothing to fear, for not only is your **head** in the right place it is because your **heart** is where it should be. Do you see? They need to be together, and they are. With your **heart** being in the right place, you see, it is then fed **through** your mind, rather than the other way around. So you **first** have your **heart** feeling, you feed that energy and that knowing through the mind which can then **understand** what is happening...do you see? So, what I am saying is just have **no** fear, for there is no need. Not only do you have guidance from above, but you actually have **help** on Earth, too.

Now, can I help you with your questions? I know there is more you are needing. What are you needing to know? You both know I will not be a fortune teller; I **cannot**...you do not **want** me to and it would not help you. For you see our goal, **all** of us, is to guide and to help. But by being a fortune teller...that is not going to help you in any way. And since we all Love and want the **best** for you, we will disclose what **is** best, do you see? It is not because we are trying to be mean... it is because **we** want the best for you and some things need to be **learned** on your path. It is there to be **learned** by you, not **told** by me. And **that** is what you need to remember. Sometimes you get **fussy** about that, but it **truly** happens the way that it must. Just remember to keep the joy alive. Keep the laughter flowing, for it is the **laughter** that will help **heal** everything; the laughter and the Love. Love heals all, but laughter is such a wondrous gift! Keep it moving, keep it flowing, keep it going! And you know, it is contagious! Laughter is as contagious as a Loving smile! So feel free to

324

laugh out loud! And keep the joy in your life and your heart and simply continue to move forward.

Charlie, it is **important**, now, for you to **erase all of the tapes** from your childhood that **told you that you were not enough**. You must learn to be **good** to you. **You** are a child of God, My Dear. And as it has been said to you before, simply **be**. By **being**, you will be at the right place, you will say the right things and you will do what is right. Do not worry about if you say too much, do too much, or if you are in the wrong place or if you are living in the wrong place. You see…there **is** no wrong. I **promise** you, I promise you. Do **not** worry about the trivial. Do not **worry** at all…simply **be**. Charlie, things **will** happen for you so you do not **have** to worry. Just continue working through what you are working through. Just **open** yourself up and say, "**I am ready to receive. I now know how to give to myself, and so I am ready to receive. I want to have what is truly mine. I want to have it all and I am ready to receive. I have learned to receive gifts from my friends. I have learned to give gifts to myself. I am ready to receive. I am ready to be who I am. I am wanting to be who I am; that successful person who is in charge of her own power. I can be what I truly want to be and I will be that; Loving, good and kind. And by being the Loving, good and kind person, I will help those along the way that need my help. And I will do so in every way possible that I am capable of doing. I now know the more I give, the more I get; not physical things but of myself. I will do all I can and then I am ready to receive. I am ready to open myself up to the Universe to be given all that I want and need and more. And I can and will be in charge of my own personal power. And my own personal power is surrounded by Love and Light! And knowing that, I can be who I am.**" Did you get all of that, Charlie?

Charlie: Yes, thank you.

Sue, stop **worrying** about the trivial…a house here, a house there…get **off** it. It is simply **not** important. All **will** happen as it should. And when a buyer is **right** the buyer will be here. All **will** happen as it should. Remember, **you** might not have lessons to learn but **your husband** might. And you are walking a path **next** to one another when it comes to selling things you own together. Just remember **not** to worry and **truly** not to worry. For **all** will happen as it should. But he **does** have some learning ahead of him; so prepare yourself for **his** learning and remember not to say **anything** to him unless asked…that will be **imperative**. That will be **imperative**! Keep your mouth **shut**! Both of you have learned that it is best **not** to give advice unless **asked**. Once the right Light goes on around you, you will **know** when it is time to open up. Sue, you did so with a client, yesterday. You know when there are **certain** words said and there is a **certain** feel in the air, that it **is** time to open up and disclose things that you don't disclose to a gentle acquaintance that you don't know…unless you **are** asked. So, I just tell you both to **be aware**. Be aware and alert. Pay **attention** to what is around you. Continuously, continuously **protect yourselves**!

I want you **both** to realize that you have **plenty** of protection around you. Your poor planet, is in **desperate** need of Light. It must be Lightened up and so **additional** help has been granted and has joined you. And the entire Universe is aware of the need. So **please** do not think you are in this by yourselves…you are not! You are **not** in this by yourselves! And yes, there **are** dark entities on your Earth, too. But I promise you; it is the **Light**…the **Light overcomes all**!

Think about it. **Think** about yourselves. You are Light entities, but **put** yourselves in your human place. When you are in your human mind and you are in a dark room, are you not **drawn** to the light you find? Of course…if there is a light in the hallway, if there is a light coming from anywhere, **that** is where you are drawn. Trust me. The darkness is **also** drawn to the Light; sometimes out of curiosity, sometimes to overpower, but there **is** no overpowering! They just don't understand, but there **is** no overpowering; it **cannot** and **will not** happen.

You have been told by many, **protect** yourselves at all times. Protect constantly! Do not only put the Bubble of Light, the Bubble of Protection, around **you**, but put it around **all**! Put it around yourself in your car. Put it around those you Love. Put it around your family. Put it around **everyone**! Try your very hardest to keep **constant** protection. It **is** important now. It is **imperative**! We are **always** here for protection, too. It is **not** as though you are left on your own, for you are **never** left on your own! But you both still have **much** ahead of you and so I just challenge you, please, to remember to **do** so, daily. And if you **think** about it once an hour, do it **again**…just be continuous.

For you see, you are very, very **bright** Light entities and therefore, you are **attractive** to those that are **not** of your Light. Just keep **constant protection** around you and **recognize** that which you should not be around. Recognize those negative energies, that **are** flowing from certain people, that you do not **want** as a part of you or your aura. You do **not** want **that** around you. Continuously **send** it Light and Love. Know the importance of that. You see, by **sending** a dark or negative entity Light and Love, you **throw off** their entire balance. You **throw off** their entire ability to try to **confuse** you with their negativity. You see you are, literally, **encompassing** the darkness with Light. And then by putting a bubble around it, it is **sealing in** the negativity to **them**, not to anyone else! Then **send it away** with Light and Love. You will confuse it, totally, and it will work.
What questions do you have today?

Charlie: I believe that you have answered them. Thank you so much.

Oh, always a pleasure! But do not be **afraid**, and I say it again, do not **ever** be afraid to think you **cannot** have a

327

channeling or meditation because you do **not** have questions. You can just say "Hello", you know, and it **is** okay! Sometimes you may find information that you didn't expect.

Now, I will share some additional things with you. You are very intent, at this time, on **recording** everything and you are doing so at our instruction or advice. But I tell you, the **majority** of information that you have learned is on your tapes, and it is all **basic** and it is all **there**. There is **very little** that you will hear now, that does not address the personal. So, therefore, it is your **choice** to record or not to record. All of the **basic information** that we have given you, we have given you in different forms and in different analogies but it is **all** there.

You recognize that as you listen to a tape once or twice or even three times, you **hear additional information**. That **will** be continuous. Listen to your tapes. The current tapes you are doing address more the **individual** and personal aspects of your lives. It is your **choice** to record or **not** to record. It is your choice to listen and feel whether or not there is information there that **can** be shared with others or that would be beneficial for others to hear. Very often, it may not. It simply may be comforting to **you**…it may not be instrumental in helping another grow. Do you understand?

Charlie: Yes.

It is very much **your** choice. And there is **no** need to **wait** for a recorder. You are so funny! But you can talk to me **always**…with a pen, with channeling, in a dream…I am **always** here, I am **always** listening and I **always** Love you. The Creator is very proud of you **and** me! I learned **much** through you, and I am **continuing** to learn through you. Thank you for sharing and guiding me and helping me learn patience. I thank you **so** much! I am **so** grateful!

Now, I share with you, there are **many** Angels around you, surrounding you. You, literally, have a **house** full. If you could see your house from another planet or from the sky itself, in the eyes of an Angel, you would see that your house is **aglow**. You would see the bright **aura** of the lovely Light that is coming from the block you are on. It is shining and it is lovely!

I, gently, put a **protection** around **you**, your **home** and your **cars**. Enjoy your evening. Know we **Love** you. Know we are here. **Know** you will be guided. **Know** you are Loved. **Know** you are protected. And yet, we **continuously** encourage you to do a **personal** protection for yourselves and those you Love. I **know** I am being redundant, but **that** is how **important** it is. With much Love and Light I say good-bye to you tonight and I tell you to have sweet, Loving dreams. Love to you. Goodnight now.

Thank you. Thank you.

-51-
Protect Yourself & Spark Hearts

November 1, 2001 at 12:15 P.M. Charlie and Sue
Prayer for protection and gratitude and The Language of Light was
spoken...

Good afternoon, My Darlings. It is I; it is Michael. And I share with you this...there are **many** Archangels. All of the Archangels are here with me right now. We come here especially to again **help** you and tell you it is **imperative** that you protect yourself; you **physically** and **emotionally** protect yourself! You always have **us** protecting you, but **you** must be **aware**, as you have been told. Please be **aware** of all that is happening **around** you; the **people** that are in your presence, **everything** that is happening **around** you. One reason we have asked you **not** to have your cocktails, and you **so** enjoy them, is it does **let down** your guard. You need to **pay attention** now, please. We are **imploring** you to pay attention! We **tell** you this with Love. We **tell** you this trying to be helpful. We **tell** you this trying to guide. We **Love** you so! Some things we can help you with, and other things we **tell** you, **you** must do on your **own**. And so please, please **pay attention**!

This is not meant to frighten you in **any** way, for **you** do not live in fear. You live in Love, and we want you to **stay** in the Love surrounding you, in the atmosphere that you so enjoy, in the atmosphere that brings you pleasure. You see, we are not **asking** you to stop those things, simply **pay attention**. It is **not over**, so please keep your wits about you. Have fun, live in joy and live in Love. That is what you **are** to do. That is who you **are**...you are Light and Love. And you cannot **stop** being that and you cannot **stop** doing things that provide you with the happiness you have...we just simply ask you to please **be cautious**, please. We will **never** leave you and we are here at **all** times surrounding you. You have **armies** surrounding you. You have armies **protecting** you. But some things you must pay attention to and simply be **aware**, that is all. Pay attention to the negativity. Pay attention to those people that you **do not like** and follow your discerning attitude; **follow** your discernment. **Follow** your gut-level feeling! Listen to yourselves for by **doing** so, you are listening to **us**. You are **listening** to what we are saying and whispering in your ear! Protect the interior of your cars as you enter, and the exterior, also. Protect the interior and exterior of your homes and your entire entity. **There is no over-protection**. You **cannot** do too much. And **by** doing this, it is simply helping you and you are **clearer** in hearing what we say to you. For you **remove** any and all negativity that might be between us; or any fog, as you might say. For you simply **clear** the path by doing so.

Now My Dears, I **never** try to frighten you. That is **never** my goal. I Love seeing you in total and complete happiness and joy at all times. Do **not** live in fear. There is fear **all over** your world right now, and it will not stop; it will increase. So the **increase** in fear brings the **increase** in the darkness and the negativity. And so you see, your **Light** is needed more and more. **Keep** yourself in a Light space. **Keep** yourselves in the Light that you are! When you wake up in the morning, thank the Heavenly Creator for **all** He does for you and He will give you **additional** Light. Again, do your meditation...as you feel Heavenly Creator's Light directly through your **crown** chakra and **each** chakra and through your very being; for it **enlightens** your very aura.

Again, **protect** yourself with the Light that is **in** you. Protect **yourself** against the negativity. As I share with you, My Dears, the negativities **will** get worse and worse! Not to **frighten** you; simply to help you **keep** your Light shining as bright as it should and does. For you see...we **need your Light** to shine and shine and shine! So we are **not** telling you to **stay out** of the activities that you need to be in. You **need** to be there for you **need** to be the Light that shines. For you **need** to be **in** the space that you need to be **in**...not in closed door... not in the **house** by yourself in **fear**. No, no, **that** is not you! For it is **your Light** that needs to be shared! It is **your Light** that will bring the Light out in others; it will **spark the heart**.

So **you** will **spark the heart** of those that forgot what Light is; that are **shivering** in fear and that are **trying to hide** in the darkness. But **you** will bring the Light **into their darkness** until they turn their **own** Light on, and **that** is what your job is. You will be **turning on the Light** in the hearts of others who choose to **hide** in the darkness, in fear. You will bring them out of the darkness by turning their **own** Light on for them...not that you **physically** turn their Light on...you will show **them** how to turn **their own** Light on. And **that** is what you will be doing. And, therefore, how could you **do** that if you are behind closed door? You cannot! So we encourage you to protect yourselves in **every** way you know, and to **get out** amongst the people! And **get out** in the groups that you know and amongst people you don't know. You will be **called** out, more and more, into **groups**. You will be **called** out to be in groups. You will be **speaking** in groups. You will be **teaching** in groups. You will be **sharing** in groups.

And they will **not all** be the Light-filled people. There **will** be negativity. There **will** be darkness. And that is **why** we share with you how **important** it is to **protect yourselves**. For you see... you will be helping **many** and that is how it will **be** and that is what you shall **do**. And it will **all fall into place** upon your very path. And it is good; and it **will be** for it is **on** your path now. And so we tell you to **protect** yourselves at all times. For you could be **overtaken** by darkness because you are not **expecting** it. You are not **allowing** it, but you are **not expecting** it. And that is why we share with you how **very** important it is to constantly, constantly be protected.

Drink as much **water** as you can for it is a **cleansing**...it is a **clearing** for you. It is best to have the **cleanest** water you can, and drink a lot, please. For not only will it keep your body cleansed, it will **help** keep you alert. It will **help** keep you constantly hearing, constantly listening, constantly on the alert...not **just** for negativity, not to misunderstand, but also for your **Light** beings, also for us. For we are **there** in many different ways, shapes and forms. And when you **recognize** us...chuckle! And **we** will chuckle, too. For we **so** Love it when you recognize us! It is **so** fun to watch you! It is **so** fun when you remember something...and **recognize** it was us! Yes, it is delightful! Please remember we are **not** trying to spread fear in your life for that is **not** what we do and that is **not** what we choose and that is **not** what we want you to think. What we **want** to do is protect and Love and guide. So please understand the **intent**. Love is **surrounding** you. Protection is all **around** you. Many Angels, armies of Angels, **protect** you at all times. Now, are there questions?

Charlie: Are we protected by the **intention**, or is there something more we need to be doing?

Absolutely the **intention**! It is through the intention and the **visualization**...visualization is **extremely** important, so visualize! **Visualize** the Light coming through your crown chakra. **Visualize** your Bubble of Protection around yourselves; around the **interior** of your home, your car, and then around the **exterior** of your home and your car. In your visualization, visualize **protection** around your Earth. Protect your Earth. Visualize the **Light** that we are trying so hard to give you. We are there to help. And when you get in despair, reach your hand **up** for we will help you up. **Ask.** Your Creator is **there** for you. He **Loves** you so! He has **sent** us to help you. He wants you to **know** all you can **ask** for, you can **have.** As much as you can **imagine**, you can **have** and you can **do.** So imagine the **best**, for that is what you can **have** and that is what you can **do. Imagine** how **creative** you can be in spreading Light around your Earth! **Think** about that. You have the Internet. You can do **so** much good. You know so **many** people. There are **many** things you can do and share to spread the Light; to spark the heart to begin the **Light beam** that **shall** and **will** be felt around your world. Not just your personal world, I am talking about your **planet**, your **Earth**, your **world**. It is so, so **important**! **Heal** your Mother Earth. She is **hurting**. And all through the Universe **help** is being sent by **all** the Light beings.

Yes, you can **protect** your children, but I must share with you they all have their **own** wills. They can do what **they** choose. But by protecting them with a Bubble of Light, what you are **really** doing is asking **extra** Angels to whisper in their ears. You are **asking** them to be cautious. If their will is that that **chooses** to be shut down, then it is very **difficult** for us to do work with them. But always we are **there** Loving them and protecting them. It is just hard for them to **hear** us when walls are built up; and walls are **not** built by you, they are built by them. Pray for them continuously. Just as you have had a difficulty in learning to Love your very **own** being and Loving **yourself** completely, you taught others to Love **themselves so well** that **they** have a difficulty Loving others as much as they Love themselves. And **you** have trouble Loving **yourself** as much as you Love others. Fill **yourself** up with Love. Love **yourself**! It is no different than being **zapped** of your energy. You see you get zapped of Love. You have Love being **taken** from you because you have so willingly **given** it and you constantly **give** it to all. You constantly **give** it to your children and your grandchildren and your partners.

Enjoy being **where** you are. Enjoy **being** who you are. Enjoy **knowing** that you have Loving protection **continuously** and enjoy **knowing** that all are here. Michael is **always** here, as am I, as are **all** the Archangels. When you call us we are **here** for we are **always** here... but we "tune in", shall we say, when **asked**. And we **thank** you for inviting us and we **thank** you for meeting us. You see not all are **aware** that they **have** us available at their beck and call. We **are**!

And the Heavenly Lord looks down upon you and He smiles and He Loves you! As Light and Love are gifted to you at all times continuously for you see, you give it away. But we say to you do **keep** enough for yourself! If you feel that you are depleted, simply **ask**... for you see, you can have all you ask for. It is at your beck and call. It is there. It is at your feet, it is at your crown, it is **surrounding** you! Simply **ask** and it **shall** be given. And now I must say it is time for us to let you go back to what you need to do. If there is anything else we can help you with, simply ask. Do you have any more questions before we say good day to you?

Charlie: No, thank you very much.

The **best** part is **knowing** that you can ask questions **all** the time...all day long...all night long. It doesn't matter what **time** of day it is. It doesn't matter **how** you ask; whether you physically look up and say, "Excuse me, I need some help here," and we will help. Or if you choose to write or if you choose to sing or if you choose to think or dream, we are here. **Know** we are here. Know again, that we **protect** you for we Love you so! The Heavenly Creator has given you all you want and need. And with this I say, have a lovely afternoon and know you are **covered** in protection and Love and Grace. Good-bye now.

Thank you. Thank you.

52

Denis' Automatic Writing About Success

11/23/2001

Dear God the Creator,
Good Morning!

Please help me to understand the answers to the following questions:
1- What are the ingredients of success for a man?
2- What does it mean to be "Successful"?
3- How do You measure success in a man?
Thank you for your help and Divine Guidance on this topic.

Love,
Denis

11/23/2001

Dearest Denis,

This is a very profound topic and there is much confusion on Earth about the meaning of success.

First-   Most people equate success with job-related topics and with money. These are accomplishments and nothing more.   Let's go deeper than career matters. Let's look at "Purpose" and "Intent".

When you made the decision to come to Earth School, you identified the subjects that you wanted to learn about; some very broad and some very specific.

You chose to accept a human body and you agreed to temporarily forget your history and your identity to take on a new one (name, etc.). Your challenge was to work your way back...that is to remember your purpose to and

to remember who you are and your connection to Me. The substance of all connection is Love and the conduit of all connection is Compassion. Some of you realize these things faster than others. Success is measured by the progress toward this remembering and realization and by the utilization of Love and Compassion.
Some examples of successful progress are:

1- Remembering who you are.
2- Remembering your purpose on Earth.
3- Acting with harmony in both of the above.
4- Realizing that Love is the key to all success.
5- Realizing that Compassion is the opportunity to share this Love between yourself and others and to provide the caring and helping that exemplifies this Love.
6- Being observant to Life's Lessons and absorbing the knowledge that comes from this observation.
7- Allowing yourself to live in the moment and feeling <u>everything</u>*... savoring is a better term. I want you to savor everything!*
8- By doing everything you do (work, play,etc.) with Love, you are able to accomplish much more in your lifetime.
9- By encouraging others and helping others and enriching others.
10- By allowing others to be "Who they are" and not judging them on their path.
11- By not criticizing others. Allow them to learn their lessons.
12- By seeking Joy everywhere.
13- By appreciating Nature.
14- By accepting My Love for you and realizing that we are ONE. That is to say by accepting your Love for you and by realizing that I Love no one more than another

and no one less and by realizing that you are all connected to Me and to each other.

As you see, success is not just a "job or career thing". It is a "personal journey along your path thing". Enjoy the trip!

I Love you!
God

53

A Grateful Recap...No Need To Record Anymore...

December 3, 2001 at 5:10 P.M. Sue and Charlie
Prayer and speaking of The Language of Light...

Well good afternoon! How are you doing today? Yes it **is** a happy, good day! Welcome each day with just that. Wake up in the morning and **welcome** it. Be joyful and be happy in your heart. I see with both of you, that you are having a little bit of **dismal** feeling. You are not acting your happy selves. I share this with you...please be happy and joyful, for that is what your life is to be...happy and joyful! Yet what I **see** in both of you is that **you** are seeing the things that are in the future path of both of you.

You are **seeing** things that are in the future of your families, of your state and country and of the world itself. Well, My Dears, have **no fear** for fear has **no** place in your Loving, good hearts. What you are feeling is the completion of a year and with that completion, you **worry** about that which has not yet taken place. Well, you are right...there **are** more things to come before the year is ended. And you are right...they **will** be difficult for you to see the joy and happiness in them. But I tell you this...**all** that **must** happen is happening for the good and best and highest good of **all**. **Know** this! And if you **know** this and **believe** this in your heart, you will be joyful. For you see, if you **know** all is happening for the highest and best good of **all**, it is **easy** to be joyful!

So you see by what I am saying to you, it is **not** time to let down your guard. It is time to **stay protected**, as you both are learning **well** to protect yourselves. Continue. It is not time to **stop** that and it will **not** be time for a long time to come. It should be a part of your very morning prayers to complete your protection and your Bubble of Light. For you see, it is simply a good habit. It does **not** mean there is **fear** in front of you. It simply means that you are totally surrounded by Love and Light. It simply means that you are totally protected and this is good. You need to **continue** to do so. And you need to continue to pray and to ask for guidance; but in doing so, you must **allow** yourself to be **led**! For you see, remember that old saying, "we can lead a horse to water"… well My Dears, start **drinking**! We have led you and now it is **time** to drink.

You keep asking for more, and yet we say to you it has **all been given** and it is time to **apply**. You need to **apply** all you have learned and you are doing well with this. You are applying things well. It is wise to **re-listen** to tapes. For in doing so, you **remember**. And in doing so, you **help** each other and you **continue** to grow. For you see, **some** of the knowledge you were given, you were not **yet** prepared to understand and you were not **yet** prepared to comprehend; and now you are.

And **now** when you listen to it you say, "I always hear something **new** when I hear a tape." Well, My Dears, you have **heard** it before…you were just unable to comprehend it, which is what we have told you about **other** people who will ask you questions. If you give too much information it is not a problem. They simply will **not** remember for they cannot **comprehend**. It is no different than you, My Dears. For you see, you are only **capable** of ingesting so much and then it is **too** much. For it is like feeding a baby. When you feed a baby five jars of baby food, it is too **much** and they can take in no more. They need to digest the information, or the food given… and in **your** case information given… before you can be given more. Do you see?

We have told you both that **many** will be leaving this planet. They are, and it is not over and it may **not** be over for a very long time. And there are many things that will come in **front** of you; directly on your paths. They will be minor mountains to climb but you **can** climb them for you have much help. Don't worry. Simply **ask** for the help that you have in front of you. Keep your **faith** in tact and do **not** have fear. Fear is

340

not a part of you. Do **not allow** others to put fear in front of you and do **not listen** to those that are fear-based. **You** are not fear-based. **You** are **Love-based**.

Do not **worry** about what others think. Who **cares** what others think? You have **never** cared before…or at least not to the extreme that you are all of a sudden worried about. It is **not** important. **Be who you are**. And that is what we have **told** you over and over. **Be** the Love-based person that you both **are**! Remember you are **surrounded** by Light and Love and you always will be. Remember you are **protected** by thousands of Angels all around you and you **always** will be. There is **no room** for fear in your life! Do not **listen** to others if that causes fear. Do not allow your **head** to take over what your heart **knows**. I am not telling you that you do not face loss in front of you... you do. It is not **your** loss; it is their **gain**. Do you see? It is not a **loss** at all!

You must change your perception for **you** can be an amazing Light to those that **do not** understand the Light and Love from above and that there **is no death** at all. It is simply a change of place. **There is no death**. It is just re-establishing a Soul in another dimension. **There is no death!** It is simply a **release** of all pain that was felt, to a **pain-free,** Light environment that is **beautiful** and **happy** and **good**! And so why would you wish another **not** to have that? I don't believe **you** do. I believe **you** wish that for **all**! I believe **you** wish that for **everyone** that you know! I know that you wish that for yourself, someday. You know it is not your turn, yet. For you see you are **so needed**, as we have told you.

You **believe** you are such a **small spark** on this big planet, but I tell you, you are **not**! You are very, very bright! You bring **so** much Light and you are needed. And you **are** where you are needed and you will **always** be where you **are** needed, for that is where your path will take you. Do not **worry** so about tomorrow…as I see that again and again on both of you. The **birds** do not worry about the worms they catch in the morning; and so why are **you**? The **birds** do **not** worry about when the rain falls. The **fox** has no **fear** of when the snow falls. The **elk** are **not** frightened of winter, spring, summer or fall. They simply **are**. They have **no fear** because fear has **no** place in their heart. They **know** they are taken care of and when their turn is up Nature takes over, as it does with you. Please, please **abide** by the Laws of Nature and **encourage** others. Remember though...you are **not** to give advice unless asked...and that is another lesson we have discussed.

It is, again, **imperative** that you pay attention! Pay attention to **that** lesson and many others. Simply pay **attention** for as you pay attention, you will notice more and more. In the fall you were very taken back by the **beauty** all around you. You were taken back by the beauty of the gorgeous sunset, with the clouds in the sky, with the leaves on the trees. You paid **attention**. You paid attention to Nature that surrounded you. Well, I share with you...**that** will not change. Nature will surround you **continuously** and the beauty will be different. But please recognize that beauty. And remember the beauty **is** in the eye of the beholder. And if asked of you, **share** the beauty you see, for others may not be **able** to find the beauty as you can. But you can...for **you** see beauty in all.

And so you see, in the near future, as in the days that follow, **that** will be your lesson. You will **see** the beauty. You will **find** the beauty. You will **share** the beauty. You will be asked, "How can you see **beauty** in this?"...and you will share. And that is so **important** for you see, by sharing these things, it is how you spread the Light. It is how you spread the Love. It is how... again... a **heart** recognizes another heart. It is how you open the doors that **need** to be opened for another. It is how **another** will **spark the heart**. And that is what **needs** to happen and that is what your **job** is right now. And that is what **will** happen!

We are just sharing with you...so that you don't feel you were left out in the cold. You are **not** left out in the cold; you can talk to us **any** time you choose. We talk to you **all** the time and we will **never** leave you alone. We tell you... **everything** that is in your path is for a teaching or learning purpose. Sometimes it is important for you to just simply relax and enjoy, too. You do not **always** have to be wondering if you are teaching or learning. You both get hung up on the **trivial** sometimes. So sometimes it is wonderful to just stop and **be**. Just **be**. By **being who you are,** you are perfect. And you **say** the perfect thing and you **do** the perfect thing and you **are** simply perfect.

As your Holiday Season begins, many **other** things will come to an end. Do not see it as an end. For very often the end is truly a new **beginning**. For in a circle there is **no end** and there is **no beginning**. It is perfect and it is round and it is complete.

Now I say to you, do you have questions? For there are many Angels here and they are **all** Loving you and they are **all** protecting you and they are **all** sharing with you that whatever you need you **have** at your beck and call. And if you need **advice**, we are here. And if you need **help**, we are here. Do you want advice today?

Charlie: Yes, we always want advice and help and guidance from you, and we appreciate it so much. I know that you know what is in our hearts, and if there is any advice that you have that can give us clarity or comfort, we appreciate that very much.

That is what I **hope** we have done. For I have said simply **be**. **Be who you are**. For by **being who you are** you are perfect. You are both very **good** at this point in your Spiritual growth. You have fine discernment. You truly **don't** need our help any longer. You **know**. Unfortunately, sometimes...you have a hard time determining whether you **want** something so badly, that you cannot **know** what is right and perfect and best for you; for **your** highest and best good. So I share with you...no matter **what** you choose, you are at a point that, if the decision you make is a decision that will take you on a **longer** road, you will get back on the right road. And not to worry…**you cannot be taken off your path** at the point you are both on.

You can't **possibly** be taken off the path. For you see, your path is **so** wide and it is **so** clear. And those small, little hills that are in the middle of your path are there because you **need** them to be… for your growth. And so it is about **learning**. But they are **not** mountains and they are not awful. And if you choose, you could even walk **around** them. It would just take you a bit longer than if you went right **over** them. For you've got Angels that will **fly** you over them. It is simply a matter of how you **deal** with it, that's all. You will fly over or you will walk around. Either way you will **end up** on the other side. You see? Your path is very wide and it is lined with beautiful flowers. And it is lined with Angels who will not **let** you get off your path. They have very strict instructions to **help** you, but you will need very **little** help. Sometimes you get caught up in your **humanness**…and guess what…it is because you are human!

And so I tell you not to **worry**, not to **fear**. There is very little, at this point, that we can help you with, except to **encourage** you. We have told you **all there is** to tell. We have given you **all** the information you need to complete your Life Goals and your Spiritual Goals. There will be **minor little** things we can help you with, but trust me; they are so **very** minor because you have **learned all there is to learn**.

You have learned about **protection**. You have learned about **judgment**. You have learned about **Light** and **Love** being the most important things in your life! And you have learned about **Love, Love, Love**! You see **Love is it**. That is **all** that **really** matters. You have learned about **listening to your heart** and stepping **outside of your mind** so your heart can take over. For it is your **heart** that **knows**…it is your Spirit! And you **know** you have all the help that you could possibly need or want! And you **know** that your job is to help others and you **do** and you **will**. You are at a point that you **help** people without **recognizing** it anymore. And you see, that is where you are to be. You don't even recognize it because you are simply **being who you are**! And that is what makes you so **great**, and **that** is what you will continue to do.

The Creator is proud of **every** move you make and Loving **every** word you speak and **every** breath you take and **everyone** you help! You know **you can channel** at **any** time...you don't need to be together. You can **write**. You can record if you choose, but it is **no longer necessary. For all the information has been given you that is needed**. And eventually...not yet, not today...but eventually...you will go through those tapes and you will outline those tapes and you will **write a book** together. We will tell you **when** that time is... you will **know** when it is time.

You are now learning through **experience**. You need to get **out** there. And you will experience more and more and different **people** will be put on your path and you will **learn** from them and you will **teach** them. And so we tell you have a wonderful, **happy** journey! And look at is as a lovely traveling adventure! Have **no fear** of the future for you know **everything** is under control. It is to happen as it **will**, as it **should**, as it **must**! And if it is not for **your** teaching and **your** learning, it is for another's. **Know** this. Let **go** of all fear and **follow** your little Lights. Let your little Lights **out** and let them **grow** and let them **grow** and let them **glow**! Let the **Light of God** be your leader! For He **is ALL**...our leader. For it is The Creator whose very, very, beautiful, deep, wonderful Light keeps us **all** aware and growing and Loving. You will **never** lose track. You will **never** lose the **sight** of the **Light**.

So do you have specific questions?

Charlie: I don't think so, thank you.

345

Then I share with you, have a lovely, wonderful evening. Enjoy your **friends**. Enjoy each **other**. Enjoy your **family**. Have no fear of what gifts to buy. Concentrate more on the Loving **relationships** that you want to feed and that you want to grow. Take a look at what it is **you** want with the Love you have to offer. Concentrate on what **you** can offer rather than what **another** can give. If you do **that** you will **be happy forever and ever**!

Now, My Dears, I share with you…have a lovely evening. Have a lovely day. Have a lovely night. Have a lovely December. Have **fun** on your party nights and **know** we are **with** you. And know **you** are not the **only** ones partying! Look up and **see** us and **we** will be the choir that is singing the praises! And **we** will be the instrumental group playing in the band! And we will be **there** with you always, sharing, singing, praising, blessing and **always** protecting.

And so, My Dears, in friendship and in Love and in Joy and in Peace, I tell you this…have a wonderful night and have a wonderful holiday. We Love you so! Good-bye now.

Thank you. Thank you.

54

Charlene:

Denis and Sue and I all continue to channel, write, meditate and search. The information we receive, from this point, is mostly personal in nature and not always applicable to all. There are many more tapes, and perhaps, someday, there will be another book or two.

We are all continuing our learning and still share on a regular basis. This is how we stay connected to The Divine at all times. I never feel alone anymore. I know that I am always surrounded by Love and Angels and by the Light of God.

Denis and I were able to become reunited after five years of individual Spiritual Work. The trust has been restored. We were remarried, on the Island of Maui on November 4, 2003.

Sue channeled the Wedding Ceremony that follows. Enjoy!

Maui Wedding Ceremony of Denis and Charlene Hill November 4, 2003

The playing of "The Hawaiian Wedding Song" preceded the Ceremony.

We are all here together, doing something brand new that we have never experienced. We are here in celebration of Charlie and Denis' Wedding. And the six of us are here together to share with them and to celebrate. What we are doing is a totally channeled ceremony. The only thing that I have received, prior to now, is that this is totally about Denis and Charlie.

Charlie and I usually start by saying the date, and today is November 4th, and we began our ceremony at 4:44 P.M., on this beautiful day in Hawaii. We invite our Heavenly Creator to join us today, along with our Spiritual Guides and The Archangels and all of the Angels. We ask that blessings be put upon all of us as we get the messages that are needed for Charlie and Denis and for all of us to share together.

The Language of Light was spoken...

The Spirit of God is with us now, and the Spirit of God is **always** with us. And today, is Celebration of Charlie and

Denis. This is a Marriage. This is a Wedding. But it is far more! It is **much** more!

Charlie, you have suffered over several years...through the separation of a marriage that the two of you made **far before** you ever joined this Earth and incarnated. The two of you have had a relationship for many, many, many years. You have grown together emotionally, Spiritually, physically. You have had children together. You have shared your Loves, your hates. You have shared your **growth** and you have shared **all** that you have become. And it became very **obvious** that for you to continue the growth... for the path that you were on and **asked** to walk... that you must separate.

So this is **more** than a Wedding or a Marriage. This is a Re-birth of a Union. This is a **Re-union**! This is the beginning of your lives together. For after today, your lives will **never** be the same! As you separately walked a path that only **you** could walk alone, you grew. You grew lifetimes! Denis, you **knew** that this was something **you had** to do to continue on and to grow. Charlie, you knew it, too, but you **hurt** through it. You **forgot** what you had agreed to do.

And now the Beginning is **here**! Today you begin a **new** walk on a **new** path **together**, as you will share new things. For here, at your Wedding, not **only** are the Angels from the Angelic Realm **all** here! Not **only** is The Heavenly Creator sending down Rays of White Light that are for you, **forever**, for **now**, for **always**!

And here is a New Beginning, not **just** for you, Denis and Charlie. You have only been **instrumental** in this Beginning, which is your lives. And **now** it is a New Beginning for **All**! For **through** this, you will develop a new Marriage Counseling that **you alone** will be responsible for; for you have **created** something **new**! And you have **proof,** in your own lives, what **Love** will do! You have **proof** in your own lives what **God** can do when you **allow** Him to intervene!

And now a New Beginning is for **All** to see and **All** to feel! It is a Reunion for those who **choose** for that Reunion to take place. For you must **Re-birth** to start again. And so you **shall**...and so it shall **be** and so it **is** now!

And you have made the most **beautiful Paradise,** the place of your New Beginning! For it is **here** where the flowers are fragrant and beautiful and grow! And the **colors** are vibrant, as they always are in your **dreams** and in your **pictures**! And now they are **here** for you to see and feel and know! And **this** is God's Creation for **you**! As you refer to this ocean as **your ocean**, Charlie...it **is**! And it will **always** be! It is **yours** to take, to keep, to Love! It is yours to witness the growth, the New Beginning and understanding. For take a look at the ocean itself and know what you must take from it. For from it you will take The Everlasting Flow of Life! And that is **exactly** what it is!

As your new lives **begin** anew on this day that you have chosen, it is perfect, for All is perfect! And it is a New Beginning for you, for your lives together, but **more** than that. For it is the Beginning of your Spiritual Life...of the changes that you are making on this plane and others! For you will be very instrumental in directing your children, your friends, and others, to grow as **you** have grown... separately and together. You can **teach** the things that you have alone have learned...separately and together! And you can teach **how** those things changed your lives; renewed your Marriage and Love for each other, which only **can** be done with the Grace and the Light and the Love of God!

And now as I look about, I see the **thousands** that are here to greet you and to rejoice for you and to Love you! You have all the help you have ever needed and will ever need. But now... there is a **Celebration**; a Great Celebration of a Ceremony! It is the Ceremony of your Beginning Anew and the intertwining of your lives and your paths! It has begun and it will **stay** that way! For you will finish your lives on this planet together, working for God! You have **much** ahead of you.

And as in **all** Weddings, the thousands that are here to greet and celebrate have brought many **gifts**. And let us share with you now, the gifts that have been brought.; for you know that you have **many** gifts already...and now to utilize them! With your human ears you now have a clarity to **hear** things that you could not hear before! With your human eyes, you now have a clarity to **see** things that cannot be seen by those human eyes, but by the **third** eye that has opened up. And you will see many, many things! You will see things that **others** **cannot** and **you** will know! And you will follow **direction** through this. And you will create new things through this...on this plane and others; in your **personal** life, as well as in your New Lives...teaching! You will be relocating, and it will be **all** that you wanted ever! And you will **have** all the things that you have asked for. You have been told, more than once, that your prayers are **heard** and your prayers are **answered**!

You have known that you have **not** had the completion that you knew you needed. You **knew** there was more, but couldn't find what that "more" was. And so I share with you now. It is the **lives** that you are entwining, and the lives that you will be **assisting** and the Light that you will be **sharing**. As **you** are spreading The Light and The Love in a way that **no one** has done before!

Now, I tell you. You have always said, "What do I **do** and where do I **go** and what should I **say**?" There **is** nothing to do, nothing to say. It will all be put on your path, and **on** your path you will know it is **perfect** for it will happen easily and it will come **easily** to you. You have been told by more than one that if it is a **struggle**, it is not meant to **be**. There will be no more **struggles** in your lives! There will be **no** more struggles! For it will be **so** pleasurable to you, it will not be

work for you! It will be fun, and joyous and glorious! And you will know that **this** is what you were **meant** to do and be!

And now you **understand** why you had to walk those separate paths to come together to be whole. For you **accomplished** more in your alone time than you have accomplished in **lifetimes**! For, sometimes, you must listen **only** to your Inner-Self...for your Inner-Self is **God-directed**! For it is **God** who is speaking to you! And you get static and cannot hear if you are too busy listening to others. And now it is **complete**, and it is **true**, and it is **perfect**! And as you complete this Reunion and Celebration, the Heavens are opened up! And they are rejoicing and singing praises! For **you** have **completed** a struggle very few have completed! For you have **altered** the lives of those you do not even know! Because you listened! And you did **exactly** as your heart told you to do. And now you will continue doing that, and you will continue that for the rest of your lives.

And you say, "Why? Why do I not have my home in Denver?" Because that is not your home! And you say, "Why?" and you will soon know **all** the answers to your "whys". And you will soon have **all** of the answers to every question you had! For you have completed that which **had to be done** for you to grow!

And The Light of God is upon you...as you are being **showered** in beautiful, White-Silver Light! You are being surrounded, not **just** by the Angelic Realm and not **just** by the Guides that you have invited to join you, but you are being surrounded by others that have passed before you. Those that you **know**, that know you. Those that know your Spirit and your heart. Those that **knew** the path you chose before you walked it. And they are here celebrating **all** that you have done, and the **completion** of all that you are and the knowledge of what you will be! The knowledge that the growth has continued... the growth has been **unlimited**! **It is unlimited**!

And now, in this moment, pay attention! Pay attention to Nature all around you. **Feel** the wind. **Smell** the air; smell the salt-air! **Feel** the humidity in the air. Know that God and His Creatures are **here** all around you, rejoicing here on Earth, and in **your ocean**, Charlie! And **know** that these words that are being said to **you**, are heard by **All**. All that **choose**. And know that the **meaning** of the things that have been said to you, will come little by little, and be **reborn** in your ears, as you are needing them to be. Know that you are **never** left alone, and know that God has **blessed** you with many, many, many gifts. And you will begin **using** these gifts as your life together changes...and it will **change** very quickly. It will not just change personally. You will be making many, many changes that you never thought or **dreamed** that you could! You will be placed and put in places that you **never** ever **dreamed** you would go! And you will be **helping** people that are foreign to you and different to you. And you will be a Blessing to many! Your choices are few, for all **will** be placed in your lap.

And I say **Rejoice**, and **Rejoice**, and **Rejoice**! Listen to the **songs** that are being sung in your honor! Feel the **presence** of those that are surrounding you! You are starting a New Beginning. And you are being **led** to that, not just by God, Your Heavenly Creator; not by just Mother/Father God, who is in charge of All; but He has given you an **army**! And All will be as **perfect** as it is today! It will be perfect! And all will **happen** in the way that it should!

There is **no more fear** in your life. There is **no more anxiet**y. There is **Joy**, and there is **Love**, and there is **Happiness**! As the Lights of your very **Souls** shine through! There is no darkness in your world...in you two...in **your** world...in your lives. You will bring the Light **into** the darkness of others! And you will "**spark that hear**t", as you have done in the past! And now it will be on a greater, greater scale...as **you are lighting Souls all over**! As the **music** plays!

Denis and Charlie, this is **your** day! This is all about **you**! This is **your Happiness**! This is **your Completion**! For you see, in a circle a **beginning** is also the **end**; and the **end** is, truly, the **beginning**. There is **no** beginning and there is **no** end! **It is a circle.**

And now, if you would like to ask questions, you may. There are **many** here to help and answer. And, yet, it is just a **celebration**, a **jubilee**, a **party**! A celebration of The New Beginning! As you may not understand the **glory** of it, but those on the other plane do! And so, **see** the thousands that are celebrating for you!

Charlie...I don't believe we have any questions. Thank you so much!

The Silver-Lining is no longer a lining. It is **pure** and **complete**! For now it is only silver and **gold**! There are no more **clouds** in your sky! There are no more **weeds** in your garden! Only the **beauty** that you feel today! This will **stay** with you forever! This will **stay** with you for the completion of your life on this planet! And you will **always** have that ability. When no one else can see the flowers blooming, **you** will always have that ability! When no one else can see the sunshine through the clouds, you will **only** see the sunshine! And when no one else can see the Lightness through the dark, you will **only** see the Lightness! May your Joys be **full** and **complete**, and many, many, many! You will be passing-on these Blessings to All!

And with this I say, now you start **your** Celebration! Remember what was said to you, and remember that as the questions come up, those answers are **always** given. Always, always! You will be able, now, to **hear** with **clarity** that you did not have before. You will, now, be able to **see** with a **clarity** you could not see before. God has showered you with **many** gifts. They will be revealed to you and you will **recognize** them as you listen and utilize them. And with this I say, have a wonderful, wonderful day! And complete the

Celebration for the Rest of Your Life, **through** the rest of your life! **For each day and each moment is to be celebrated!** **Know** this and **remember** this!

As Love surrounds you, always **has** surrounded you, and **will continue** to surround you! Blessings to All, as you go in Love and Light! We will be celebrating **with** you through the day and through the night. And now, time for **you** the celebrate the lives...**all** of the lives which you are bringing into a new understanding. Now have fun and **Love**!

Thank you! Thank you! Thank you!

Thank you for taking the time to read these words. Know that you can go directly to God for your personal answers at any time. God Loves you and is waiting to hear from you.
     You may contact us at: chill@estreet.com

We continue to stay in constant communication. There will probably be more books in the future. Love and Light to you!

Archangel Michael's Instructions for Centering

This is a conscious choice:
I tell myself and all the Angelic help I have that I am choosing to Center myself, and I ask them to help me Center myself.

Then I say to myself, " I hear consciously. I ask God the Creator to help me and assist me as I Center myself, as I concentrate on my self needs; as I concentrate on my self wants that are for the Highest and Best Good at all times.

And I ask for all fog to be removed from me, and I ask that all self- doubt be removed from me.
For I want to be the greatest at doing God's work.
For I know how GREAT His work is, and I know I am doing it with the Love and Protection of God.
And I know that Michael is protecting me at all times.
And I, hereby, Center myself in doing God's work.
And I open myself up to all that is available to me.
And I ask that God put everything carefully and easily on my path for me to see,
And I ask that clarity be given to me as it is put in my path and that as I see it I recognize it.
And I take in all the Love and Light that God has given.
And I grow and I progress and I stay in the Center of my path for the Highest and Best Good of All.
For I know who I am and I know what I need and I know I have it because God promised and I believe Him."

Do this every morning, and do this every night...Do this at all times. This is how you stay centered, and protected at all times.

This page may be copied and placed where you can see it every day.

Made in the USA
Charleston, SC
14 July 2012